Applesoft BASIC Programmer's Reference Manual

Addison-Wesley Publishing Company, Inc.
Reading, Massachusetts Menlo Park, California New York Don Mills, Ontario Wokingham, England Amsterdam Bonn Sydney Singapore Tokyo Madrid Bogotá Santiago San Juan

This manual was written for Apple Computer, Inc. by

Scot Kamins
Technology Translated, Inc.
San Francisco, California

Simultaneously published in the United States and Canada.

ISBN 0-201-17756-0
ABCDEFGHIJ-DO-8987
First printing, July 1987

WARRANTY INFORMATION

ALL IMPLIED WARRANTIES ON THIS MANUAL, INCLUDING IMPLIED WARRANTIES OF MERCHANTABILITY AND FITNESS FOR A PARTICULAR PURPOSE, ARE LIMITED IN DURATION TO NINETY (90) DAYS FROM THE DATE OF THE ORIGINAL RETAIL PURCHASE OF THIS PRODUCT.

Even though Apple has reviewed this manual, APPLE MAKES NO WARRANTY OR REPRESENTATION, EITHER EXPRESS OR IMPLIED, WITH RESPECT TO THIS MANUAL, ITS QUALITY, ACCURACY, MERCHANTABILITY, OR FITNESS FOR A PARTICULAR PURPOSE. AS A RESULT, THIS MANUAL IS SOLD "AS IS," AND YOU, THE PURCHASER, ARE ASSUMING THE ENTIRE RISK AS TO ITS QUALITY AND ACCURACY.

IN NO EVENT WILL APPLE BE LIABLE FOR DIRECT, INDIRECT, SPECIAL, INCIDENTAL, OR CONSEQUENTIAL DAMAGES RESULTING FROM ANY DEFECT OR INACCURACY IN THIS MANUAL, even if advised of the possibility of such damages.

THE WARRANTY AND REMEDIES SET FORTH ABOVE ARE EXCLUSIVE AND IN LIEU OF ALL OTHERS, ORAL OR WRITTEN, EXPRESS OR IMPLIED. No Apple dealer, agent or employee is authorized to make any modification, extension, or addition to this warranty.

Some states do not allow the exclusion or limitation of implied warranties or liability for incidental or consequential damages, so the above limitation or exclusion may not apply to you. This warranty gives you specific legal rights, and you may also have other rights which vary from state to state.

Applesoft BASIC
Programmer's Reference Manual

Contents

Figures and Tables

Preface

About This Manual

This is a reference manual for the Applesoft BASIC programming language as implemented on the Apple® II series of computers. It is intended for readers who have had some previous experience with programming, either in BASIC or in some other programming language. It assumes that you are familiar with the material in the owner's manual for your computer and, if you are a novice programmer, that you have read the *Applesoft Tutorial*.

Purposes of This Manual

This manual has four purposes:

- To serve as a complete reference manual on the Applesoft BASIC language for the experienced programmer;
- To provide clear enough explanations and examples so that a new programmer can learn the details of any statement quickly and easily;
- To allow any reader, even one who is not trying to learn Applesoft in detail, to get a general feel for the language;
- To provide an introduction to program planning, design, and development for the programmer-in-training.

This manual is decidedly not a tutorial. Experienced programmers can learn a great deal about Applesoft by reading it from the first page straight through to the end, but it wasn't designed to be used that way.

How This Manual Is Organized

This manual has eight chapters, fifteen appendixes, a glossary of terms, and a quick reference card. All of it is designed to help you get the most out of Applesoft. Here's a description of what each chapter and appendix is about:

- Chapter 1, "General Information," contains information every Applesoft programmer needs. It discusses the programming environment in which Applesoft operates and tells how to create, modify, execute, and store Applesoft programs.
- Chapter 2, "Variables and Arithmetic," deals with some of the most fundamental concepts of Applesoft programming: variables, arithmetic expressions and operators, arithmetic precedence, Applesoft's built-in functions, and how to define and use your own functions.
- Chapter 3, "Control Statements," covers the various statements available to direct the flow of program execution. It includes information on unconditional and conditional branching, loops, subroutines, error handling, and program termination.
- Chapter 4, "Arrays and Strings," completes the material on variables begun in Chapter 2. It includes information on the definition and use of arrays in Applesoft and on the various string manipulation facilities.
- Chapter 5, "Input/Output," describes Applesoft's facilities for getting information into and out of programs and for formatting the way information is presented on the display screen.
- Chapter 6, "Graphics," tells how to create, change, display, and store low- and high-resolution graphic designs. There is an extensive discussion on creating and using shape tables, with examples of animation sequences. MouseText, a set of graphics you can use in text mode, is also covered.
- Chapter 7, "Utility Statements," contains information on a variety of miscellaneous Applesoft facilities for low-level control of the programming environment: directly accessing specific memory locations, controlling the limits of program space, and tracing the execution of a program for debugging purposes.
- Chapter 8, "Bringing It All Together," is more tutorial than any other chapter in the manual. It describes and demonstrates a method for planning, designing, and developing efficient, bug-free (well, *relatively* bug-free) programs.
- Appendix A, "Summary of Applesoft Statements and Functions," gives an abbreviated description of each Applesoft statement and function, together with a reference to the chapter, section, or appendix where you can find more detailed information and examples.
- Appendix B, "Syntax Definitions," defines terms used in the formal syntactic definitions of Applesoft statements given in Appendix A. In the body of the manual, statement syntax is shown by example rather than by formal definition; most readers can safely avoid the formal definitions altogether.

- □ Appendix C, "ASCII Character Codes," contains a complete listing of the ASCII characters; it is an adjunct to the comments on ASCII in Chapter 4.
- □ Appendix D, "Reserved Words in Applesoft," is a list of words (some of them rather odd-looking) that cannot be used in variable names.
- □ Appendix E, "Error Messages," describes the meanings of the error messages that Applesoft displays on the screen. Each description includes an explanation of why the error occurred; in some cases, there are suggestions for debugging.
- □ Appendix F, "Peeks, Pokes, and Calls," deals with low-level access to features of the Apple II computer via Applesoft's PEEK function and POKE and CALL statements. There are sections on screen text, the keyboard, graphics, miscellaneous input and output, and error handling.
- □ Appendix G, "Hints for Program Efficiency," offers techniques for cutting down the size of programs and for speeding up program execution.
- □ Appendix H, "Implementation Details," contains information of interest mainly to the advanced programmer. Included here is a memory map with a list of pointers and their descriptions, information on Applesoft's methods of internal storage allocation, an outline of its usage of special locations in page 0 of memory, and a list of the tokens it uses for internal representation of keywords.
- □ Appendix I, "Display Formats for Numbers," describes how Applesoft displays numbers on the screen, and gives the ranges of numbers the system is capable of handling.
- □ Appendix J, "On-Screen Editing and Cursor Control," contains tables summarizing Applesoft's on-screen editing features.
- □ Appendix K, "40/80-Column Display Differences," is a table showing the differences in Applesoft's behavior when it is displaying 80 as opposed to 40 columns of text.
- □ Appendix L, "Comparison With Integer BASIC," gives charts showing the differences between Applesoft and Apple Integer BASIC and discusses how to convert Integer BASIC and non-Apple II BASIC programs into Applesoft.
- □ Appendix M, "If You Have a Cassette Recorder," describes Applesoft's statements for using tape cassettes as a storage medium for programs and information. This applies only to the Apple II, Apple II Plus, and Apple IIe.
- □ Appendix N, "Complete Listing of the Postage Rates Program," gives the complete text of the programming example developed in Chapter 8.
- □ Appendix O, "BASIC and the Mouse", shows how to take advantage of the optional mouse accessory in BASIC programs.

At the back of the manual is a glossary of technical terms. In general, buzz words are no-no's in this manual; but any technical field has its own jargon, developed out of necessity to describe concepts genuinely having no parallel in common language. The glossary lists all such words and terms that have found their way into the manual, and a few others besides. When you run across a term you're not familiar with, look it up in the glossary.

A tear-out quick reference card, designed to act as a memory aid, gives an extremely brief description of each statement, function, operator, and variable type in Applesoft BASIC.

How to Use This Manual

Here are some suggestions on how to use this manual, depending on what you want to accomplish.

As a Reference Book

There are several ways you can use this book as a reference:

- Look up the feature of interest on the quick reference card; each statement, function, operator, and variable type is listed there in an extremely abbreviated form as a memory aid.
- Look up the feature in Appendix A, "Summary of Applesoft Statements and Functions." Each statement and function is described briefly, and a reference is given to the chapter, section, or appendix where it is discussed in detail.
- Look up the feature in the index. There you'll find page numbers of the places in the manual where it is mentioned.
- Look in the appendixes at the back of the manual for quick reference on specific facts.

To Learn the Applesoft Language

If you are not familar with Applesoft, you can follow this procedure to learn it:

1. Read Appendix A, "Summary of Applesoft Statements and Functions," to get a quick feel for each of the features in the language.
2. Read through each chapter and enter and run the sample programs. Then try modifying them to check your understanding and gain hands-on experience.
3. Enter, run, and modify the sample program in Chapter 8.

To Learn Program Planning

If you already know something about Applesoft and want to increase your programming skill and efficiency:

- □ Read through Chapter 8 and experiment with the program developed there.
- □ Develop your own programs based on the methods presented in Chapter 8.
- □ Restructure someone else's program using the methods in Chapter 8.
- □ Read Appendix G, "Hints for Program Efficiency," at the back of the manual.

Conventions Used in This Manual

Throughout this manual you'll encounter the following conventions:

The term *Apple II* is used generically to refer to all models in the Apple II series of personal computers (original Apple II, Apple II Plus, Apple IIe, Apple IIc). Comments referring specifically to the original Apple II are clear from the context.

When numbers (such as memory addresses) are preceded by a dollar sign, such as $9600, that means they are in hexadecimal notation. Numbers without a dollar sign are generally in decimal, unless otherwise stated.

Computer terms you may not know are in **boldface** type. All boldface words are defined in the Glossary.

Every section that explains an Applesoft statement or command begins with an example or examples of correct syntax. For instance, Section 3.3.2, "The Next Statement," begins with these examples:

```
NEXT
NEXT INDEX
NEXT J,I
```

▲Warning Warnings like this indicate potential serious problems.

Important! Text set off in this manner—and with a tag in the margin—presents important information.

II, II Plus, IIe Text set off in this manner presents information specific to one or more models in the Apple II series of computers. For instance, the tag opposite this paragraph indicates that the text concerns the Apple II, Apple II Plus, and Apple IIe.

Marginal notes define computer terms and point you to additional information about a topic.

By the Way: Text set off in this manner presents sidelights or interesting pieces of information.

Where to Learn More

The following sources contain further information about the Apple II series of computers in general and the Applesoft programming language in particular:

- The owner's manual for your particular Apple computer covers the basics of the system and includes a special section on your computer's keyboard. It also contains a list of books and magazines of special interest to Applesoft programmers, as well as a short guide to the rest of the documentation that comes with your computer.
- A keyboard introduction disk comes with all disk-based Apple II systems. It contains an interactive tutorial program giving you hands-on practice with many of the concepts discussed in your owner's manual. It's a must if you're new to computers.
- *BASIC Programming With ProDOS* tells how to create and read text files on disk, and how to save your Applesoft programs on disk, using the ProDOS operating system. This manual includes a disk of programming examples, as well as the Applesoft Programmer's Assistant—a collection of time-saving tools.
- The *Applesoft Tutorial* is an excellent guide for beginning programmers. It provides introductory, step-by-step guidance for the new programmer and has a special chapter on editing Applesoft programs.

- *Apple Backpack: Humanized Programming in BASIC*, by Scot Kamins and Mitchell Waite (BYTE/McGraw-Hill Books) teaches programming in a friendly and easy-paced way for people who are not computer experts.
- The reference manual for your Apple computer contains a wealth of information about the more technical aspects of the system's operation, with lists of various programmer-accessible system flags, pointers, and soft switches.

Chapter 1

General Information

BASIC: Beginner's All-purpose Symbolic Instruction Code

Applesoft BASIC is a very extended version (in computer parlance, a superset) of the BASIC programming language. It includes many more features than either the original BASIC, developed at Dartmouth College in the 1960s, or the standard version of the language, as defined by the American National Standards Institute (ANSI). The extra features allow your programs to use the special capabilities of the Apple II, such as color graphics, animation, and hand controls.

This first chapter introduces the Applesoft language and the environment in which it operates. Here you will find information on how to create, modify, execute, and store Applesoft programs.

- Section 1.1, "Statements, Lines, and Programs," deals with the fundamental units of Applesoft programs. It tells how to type Applesoft statements for immediate execution and how to create and modify programs in the computer's memory.
- Section 1.2, "Operations on Whole Programs," introduces Applesoft's commands for displaying a program on the screen, writing it to an output device such as a printer, executing it, saving it on a disk, and retrieving it from a disk.
- Section 1.3, "Interrupting and Resuming a Program," tells how to suspend or cancel the execution of a running program and how to resume execution after an interruption.
- Section 1.4, "Editing What You Type," briefly describes Applesoft's facilities for correcting typing errors and editing text on the screen.

1.1 Statements, Lines, and Programs

The basic unit of an Applesoft program is the program line, which can contain one or more statements specifying actions you want the computer to perform. Most Applesoft statements are identified by one or more keywords, special words that Applesoft recognizes as denoting a particular type of statement.

You can type a program line whenever you see Applesoft's prompt character, a right bracket ( ]), displayed on the screen followed by the cursor. Each line you type must end in a press of the RETURN key (but see Section 1.1.4 about multiple statements per line). Depending on what you type, the statements in the line are either executed immediately or deferred for later execution as part of a complete program.

Uppercase Versus Lowercase: If you have an Apple IIc or an enhanced Apple IIe, it doesn't matter whether you type the names of variables or Applesoft commands in uppercase or lowercase letters; they're automatically converted to uppercase when you list the program.

However, the Apple II, Apple II Plus, and earlier Apple IIe computers require that you use uppercase letters. For the sake of consistency, uppercase letters are used in this manual.

By the way, earlier Apple IIe computers can be upgraded to enhanced Apple IIe's. See your dealer for details.

Notice that a program line is not the same thing as a line of text on the screen. If the cursor reaches the end of a screen line while you're typing a program line, it wraps around to the beginning of the next screen line and continues displaying what you type. A program line can be up to 239 characters long (including line numbers) and ends only when you press RETURN.

Extra-Long Program Lines: Actually, you can type as many as 255 characters in a program line (including the line number and any spaces), but all characters after 239 are ignored. If you type more than 255 characters, Applesoft displays a backslash character (\ ) and cancels the entire line. It then redisplays the prompt character ( ]) followed by the cursor, and you have to retype the entire line from the beginning. As a warning, Applesoft beeps with every character you type beginning with the 245th in a line.

It's usually a bad idea to type program lines this long. In practice, you should keep your lines well below 239 characters in length.

1.1.1 Immediate Execution

If you want Applesoft to execute a statement or program line as soon as you type it, just type the line and press RETURN. For example, if you type

```
PRINT "HELLO"
```

Applesoft immediately displays the word `HELLO` on the screen, on the line following what you just typed.

1.1.2 Line Numbers and Deferred Execution

If you want Applesoft to save a program line to be executed later—that is, if you want it to defer execution—then precede the line with a line number:

```
10   PRINT "HELLO"
```

Line numbers must be in the range 0 through 63999. Applesoft uses the presence or absence of line numbers to determine whether the line you type is to be carried out immediately or deferred (stored for execution at some future time).

A sequence of deferred-execution lines, each preceded by a different line number, is an Applesoft program. Program lines are stored in the computer's memory in sequential order, from the lowest-numbered line to the highest.

1.1.3 Adding Lines to a Program

To add a new line to a program, just type the new line preceded by a line number indicating where in the program you wish to insert it. It makes no difference in what order you enter program lines; Applesoft puts them in the proper order for you.

> *Helpful Hint:* Instead of using consecutive line numbers (0, 1, 2...), it's usually more convenient to leave intervals of 5 or 10 or 20 between the line numbers in your program. This makes it easy to insert new lines, if necessary, in between the old ones.

1.1.4 Multiple Statements on the Same Line

Applesoft allows you to put more than one statement on the same program line. Use a colon (:) to separate the statements:

```
40   PRINT "COME OUTSIDE" : PRINT "AND PLAY"
```

You can type as many statements as will fit within the limit of 239 characters per line.

A Drawback: Although using multiple statements on the same line can speed up the execution of your program, it can also make program editing difficult and time consuming. This example, for instance, has two statements on the same line. In order to change the word `OUTSIDE` in the first statement to `INSIDE`, you would have to retype both statements. But if each statement were on its own line, you would have to retype only the one statement you wanted to change. This may not seem like much of a time savings; but when you multiply three or four seconds by the dozens of edits you might need to make in developing a typical program, the savings can become considerable.

1.1.5 Deleting Lines: The DEL Command

```
DEL 100, 200
```

The DEL command deletes (removes) a range of consecutive lines from the program currently in memory. The line numbers of the first and last lines to be deleted follow the keyword DEL and are separated from each other by a comma. All program lines between and including the two specified line numbers are deleted from the program. This example, for instance, deletes lines 100 to 200, inclusive.

If either line number is out of the range of lines in the actual program (for instance, if the command is DEL 100, 200 and the highest existing line number is 150), then all existing lines within the specified range are deleted. If DEL specifies a range of lines that doesn't exist, or if the second line number is smaller than the first, the command has no effect:

```
DEL 200, 100                    Nothing happens.
```

A single number with a comma also has no effect:

```
DEL 35,
```

A single number without a comma causes a syntax error:

```
DEL 35                          Syntax error.
```

To delete a single line from the program, simply type the number of that line and press [RETURN]:

```
150 [RETURN]
```

Dash Not Allowed in DEL Command: Unlike the LIST command (see Section 1.2.3), you cannot use a dash (—) to separate the line numbers in the DEL command:

`DEL 60 - 100`	Causes a syntax error.

The DEL command is normally used in immediate execution. You can also use it from within a program, but as soon as it is executed the program stops with no error message:

`20 DEL 135, 250`	Removes lines 135 through 250 from program; halts program execution.

1.1.6 Changing Lines in a Program

To replace an existing line of your program, simply type the new line using the same line number as the existing one. What you type replaces the old line under the same line number; the old line is forgotten.

To alter an existing line, either retype the line or use your computer's editing facilities, discussed in Section 1.4 and in Appendix J.

1.1.7 Annotating a Program: The REM Statement

```
REM  TEST FOR ERROR
```

One rule of good programming practice is to include comments in your program, explaining or clarifying to a human reader how the program works. Applesoft's REM (for remark) statement allows you to include such remarks within the body of your program. It consists of the keyword REM followed by any explanatory notes you care to include. An example of a REM statement is

```
0  REM  MONTHLY BUDGET PROGRAM
```

This statement is included in the program strictly for the benefit of the human reader. When you list the program, the REM statement appears just like any other statement. But when you run the program, Applesoft ignores everything following the keyword REM on the same line and just goes on to the next line. See Chapter 8, "Programming: Bringing It All Together," for some tips on using the REM statement.

1.2 Operations on Whole Programs

This section describes Applesoft's commands for manipulating whole programs:

- NEW (see Section 1.2.1) clears the current program from the computer's memory so you can start typing another.
- CLEAR (see Section 1.2.2) resets all variables and internal control information to their initial settings, without affecting the Applesoft program in memory.
- LIST (see Section 1.2.3) displays the current program on the screen or writes it to an output device such as a printer.
- RUN (see Section 1.2.4) executes the program currently in memory. It can also be used to load and execute a program stored on a disk.
- SAVE (see Section 1.2.5) writes the program currently in memory onto a disk or a tape cassette for future use.
- LOAD (see Section 1.2.6) reads a program into memory from a disk or a tape cassette for execution.

You can use all of these commands for immediate execution. You can use some of them from within your Applesoft programs as well.

1.2.1 Clearing Memory: The NEW Command

```
NEW
```

The NEW command clears the current program from memory, resets the values of all numeric variables to 0 and those of all string variables to the null string, and prepares Applesoft to accept a new program. If there are no programs and no variables in memory, NEW has no effect.

When you sit down to start typing a new program, always begin by typing NEW. Otherwise, you might find that you're not typing a new program at all, but just editing the first lines of a program already in memory.

Although NEW is usually used in immediate execution, you can also use it in deferred execution (from within a program):

```
100  IF A$ = "RATS" THEN NEW
                                    NEW in conditional statement.
999  NEW                            NEW on its own line.
```

▲Warning

hang: for a program to spin its wheels indefinitely, performing no useful work

Using NEW in deferred execution can do strange and unpredictable things to Applesoft's innards, causing subsequently entered programs to hang. If you use NEW from within a program, it's a good idea to warn your user to restart the system before typing another program:

```
100  IF A$ = "RATS" THEN PRINT "PLEASE
     RESTART YOUR SYSTEM BEFORE TYPING
     A NEW PROGRAM." : NEW
```

1.2.2 Resetting Variables: The CLEAR Command

```
CLEAR
```

null string: a string containing no characters

The CLEAR command resets the values of all numeric variables to 0 and those of all string variables to the null string; it also resets Applesoft's internal control information to its initial state. It has no effect on the contents of the program lines in memory.

Although CLEAR is usually used in immediate execution, you can also use it in deferred execution (from within a program):

```
100  IF Z$ = "NUTS" THEN CLEAR
                                CLEAR in conditional statement.
999  CLEAR                      CLEAR on its own line.
```

▲Warning

subroutines, control stack: see Section 3.4

Be careful where you execute CLEAR. Since CLEAR resets Applesoft's internal control stack, using it in the midst of a subroutine or in a FOR/NEXT loop can interfere with the orderly flow of program execution. The following program, for example, crashes in line 40 with a `NEXT WITHOUT FOR` error:

```
10  FOR X = 1 TO 10       Tries to loop 10 times.
20  PRINT X
30  CLEAR                 CLEAR resets control stack
                          (among other things).
40  NEXT X                Program fails here—doesn't know
                          it's in a loop.
50  PRINT "HI!"           Program won't get this far.
```

1.2.3 Listing a Program: The LIST Command

```
LIST
LIST 100
LIST 100,
LIST 100 -
LIST - 200
LIST ,200

LIST 100, 200
LIST 100 - 200
```

The LIST command displays on the screen all or part of the program currently in memory, or writes it to the current output device as specified in the last PR# statement. (See Section 5.2.1.) For example, if there is a printer connected to slot 1 or port 1, and if the statement `PR# 1` has been executed, then the program listing is sent to the printer.

To list the entire program, just type

```
LIST
```

and press [RETURN].

You can list a portion of the program by specifying the first and last lines you want to list, separated by either a comma or a dash:

`LIST 100, 250`	Displays lines 100 through 250.
`LIST 100 - 250`	Also displays lines 100 through 250.

If none of the lines in the specified range are in memory, nothing is listed. If the specified range is greater than the actual range of lines in the program, Applesoft lists the entire program.

If you specify only one line number *preceded* by a comma or dash, all lines from the beginning of the program through the specified line are listed:

`LIST ,100`	Displays from beginning of program through line 100.

If you specify only one line number *followed* by a comma or dash, all lines from the specified line through the end of the program are listed:

`LIST 100 –`	Displays from line 100 through end of program.

If you just specify a single line number, only that line is listed:

`LIST 100`	Displays line 100 only.

An Exception: You cannot list line number 0 by itself. You must use a form like

```
LIST 0,1
```

▲Warning Always be sure to type the keyword LIST before the number of the program line you want to list; typing a line number not preceded by a keyword *deletes* the specified line from the program. (See Section 1.1.5.)

Although the LIST command is usually used in immediate execution, you can also use it from within a program:

`150 LIST`	Lists entire program.
`235 IF Z = X THEN LIST 10, 75`	Lists lines 10 through 75 if variable Z holds same value as variable X.

1.2.4 The RUN Command

```
RUN
RUN 275
RUN MONTHLY.BUDGET
```

The RUN command instructs Applesoft to execute the program currently in memory. If no line number is given, execution begins at the beginning of the program; if the RUN command includes a line number, execution begins at the specified line:

`RUN`	Executes program from beginning.
`RUN 500`	Executes program from line 500.

If you attempt to run a program from a specified line number (as in `RUN 500`) and that line doesn't exist, the message `?UNDEF'D STATEMENT ERROR` is displayed and program execution halts.

Although RUN is normally used in immediate execution, you can also use it from within a program:

`150 IF A = 0 THEN RUN`	If value of A is 0, then executes program from beginning.
`235 RUN 600`	Executes program from line 600.

You can use this technique, for example, to restart a game or to avoid executing some code with low line numbers.

▲Warning Whenever the RUN statement is executed, it resets the values of all numeric variables to 0 and those of all string variables to the null string before executing the first program line. If you have assigned values to any variables in immediate execution, those values are forgotten. This happens even if there is no program currently in memory.

If your computer is equipped with a disk drive and the disk operating system is active, you can use the RUN command to load a program into memory from a disk file and then execute it. To do this, follow the keyword RUN with the filename under which the program is stored on the disk. For example, if the program you want to run is stored in a file named AWAY, first make sure the disk containing that file is in the disk drive, then type

```
RUN AWAY
```

and press RETURN. Applesoft (and the disk operating system) does the rest.

If you try to use this form of the RUN command with no disk drive connected to your computer, or without the disk operating system loaded and active, you'll get a syntax error.

Where Else to Look: For more information on disk drives, disks, files, and filenames, see *BASIC Programming With ProDOS* and the manual that came with your disk drive. If you received DOS with your disk drive, this is the *DOS User's Manual*. If you received ProDOS, it is the *ProDOS User's Manual*. If your computer is an Apple IIc, it is the *System Utilities Manual*. For related Applesoft commands, see Sections 1.2.5 and 1.2.6. For information on using a cassette tape recorder in place of a disk drive, see Appendix M.

1.2.5 The SAVE Command

```
SAVE
SAVE MONTHLY.BUDGET
```

On systems equipped with a disk drive, the SAVE command writes the Applesoft program currently in memory to a file on a disk. The keyword SAVE is followed by the filename under which the program is to be saved. The copy of the program in memory is not affected in any way. For example,

```
SAVE MY.CHILD
```

stores the current program on disk under the filename MY.CHILD.

Attempting to use this form of the SAVE command with no disk drive connected to your computer, or without the disk operating system loaded and active, results in a syntax error.

II, II Plus, IIe

If you issue the SAVE command without specifying a filename, Applesoft attempts to write the program in memory onto a tape cassette. If no cassette recorder is connected, the computer seems to hang for a while; the actual time that passes before you regain control depends on the length of the program in memory. You can regain control immediately by pressing [CONTROL]-[RESET] (see Section 1.3.2).

Where Else to Look: For more information on disk drives, disks, files, and filenames, see *BASIC Programming With ProDOS* and the manual that came with your disk drive—the *DOS User's Manual*, *ProDOS User's Manual*, or *System Utilities Manual*. For related Applesoft commands, see Sections 1.2.4 and 1.2.6. For information on using a cassette tape recorder in place of a disk drive, see Appendix M.

1.2.6 The LOAD Command

```
LOAD MONTHLY.BUDGET
```

On systems equipped with a disk drive, the LOAD command reads an Applesoft program from a file on a disk into the computer's memory for execution or editing. The keyword LOAD is followed by the filename under which the program is to be found on the disk. For example,

```
LOAD THE.DICE
```

loads the program into memory from the file named THE.DICE.

LOAD does not execute the program it retrieves; it merely reads a copy of the program into memory. You can then execute the program, if you wish, with the RUN command. The copy of the program on the disk is not affected in any way.

If the disk in the disk drive doesn't contain a file of the specified name, the error message `FILE NOT FOUND` is displayed. If there is no disk drive connected to your computer, or if the disk operating system isn't loaded and active, you get a syntax error.

On systems capable of cassette tape storage, if you issue the LOAD command without specifying a filename, Applesoft attempts to read a program into memory from a tape cassette. If no cassette recorder is connected, or if the tape in the recorder doesn't contain a program to load, or if the recorder is turned off, the computer hangs forever looking for a program that isn't there. When you get bored waiting, press CONTROL-RESET to regain control.

Where Else to Look: For more information on disk drives, disks, files, and filenames, see *BASIC Programming With ProDOS* and the manual that came with your disk drive. For related Applesoft commands, see Sections 1.2.4 and 1.2.5. For information on using a cassette tape recorder in place of a disk drive, see Appendix M.

1.3 Interrupting and Resuming a Program

If a program starts to run away from you, (for example, if it gets into an endless loop), there are various ways of interrupting it and regaining control.

1.3.1 Suspending Screen Output

Sometimes a program's output, or its listing, exceeds the number of lines available on the display screen, causing the output to fly by on the screen too fast for you to read. To suspend screen output temporarily, you can press CONTROL-S (press S while holding down CONTROL).

CONTROL-S doesn't permanently discontinue the display of text; pressing any key, including another CONTROL-S, causes screen output to resume. You can then suspend it again with another CONTROL-S. To permanently discontinue a program or a listing, use CONTROL-C.

Helpful Hint: Experienced programmers looking at listings of long programs keep CONTROL continually pressed; they press S whenever they want to either suspend or continue the listing.

1.3.2 Interrupting Program Execution

Applesoft gives you two ways of interrupting the execution of a running program or canceling a listing. Pressing CONTROL-C interrupts the program in such a way that it is usually possible to resume execution from the point of the interruption. Pressing CONTROL-RESET is somewhat more drastic, and often leaves the system in a state from which the program can't be resumed with a CONT statement (see Section 1.3.3).

1.3.2.1 CONTROL-C

Pressing CONTROL-C (pressing C while holding down CONTROL) cancels the execution or listing of a program and returns Applesoft to its command level, displaying the prompt character ( ]). You can then resume execution of the program, if you wish, with the CONT command.

> ***Canceling a Program Waiting for a Response:*** To cancel a program that is waiting for a response to an INPUT statement (see Section 5.1.2), press CONTROL-C and follow it immediately with RETURN.
>
> CONTROL-C does not interrupt a program waiting for a response to a GET statement (see Section 5.1.3). Unlike the INPUT statement, GET assumes that CONTROL-C is a valid response and assigns the ASCII code for the character CONTROL-C to the specified variable. To allow a program halted at a GET statement to be interrupted with CONTROL-C, use this form in the program:
>
> ```
> 250   GET A$                          Waits for user to press a key
> 260   IF A$ = CHR$(3) THEN STOP
>                                       If user presses CONTROL-C
>                                       (ASCII code 3), then stops
> ```

▲Warning In certain situations, using CONTROL-C can disconnect the disk operating system. See the disk operating system manual for information on this point.

1.3.2.2 CONTROL-RESET

In most cases you can immediately and unconditionally stop the execution of any Applesoft program or command by pressing CONTROL-RESET (pressing RESET while holding down CONTROL). The program in memory remains intact, but some of Applesoft's internal "housekeeping" information is changed; as a result, it may not be possible to resume execution of the program with the CONT command.

Controlling CONTROL-RESET*:* Your Apple II has an advanced software feature called a **reset vector**, which allows you to control what happens when CONTROL-RESET is pressed. You can use the reset vector to make the program continue as if nothing had happened, branch to some other portion of the program, or do whatever you choose. To use this technique you need to be familiar with the Apple II's built-in Monitor program: see your computer's reference manual for details.

1.3.3 Resuming Execution: CONT Command

```
CONT
```

The CONT (for continue) command is used to resume execution of a program after it has been interrupted by a STOP (see Section 3.6.1) or END statement (see Section 3.6.2) or by pressing CONTROL-C. Execution resumes at the first statement *after* the STOP or END, or at the point in the program where execution was interrupted by CONTROL-C (see Section 1.3.2).

CONT won't work if

- the program has been stopped because of an error
- an error has occurred in immediate execution
- an INPUT statement has been interrupted with CONTROL-C
- the CLEAR or NEW command has been executed
- any program line has been edited since the program stopped running
- there are no more program lines after STOP or END.

However, you can continue the program with CONT after examining or changing the values of variables, provided you haven't edited any program lines.

Important! Resuming after CONTROL-RESET: When a program is interrupted with CONTROL-RESET, CONT may or may not continue execution. Let the programmer beware!

▲Warning The CONT command should be used in immediate execution only. If it is executed from within a program, it causes the program to hang.

1.4 Editing What You Type

This section gives a very brief description of Applesoft's facilities for correcting typing mistakes and editing text on the screen. More detailed discussions of these features can be found in your Apple computer owner's manual and the *Applesoft Tutorial.* For hands-on experience with the various keys and editing features, use the keyboard introduction disk that came with your computer.

1.4.1 Canceling an Input Line

CONTROL-X is your escape hatch. By pressing X while holding down CONTROL, you can change your mind (as long as you haven't yet pressed RETURN) and cancel a program line that you're entering or editing, or a line of input that you're in the midst of typing into a program. Applesoft displays a backslash (\) at the end of the line you were typing, to show that it's ignoring that input, and redisplays the cursor at the beginning of the next line of the screen.

- If you were typing a new program line, the whole line is eliminated and you can start over again.
- If you were retyping a previously entered program line, any changes you typed are canceled.
- If you were typing input to a running program, the line you were typing is ignored and the program waits for your new response.

CONTROL-X does not affect any previous input you've typed or program lines already entered.

1.4.2 The Arrow Keys

There are four arrow keys on most models of the Apple II keyboard:

- The [←] key works as a backspace. It moves the cursor one position to the left and causes Applesoft to forget the last character typed from the keyboard (or recopied with the [→] key;), though no characters are removed from the screen. If any pure cursor moves (see Section 1.4.3) have been used, the character "erased" may not be the one the cursor backs up over.
- The [→] key recopies the character under the cursor as if it had been typed from the keyboard, then moves the cursor one position to the right. Moving the cursor over a character with [→] is exactly the same as typing that character from the keyboard.
- The [↓] key moves the cursor down one line without erasing or recopying any characters. Neither the Apple II nor the Apple II Plus has this key.
- The [↑] key has no effect in Applesoft.

In escape mode (see Section 1.4.3), all four arrow keys lose their backspace and recopy functions and simply move the cursor one position in the indicated direction.

> ***Fast Moves:*** The Apple II keyboard's auto-repeat feature is particularly handy for long cursor moves. If you press and hold down any of the arrow keys, the cursor moves repeatedly in the indicated direction for as long as you hold down the key. (Exception: the [↑] key doesn't move the cursor unless you're in escape mode.)

Every time you press an arrow key, you send an ASCII code (see Section 4.2.1 and Appendix C) to the computer. Table 1.1 shows which codes correspond to which keys.

Table 1-1. ASCII Equivalents of Arrow Keys

Key	**ASCII Code**	**Keyboard Equivalent**
[←]	8	[CONTROL]-[H]
[→]	21	[CONTROL]-[U]
[↑]	11	[CONTROL]-[K]
[↓]	10	[CONTROL]-[J]

For Experts Only: [↑] and [↓] (not present on Apple II and Apple II Plus) can be typed by the user in response to an INPUT statement in a running Applesoft program. ([←] and [→] can't be, because they're interpreted as backspace and recopy, even in program input; but any of the four arrow keys can be typed as a response to a GET statement.) In your own programs, you can make the arrow keys mean just what you choose them to mean by having the program test the input for each arrow's ASCII value, as shown in Table 1-1. The program can take any action you want on receiving one of these codes from the user.

("The question is," said Alice, "whether you *can* make keys mean so *many* different things."

"The question is," said Humpty Dumpty, "which is to be master—that's all.")

1.4.3 Escape Mode

If you press [ESC] while the] prompt is on the screen, you put Applesoft into **escape mode**, in which certain keys take on special meanings. Some of the keys become pure cursor moves, meaning that they move the cursor around on the screen without erasing or recopying characters or affecting Applesoft's input in any way. Others can be used to clear away text from all or part of the screen, again without having any effect on the input received by Applesoft.

Letters Can Be Uppercase or Lowercase: All of the letter keys listed have the same effect whether they are typed in uppercase or lowercase on all Apple II series computers.

In escape mode, the following characters move the cursor one position in the stated direction and then *leave escape mode*. To continue moving the cursor, you have to press [ESC] again. The functions of these keys are illustrated in Figure 1-1.

Figure 1-1. Single Cursor Moves

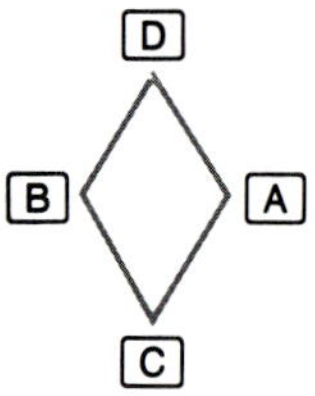

- [A] moves the cursor one position to the right.
- [B] moves the cursor one position to the left.
- [C] moves the cursor down one line.
- [D] moves the cursor up one line.

II, II Plus, IIe

Figure 1-2. Long-Range Cursor Moves

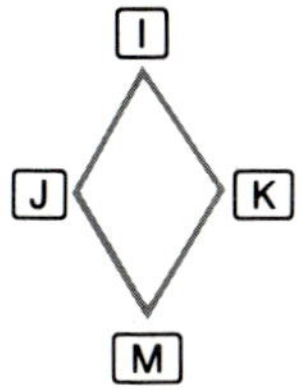

The following characters move the cursor one position in the stated direction and *remain in escape mode*. You can continue moving the cursor without pressing [ESC] again. These keys are especially useful for long-range cursor moves. The functions of these keys are illustrated in Figure 1-2.

- [I] moves the cursor up one line.
- [J] moves the cursor one position to the left.
- [K] moves the cursor one position to the right.
- [M] moves the cursor down one line.

Cursor Control Diamond: Notice that the [I], [J], [K], and [M] keys form a diamond shape on the keyboard, representing the directions in which these keys move the cursor: [I] up, [J] left, [K] right, [M] down.

Fast Moves: The Apple IIe and Apple IIc keyboards have an auto-repeat feature, particularly handy for long cursor moves. If you press and hold down [I], [J], [K], [M], or any of the arrow keys while in escape mode, the cursor moves repeatedly in the indicated direction for as long as you hold down the key.

In escape mode, the following keys clear away text from all or part of the display screen and then leave escape mode:

- [E] clears from the current cursor position to the end of the line.
- [F] clears from the current cursor position to the end of the text window. (See Section 5.2.4.)
- [@] clears the entire text window and moves the cursor to the top-left corner.
- [ESC] [CONTROL]-[E] enables displaying on the screen of most control characters. [ESC] [CONTROL]-[D] disables it. (This applies to the Apple IIc and enhanced Apple IIe's only.)

The special functions of all keys in escape mode are summarized in Table 1-2.

To leave escape mode, you can press any key except one of those listed in the table. But to avoid inadvertently pressing a key that has a special meaning, it's safest always to press the [SPACE] bar to leave escape mode.

Table 1-2. Escape-Mode Functions

Note: Table applies to Apple IIc and Apple IIe only.

Key	Function
[A]	Moves cursor right one position; leaves escape mode.
[B]	Moves cursor left one position; leaves escape mode.
[C]	Moves cursor down one line; leaves escape mode.
[D]	Moves cursor up one line; leaves escape mode.
[I]	Moves cursor up one line; remains in escape mode.
[J]	Moves cursor left one position; remains in escape mode.
[K]	Moves cursor right one position; remains in escape mode.
[M]	Moves cursor down one line; remains in escape mode.
[←]	Moves cursor left one position; remains in escape mode.
[→]	Moves cursor right one position; remains in escape mode.
[↑]	Moves cursor up one line; remains in escape mode (Apple IIe and Apple IIc only).
[↓]	Moves cursor down one line; remains in escape mode (Apple IIe and Apple IIc only).
[E]	Clears from cursor to end of line; leaves escape mode.
[F]	Clears from cursor to end of screen; leaves escape mode.
[@]	Clears entire screen; moves cursor to top-left corner; leaves escape mode.
[CONTROL]-[E]	Enables display of control characters.
[CONTROL]-[D]	Disables display of control characters.

Chapter 2

Variables and Arithmetic

This chapter deals with variables and arithmetic in Applesoft. These concepts are fundamental to Applesoft programming and appear again and again throughout this manual.

- Section 2.1, "Variables," discusses how to define and use variables, the various types of variables available in Applesoft, and the rules for naming them.
- Section 2.2, "Assigning Values: The Assignment Statement," deals briefly with one of Applesoft's most basic types of statements, the assignment statement.
- Section 2.3, "Expressions," discusses arithmetic operators and expressions and the rules of precedence that govern them.
- Section 2.4, "Functions," covers Applesoft's built-in arithmetic functions and tells how you can define your own functions.

2.1 Variables

A variable is a symbol representing a location in the computer's memory where a value can be stored. The first time your program assigns a value to a particular variable, Applesoft automatically allocates enough memory for that variable and stores the specified value at that location. Thereafter, whenever your program uses that particular variable name, Applesoft takes the name to refer to the value stored at the corresponding location. For instance, if the variable PI refers to a memory location where the value 3.14159 is stored, then the statement `PRINT PI` displays the value `3.14159` on the screen.

Applesoft has three types of variables:

- **Real variables** (see Section 2.1.2) can contain either whole numbers or numbers containing decimal fractions.
- **Integer variables** (see Section 2.1.3) can contain whole numbers only.
- **String variables** (see Section 2.1.4) can contain strings of text characters such as words or names.

In addition, Applesoft allows you to define collections of variables, called **arrays**, of any of the types listed.

Programming Tip: Applesoft converts all integer values to real form before performing arithmetic on them. Because this conversion takes time, integer arithmetic is considerably slower than arithmetic on real quantities. However, integers take up less space in the computer's memory than real numbers. In relatively small programs in which space is not a concern, you can speed up your program by using real variables instead of integers wherever possible, especially in subroutines, loops, and other sections of code that are executed many times. In large programs where space is critical, you can save space at the expense of time by using integers instead of reals, particularly in arrays containing many elements. See Appendix G for further suggestions on how to save space and time in your programs.

2.1.1 Variable Names

The name of a variable must begin with a letter of the alphabet, which may be followed by one or more letters and/or digits. In addition, the names of all integer variables must end with a percent character (%) and those of string variables must end with a dollar sign ($). The various variable types and the rules for naming them are summarized in Table 2-1.

Table 2-1. Variable Types

Type	**Suffix**	**Simple Examples**	**Array Examples**
Real	(none)	K	AGE (CHILD)
		PRICE	TAX (ITEM)
		N1	N1 (J%,3)
Integer	%	J%	YEAR% (N)
		G5%	BOOK% (COUNT)
		N1%	N1% (J%,3)
String	$	A$	SHOP$ (5)
		SAM$	DAY$ (WEEK)
		N1$	N1$ (J%,3)

A variable name can be up to 238 characters long, but Applesoft uses only the first two characters to distinguish one variable from another of the same type. Except for the suffix, all characters beyond the first two in a name are ignored, as long as they don't include a reserved word.

▲Warning

Take care not to begin the names of different variables of the same type with the same two characters. Applesoft considers the names SUM and SUNSTROKE, for example, to refer to the same variable, since they both begin with the same two characters.

Notice that this restriction applies only to variables of the same type. Applesoft considers the names TAX, TAX%, and TAX$ to refer to three different variables, even though they all begin with the same two characters, because they are of different types (real, integer, and string).

Reserved Words: Certain words used in Applesoft are reserved for special uses in specific commands; you can't use these words as variable names or as parts of variable names (even beyond the first two characters). For instance, TOTAL or SUBTOTAL are illegal as variable names, because they both contain the reserved word TO. See Appendix D for a list of Applesoft's reserved words.

2.1.2 Real Variables

A real variable can hold any numeric value, with or without a decimal point, between -9.99999999E+37 and +9.99999999E+37 (where "E+37" means "times 10 to the +37th power"). Applesoft represents real numbers to 32 bits (about 9 digits) of precision.

The name of a real variable must consist of letters and digits only. Some legal real variable names are

SAM
TAX
Q7
SUMOFALLNUMBERS

Until they are given some other value with an assignment statement, all real variables are preset to the value 0.

2.1.3 Integer Variables

Integer variables can hold only whole-number values between -32767 and +32767. The name of an integer variable must end with the percent character (%). Some legal integer variable names are

SHARE%
D5%
TAX%

Until they are given some other value with an assignment statement, all integer variables are preset to the value 0.

If a number containing a decimal fraction is assigned as the value of an integer variable, it is truncated to the next lowest whole number—*not* rounded to the nearest whole number:

`LET A% = 32.678`	Value 32 is assigned to variable A%.
`LET B% = -34.2`	Value -35 is assigned to variable B%.

2.1.4 String Variables

A **string** is a sequence of text characters (letters, digits, and punctuation marks). Just as you can write numeric constants such as 27 and 2.236 in your Applesoft programs, you can write string constants by enclosing the characters in the desired string between double quotation marks:

"NOT WITH A BANG BUT A WHIMPER"
"George Bernard Shaw"
"H234J7"
"$?*!!%"

> *Lowercase Okay:* Even though your version of Applesoft may not understand lowercase letters when you use them in keywords, it allows you to use them in a string constant, as the second example shows.

A string can contain from 0 to 255 characters; when it contains no characters it is called a **null string**. Two quotation marks with nothing between them denote the null string:

```
""
```

A string variable can hold any string as its value. Its name must end with a dollar sign ($). Some legal string variable names are

NAME$
S9$
J$

Until they are given some other value with an assignment statement, all string variables are preset to the null string.

2.1.5 Arrays: Collections of Variables

An **array** is a collection of variables referred to by the same name, usually holding a collection of data items that are related to each other in some logical or systematic way. The individual variables in the array are called its **elements**, and are distinguished from one another by means of identifying index numbers called **subscripts**.

An array can be of any type: integer, real, or string. Array names follow the same rules as simple variable names of the same type. To refer to a particular element of an array, write the array name followed by one or more subscripts, separated by commas and enclosed in parentheses. The subscripts refer to the position of the desired element within the array:

`Q (6)`	Element 6 of real array Q.
`FIGURE% (N)`	Element N of integer array FIGURE%.
`NAME$ (J - 3)`	Element J - 3 of string array NAME$.
`COUNT (SUM%, 2)`	Element (SUM%, 2) of real array COUNT.

Figure 2-1. A Typical Array

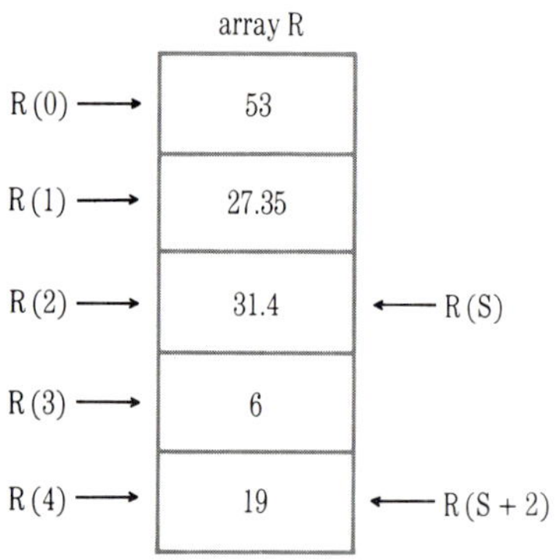

Figure 2-1 shows a real array named R with five elements, numbered 0 to 4. Element R(0) (pronounced *R-sub-zero*) holds the value 53, R(1) holds 27.35, and so on. If the value of variable S is 2, then the expression R(S) refers to element R(2), whose value is 31.4, and the expression R(S + 2) refers to element R(4), which holds the value 19.

For a more complete discussion of arrays and their use, see Section 4.1.

2.2 Assigning Values: The Assignment Statement

```
LET PI = 3.14159265
COUNT% = 0
```

When Applesoft begins running a program, it sets the values of all real and integer variables to 0 and the values of all string variables to the null string (that is, a string containing no characters). The program can then change the value of any variable at any time by executing an assignment statement.

> *Commands That Reset Variables:* The NEW (see Section 1.2.1), CLEAR (see Section 1.2.2), and RUN (see Section 1.2.4) commands also reset all real and integer variables to 0 and all string variables to the null string.

An **assignment statement** consists of the optional keyword LET, followed by the name of the variable whose value is to be changed, an equal sign (=), and an expression denoting the new value to be assigned to that variable. The equal sign means *receives the value* or *is assigned the value*; it is often read simply as *gets* ("X gets Y plus 2"). The assignment statement means *evaluate the expression to the right of the equal sign and assign the resulting value to the variable named to the left of the equal sign*. The variable holds that value until it is changed by another assignment statement or is reset by a NEW, CLEAR, or RUN command. For example:

`LET Q = 27.4`	Assigns value 27.4 to real variable Q.
`LET D3 = J`	Assigns current value of real variable J to real variable D3; variable J unchanged.
`COUNT% = A + B`	Assigns current value of real variable A plus current value of real variable B to integer variable COUNT%; variables A and B unchanged.
`S9% = 35`	Assigns value 35 to integer variable S9%.
`NAME$ = "SAM"`	Assigns string value "SAM" to string variable NAME$.

`NAME$ = SAM$`	Assigns current value of string variable SAM$ to string variable NAME$; variable SAM$ unchanged.
`BOX(5) = 36`	Assigns value 36 to element 5 of real array BOX.
`J% = A%(N)`	Assigns current value of element N of integer array A% to integer variable J%; array A% and variable N unchanged.
`SHOP$(N) = "BAKERY"`	Assigns value "BAKERY" to element N of string array SHOP$.

Keyword Optional: The keyword LET is optional in assignment statements. The statements

```
LET Q = 27.4
```

and

```
Q = 27.4
```

mean exactly the same thing.

2.3 Expressions

An **expression** is a formula describing a calculation for the computer to perform. It can involve any number of numeric variables and constants, together with operators specifying how the values of the variables and constants are to be combined. There are three kinds of operators that can be used in an Applesoft expression:

- **Arithmetic operators** (see Section 2.3.1) combine two numeric values and produce a numeric result.
- **Relational operators** (see Section 2.3.2) compare two values and produce a logical (true-or-false) result.
- **Logical operators** (see Section 2.3.3) combine two logical values and produce a logical result.

2.3.1 Arithmetic Operators

Arithmetic operators combine two numeric values to produce a numeric result. There are five of them in Applesoft, corresponding to the familiar operations of arithmetic: + (addition), — (subtraction), * (multiplication), / (division), and ^ (exponentiation). Here are some examples of their use:

`3 + 4`	3 plus 4, yielding 7.
`+144`	Plus 144 (a positive number).
`X + Y`	The value of X plus the value of Y.
`23.7 - 11.4`	23.7 minus 1.4, yielding 12.3.
`5Ø - 75`	50 minus 75, yielding -25.
`-144`	Minus 144 (a negative number).
`SUM% - 2`	The value of SUM% minus 2.
`13 * 5`	13 times 5, yielding 65.
`6 * .25`	6 times .25, yielding 1.5.
`25 * QUARTERS%`	25 times the value of QUARTERS%.
`4.8 * COUNT(5)`	4.8 times the value of element 5 of array COUNT.
`18 / 6`	18 divided by 6, yielding 3.
`6 / 18`	6 divided by 18, yielding .333333333.
`DIST / TIME`	The value of DIST divided by the value of TIME.
`DOLLARS% / 1ØØ`	The value of DOLLARS% divided by 100.
`2 ^ 3`	2 to the 3rd power, yielding 8.
`3 ^ .5`	3 to the .5 power, yielding 1.73205081.
`X ^ J%`	The value of X raised to the power of the value of J%.

> *Note:* Like most other computer languages, Applesoft uses an asterisk (*) instead of the letter x to represent multiplication.

What to Do With Fractions: Applesoft doesn't treat fractional numbers in the way that you are probably used to dealing with them. Most people would read the expression 3 3/4 as *three and three quarters.* To Applesoft, however, the same expression would mean *thirty-three divided by four.* (Applesoft ignores any spaces it finds in a number.)

It's easy to convert fractions to a form Applesoft understands correctly. Just think of 3 3/4 as *three plus three divided by four.* In other words, instead of typing

```
LET A = 3 3/4
```

type this:

```
LET A = 3 + 3/4
```

Applesoft does the rest.

2.3.2 Relational Operators

A **relational operator** tests for a relation between two values and produces a logical (true-or-false) result, depending on whether the particular relation does or doesn't hold between those two values. For example, the expression

```
A > B
```

means *the value of variable A is greater than that of variable B.* If the current value of variable A is 5 and that of B is 3, then the relation is true; if the value of B is 8, the relation is false.

Note: Relational operators are particularly useful in connection with the IF...THEN statement, discussed in Section 3.2.2.

The Truth About Applesoft: Applesoft actually uses numeric values to represent the logical values true and false: if the stated relation is true, the value of the relational expression is 1; if the relation is false, the value of the expression is 0. For example, if you type the statement

```
PRINT 6 > 12
```

in immediate execution, Applesoft responds by displaying the number 0, meaning false; if you type

```
PRINT 12 > 6
```

Applesoft displays the number 1, meaning true.

Applesoft has six relational operators (some of which can be written in more than one way):

= is equal to
< is less than
> is greater than
<= or =< is less than or equal to
>= or => is greater than or equal to
<> or >< is not equal to.

Here are some examples of their use:

`6 = 6`	6 equals 6, yielding 1 for true.
`6 = 12`	6 equals 12, yielding 0 for false.
`X = 2`	The value of X is equal to 2.
`NAME$ = "Ann"`	The value of NAME$ is equal to the string "Ann."
`6 < 6`	6 is less than 6, yielding 0 for false.
`6 < 12`	6 is less than 12, yielding 1 for true.
`PROBABILITY < .5`	The value of PROBABILITY is less than .5.
`6 > 6`	6 is greater than 6, yielding 0 for false.
`6 > 12`	6 is greater than 12, yielding 0 for false.
`AGE > 65`	The value of AGE is greater than 65.
`6 <= 6` `6 =< 6`	6 is less than or equal to 6, yielding 1 for true.
`6 <= 12` `6 =< 12`	6 is less than or equal to 12, yielding 1 for true.
`A% <= 3 * B%` `A% =< 3 * B%`	The value of A% is less than or equal to 3 times the value of B%.

`6 >= 6` `6 => 6`	6 is greater than or equal to 6, yielding 1 for true.
`6 >= 12` `6 => 12`	6 is greater than or equal to 12, yielding 0 for false.
`SALARY >= 20000` `SALARY => 20000`	The value of SALARY is greater than or equal to 20000.
`6 <> 6` `6 >< 6`	6 is not equal to 6, yielding 0 for false.
`6 <> 12` `6 >< 12`	6 is not equal to 12, yielding 1 for true.
`X <> Y` `X >< Y`	The value of X is not equal to the value of Y.
`BANG$ >< "WHIMPER"` `BANG$ <> "WHIMPER"`	The value of BANG$ is not equal to the string "WHIMPER."

2.3.3 Logical Operators

A **logical operator** combines two logical (true-or-false) values and produces a logical result. There are three logical operators in Applesoft: AND, OR, and NOT. Here are some examples of their use:

`6 <= 12 AND 6 >= 12`	6 is less than or equal to 12 and 6 is greater than or equal to 12; value is 0 for false.
`.25 <= R AND R < .75`	.25 is less than or equal to the value of R and the value of R is less than .75.
`6 <= 12 OR 6 >= 12`	6 is less than or equal to 12 or 6 is greater than or equal to 12; value is 1 for true.
`ANIMAL$ = "DOG" OR ANIMAL = "CAT"`	The value of ANIMAL$ is equal to the string "DOG" or the string "CAT."
`NOT (6 <= 12)`	6 is not less than or equal to 12; value is 0 for false.
`NOT (YEAR% > 1950)`	The value of YEAR% is not greater than 1950.

> *How OR Works:* Notice that the OR operator doesn't behave exactly the way we often use the word *or* in everyday speech. When we say "A or B is true," we usually mean that one of the two statements is true, but not both. The Applesoft OR operator produces a *true* value if either or both of its original expressions are true.

Applesoft's logical operators consider a numerical value of 0 to mean false; any numerical value other than 0 is taken to mean true. The logical operators always yield a value of 1 for true or 0 for false.

Logical operators are particularly useful in connection with the IF...THEN statement, discussed in Section 3.2.2.

2.3.4 Precedence of Operators

Operators in Applesoft have an order of precedence that determines which operations are carried out first when they are combined in an expression. Table 2-3 lists the operators in descending order of precedence. Operators shown higher in the list are carried out before those lower down. Operators on the same line of the list have the same precedence, and are carried out from left to right within an expression.

Table 2-3. Precedence of Operators

Parentheses (innermost first)	( )
Signed arithmetic and logical NOT	+ - NOT
Exponentiation (powers of numbers)	^
Multiplication and division	* /
Addition and subtraction	+ -
Relational operators	= < > <= =< >= => <> ><
Logical AND	AND
Logical OR	OR

Notice that the operators + and - have higher precedence when used to represent the sign of a number (as in +144 or -X) than when they stand for the operations of addition and subtraction.

To understand how Applesoft's precedence rules work, consider the expression

```
-2 * Z ^ 3 + Q / 5 - A * B
```

When Applesoft evaluates this expression, it begins by applying the first minus sign to the constant 2, obtaining a result of -2. Next it raises the value of Z to the 3rd power and multiplies the result by -2. Then it divides the value of Q by 5 and adds the result to that of the previous calculation. Finally, it multiplies the values of A and B and subtracts that result from the previous one.

For example, suppose the current values of the variables in this expression are as follows: Z = 2, Q = 10, A = 7, B = 4. Then

-2		= -2
Z ^ 3	= 2 ^ 3	= 8
-2 * 8		= -16
Q / 5	= 10 / 5	= 2
-16 + 2		= -14
A * B	= 7 * 4	= 28
-14 - 28		= -42

The value of the expression is -42.

Parentheses can be used to change the normal order of precedence. For example:

```
-2 * Z ^ (3 + Q) / 5 - A * B
```

Value is -3304.8; (3 + Q) evaluated as a unit.

```
-2 * Z ^ 3 + (Q / 5 - A) * B
```

Value is -36; (Q / 5 - A) evaluated as a unit.

```
-2 * Z ^ 3 + Q / (5 - A * B)
```

Value is -16.4347826; (Q / (5 - A * B)) evaluated as a unit.

The original expression above is equivalent to the fully parenthesized expression

```
(((-2) * (Z ^ 3)) + (Q / 5)) - (A * B)
```

Helpful Hint: When you're unsure of the order of precedence, use parentheses to make sure the expression is evaluated in the order you intend.

2.4 Functions

A **function** is a preprogrammed calculation that can be carried out on request. You can use functions whenever you need to perform the same calculation repeatedly throughout a program. Whenever you call a function (request its execution), you must give it a particular value to operate on; this value is called the **argument** of the function.

Applesoft offers a variety of built-in functions, discussed in Section 2.4.1, for calculating common mathematical values such as logarithms, cosines, and square roots. Section 2.4.2 covers the built-in function RND, used for generating random numbers. In addition, you can define your own functions for the special needs of a particular program—see Section 2.4.3 for details.

2.4.1 Built-in Arithmetic Functions

This section discusses the various built-in functions that Applesoft provides for calculating commonly used mathematical quantities. To call a built-in function, just type the name of the function followed by an expression in parentheses representing the argument value on which you want the function to operate. For example, suppose you need to calculate the square root of a number. Applesoft has a built-in function named SQR for this purpose; to find the square root of 3, type

```
SQR (3)
```

To find the square root of the value of variable X plus 2, type

```
SQR (X+2)
```

2.4.1.1 The ABS Function

The built-in function ABS computes the absolute value of a number—that is, the positive numerical value of the number, without regard to its original sign. For example,

`ABS (27)`	Absolute value of 27; yields 27.
`ABS (-27)`	Absolute value of -27; yields 27.
`ABS (36.8 - 23.3)`	Absolute value of 36.8 minus 23.3; yields 13.5.
`ABS (23.3 - 36.8)`	Absolute value of 23.3 minus 36.8; yields 13.5.
`ABS (C%(9))`	Absolute value of element 9 of array C%.

2.4.1.2 The SGN Function

The SGN function determines whether the value of its argument is positive, negative, or 0. It yields a result of 1 if the argument value is positive (greater than 0), -1 if the argument value is negative (less than 0), and 0 if the argument value is 0. For example,

`SGN (27)`	Sign of 27; yields 1 (positive).
`SGN (-27)`	Sign of -27; yields -1 (negative).
`SGN (36.8 - 23.3)`	Sign of 36.8 minus 23.3; yields 1 (positive).
`SGN (23.3 - 36.8)`	Sign of 23.3 minus 36.8; yields -1 (negative).
`SGN (9 * 5 - 45)`	Sign of 9 times 5 minus 45; yields 0.
`SGN (SUM - 20)`	Sign of SUM minus 20.

2.4.1.3 The INT Function

INT returns the integer (whole-number) part of its argument value, with the fractional part, if any, discarded. Note that this function makes no attempt at rounding: that is, if the argument value is not an integer, INT yields the next lower integer, not necessarily the nearer integer. For example,

`INT (27)`	Integer part of 27; yields 27.
`INT (36.8)`	Integer part of 36.8; yields 36.
`INT (-7.9)`	Integer part of -7.9; yields -8.
`INT (-62.1)`	Integer part of -62.1; yields -63.
`INT (5 * PRICE)`	Integer part of 5 times PRICE.

Rounding a Number: To make your program round a numeric value to the nearest integer, first add .5 and then apply the INT function to the result. For example, to find the nearest integer to the current value of variable AGE, use the expression

```
INT (AGE + .5)
```

2.4.1.4 The SQR Function

The SQR function computes the positive square root of its argument. For example,

`SQR (169)`	Square root of 169; yields 13.
`SQR (163.84)`	Square root of 163.84; yields 12.8.
`SQR (3)`	Square root of 3; yields 1.73205081.
`SQR (X^2 + 9)`	Square root of X squared plus 9.

If you try to take the square root of a negative number, an `ILLEGAL QUANTITY` error occurs.

2.4.1.5 The SIN Function

to convert **degrees to radians:** see Section 2.4.3

SIN computes the trigonometric sine of its argument. The argument must be expressed in radians (not degrees). For example, assuming the value of the variable PI is 3.14159265,

`SIN (PI / 3)`	Sine of PI / 3 radians; yields .866025403.
`SIN (1)`	Sine of 1 radian; yields .841470985.
`SIN (X^2 - Y^2)`	Sine of X squared minus Y squared.

2.4.1.6 The COS Function

COS computes the trigonometric cosine of its argument. The argument must be expressed in radians (not degrees). For example, assuming the value of the variable PI is 3.14159265,

`COS (PI / 3)`	Cosine of PI / 3 radians; yields .5.
`COS (1)`	Cosine of 1 radian; yields .540302306.
`COS (X^2 - Y^2)`	Cosine of X squared minus Y squared.

2.4.1.7 The TAN Function

TAN computes the trigonometric tangent of its argument. The argument must be expressed in radians (not degrees). For example, assuming the value of the variable PI is 3.14159265,

`TAN (PI / 3)`	Tangent of PI / 3 radians; yields 1.7320508.
`TAN (1)`	Tangent of 1 radian; yields 1.55740772.
`TAN (X^2 - Y^2)`	Tangent of X squared minus Y squared.

2.4.1.8 The ATN Function

ATN computes the trigonometric arc tangent (inverse tangent) of its argument: that is, the angle whose tangent is equal to the given value. The result is expressed in radians (not degrees). For example,

`ATN (SQR(3))`	Arc tangent of the square root of 3; yields 1.04719755 (= PI / 3) radians.
`ATN (1)`	Arc tangent of 1; yields .785398163 radians.
`ATN (X^2 - Y^2)`	Arc tangent of X squared minus Y squared.

2.4.1.9 The EXP Function

The EXP function calculates the mathematical exponential of its argument. The exponential is defined as the constant *e* raised to the power of the argument, where $e = 2.718281828$. For example,

`EXP (3)`	*e* to the 3rd power; yields 20.0855369.
`EXP (LOG(10))`	*e* to the power of the natural logarithm of 10; yields 10.
`EXP (A * T)`	*e* to the power A * T.

> ***Limited Accuracy:*** Although Applesoft displays the result of the EXP function to nine places, only the first six are actually reliable. For instance, in the first example above, the computed result of 20.0855369 should be interpreted simply as 20.0855.

2.4.1.10 The LOG Function

LOG calculates the natural logarithm of its argument (the logarithm to the base *e*, where *e* = 2.718281828.) For example,

`LOG (10)`	Natural logarithm of 10; yields 2.30258509.
`LOG (EXP(3))`	Natural logarithm of *e* to the 3rd power; yields 3.
`LOG (SIN(THETA))`	Natural logarithm of the sine of THETA.

If you try to take the logarithm of 0 or a negative number, an `ILLEGAL QUANTITY` error occurs.

2.4.2 Generating Random Numbers: The RND Function

The built-in function RND produces random decimal numbers between 0 and 1. The behavior of this function depends on whether the argument you give it is positive, 0, or negative.

The simplest way to use RND is to give it a positive argument. RND produces a different random number each time you call it with a positive argument. The actual numeric value of the argument is ignored; only its sign is significant:

`RND (1)`	Yields .431448496.
`RND (1)`	Yields .735966024.
`RND (99)`	Yields .345445325.

If you give RND a 0 argument, it reproduces the same result as at the previous call:

`RND (99)`	Yields .270011996.
`RND (0)`	Yields .270011996.
`RND (0)`	Yields .270011996.
`RND (99)`	Yields .139756248.
`RND (0)`	Yields .139756248.

Calling RND with a negative argument causes it to begin a new, repeatable sequence of random numbers. This is called seeding the random number generator; the particular negative value you use for the argument acts as a *seed* for the new sequence. Different seeds produce different sequences; but each time you use the same seed you get the same result. Subsequent calls to RND with positive arguments then produce the same sequence of results:

`RND (-1)`	Yields 2.99196472E-08.
`RND (1)`	Yields .738207502.
`RND (1)`	Yields .272707136.
`RND (1)`	Yields .299733446.
`RND (-5)`	Yields 3.73720468E-08; starts new sequence.
`RND (1)`	Yields .407457285.
`RND (1)`	Yields .463740324.
`RND (1)`	Yields .387195686.
`RND (-1)`	Yields 2.99196472E-08; repeats same sequence as before.
`RND (1)`	Yields .738207502.
`RND (1)`	Yields .272707136.
`RND (1)`	Yields .299733446.

Scientific Notation: The suffix E-08 in some of the random values listed above means *times 10 to the minus-8th power*, and is an example of the scientific notation that Applesoft uses to display certain numbers. See Section 5.2.3 for further details.

2.4.3 Defining Functions: The DEF FN Statement

```
DEF FN CUBE (X) = X * X * X
```

In addition to the built-in functions discussed in Sections 2.4.1 and 2.4.2, Applesoft gives you the ability to define your own functions for the special needs of a particular program. Defining your own functions can be a real time-saver: instead of writing out the same complex formula over and over again, you can simply define it once as a function, give it a name, and then refer to it by that name whenever you need it.

To define a function of your own, use the DEF FN statement. This statement consists of the keywords DEF FN (for define function) followed by the name of the function you're defining, the argument name enclosed in parentheses, an equal sign (=), and the formula defining the function.

argument: the value on which a function operates

The following examples define functions to convert temperatures from Fahrenheit to Celsius and vice versa, and to convert angles from degrees to radians and vice versa, assuming that the value of the variable PI is 3.14159265:

```
10  DEF FN FTC (T) = (T - 32) * 5 / 9
```

Fahrenheit to Celsius.

```
20  DEF FN CTF (T) = T * (9 / 5) + 32
```

Celsius to Fahrenheit.

```
30  DEF FN DTR (A) = A * (PI / 180)
```

Degrees to radians.

```
40  DEF FN RTD (A) = A * (180 / PI)
```

Radians to degrees.

For example, the definition for function FTC says *to convert from Fahrenheit to Celsius, take the value of the argument (T), subtract 32, multiply by 5, and divide by 9.*

Formula Length Limit: The formula defining a function must not exceed one program line (239 characters) in length.

The names you give to your functions must follow the same rules given in Section 2.1.1 for variable names: the name can be as long as you like (up to 239 characters), but Applesoft uses only the first two characters to distinguish one function from another. The argument variable in the function definition must be a real variable—integer and string variables (ending in % or $) are not allowed.

Be Careful With Function Names: Take care not to begin the names of different functions with the same two characters. Applesoft considers the names CODFISH and COUNT, for example, to refer to the same function, because they both begin with the same two characters. If you try to define functions with these two names, the second definition redefines the function, causing the first definition to be forgotten.

However, a program can have a function and an array beginning with the same two characters (or even having exactly the same name). This is because references to the function are written with the keyword FN, but references to the array aren't. Thus Applesoft can tell that, for example,

```
FN COUNT (N)
```

is a call to the function named COUNT, whereas

```
COUNT (N)
```

is a reference to the array of the same name.

The DEF FN statement can be executed only from within a program; you can't use this statement in immediate execution.

To call a function that you've defined with DEF FN, type the keyword FN (for function) followed by the name of the function and an expression in parentheses representing the argument value on which you want the function to operate. For example, using the functions you defined,

`FN FTC (98.6)`	Converts 98.6 degrees Fahrenheit to Celsius; yields 37.
`FN CTF (100)`	Converts 100 degrees Celsius to Fahrenheit; yields 212.
`FN DTR (180)`	Converts 180 degrees to radians; yields 3.14159265.
`FN RTD (PI / 2)`	Converts PI / 2 radians to degrees; yields 90.

Note that the keyword FN is used in calling your own defined functions, but not for built-in functions. (See Section 2.4.1.)

Chapter 3

Control Statements

Ordinarily, Applesoft program lines are executed sequentially, from the lowest-numbered line to the highest. Control statements allow you to branch to another part of the program: that is, to alter the order of execution and send control to a line of the program other than the next line in sequence. This ability to change the course of program flow is what gives computer programs their real power and flexibility.

- Section 3.1, "Unconditional Branching: The GOTO Statement," deals with the GOTO statement, which sends control unconditionally to a specified line of the program.
- Section 3.2, "Conditional Branching," discusses conditional branching statements, which allow the program to decide what to do next by evaluating an expression or testing for a condition.
- Section 3.3, "Loops," covers statements that are used in loops (portions of a program that are executed many times repeatedly).
- Section 3.4, "Subroutines," deals with the very important subject of subroutines: sections of a program that can be executed on request from elsewhere in the program to perform some particular task.
- Section 3.5, "Error Handling," describes Applesoft's facilities for detecting and dealing with error conditions that arise during the execution of a program.
- Section 3.6, "Program Termination," covers the various ways of ending program execution.

3.1 Unconditional Branching: The GOTO Statement

```
GOTO 100
```

An **unconditional branch** sends control to a specified line of the program without reference to whether any particular condition holds. Applesoft has two statements that cause an unconditional branch: GOTO and GOSUB. The GOTO statement is described in this section; see Section 3.4.1 for a description of the GOSUB statement.

The GOTO statement interrupts the normal sequential execution of program lines and forces execution to branch to (go to) a specified line number. The branch is unconditional: that is, it doesn't depend on the truth or falsity of any particular condition.

For example, consider the following program:

`10 PRINT "HELLO"`	Displays the word HELLO.
`20 PRINT "THERE"`	Displays the word THERE.
`30 GOTO 10`	Branches to line 10.
`40 PRINT "FRIEND"`	This line never executed.

This program displays the word HELLO on the screen (line 10), displays the word THERE (line 20), and then (line 30) goes back to line 10 to repeat the process. The word FRIEND never gets displayed, because program execution never reaches line 40. Instead, the program simply repeats lines 10 to 30 indefinitely, displaying the words HELLO and THERE over and over again on the screen.

loops: see Section 3.3

> *Stopping an Infinite Loop:* This program contains an example of an infinite loop. To stop the program and regain control of the computer, press CONTROL-C.

If your program attempts to branch to a nonexistent line, or if a GOTO statement does not include a line number, an error message such as ?UNDEF'D STATEMENT ERROR IN 20 appears, identifying the program line in which the error occurred. The program stops and Applesoft returns to command level.

`10 PRINT "HELLO"`	
`20 PRINT "THERE"`	
`30 GOTO 15`	Branches to nonexistent line.
`40 PRINT "FRIEND"`	

> *You Can't Branch to a Variable:* If you attempt to use a variable instead of an actual line number to specify the line to which the program should branch (as in GOTO J), Applesoft branches to line number 0, no matter what value the variable holds. If line 0 doesn't exist, an UNDEF'D STATEMENT error occurs:
>
> | | |
> |---|---|
> | `5 LET J = 10` | Assigns value to variable. |
> | `10 PRINT "HELLO"` | |
> | `20 PRINT "THERE"` | |
> | `30 GOTO J` | Applesoft tries to go to line number 0. |
> | `40 PRINT "FRIEND"` | |

3.2 Conditional Branching

A **conditional branch** decides what action to take next, depending on the truth of a stated condition or on the value of an arithmetic expression. Applesoft has three statements that cause a conditional branch:

- ON...GOTO (see Section 3.2.1) branches to one of a number of possible program lines, depending on the value of an arithmetic expression.
- ON...GOSUB (see Section 3.4.3) branches to one of a number of possible subroutines, depending on the value of an arithmetic expression.
- IF...THEN (see Section 3.2.2) either executes or skips one or more statements, depending on the truth of a stated condition.

3.2.1 The ON...GOTO Statement

```
ON X GOTO 150, 200, 310, 310, 150, 999
ON S% - 7 GOTO 300, 285, 900, 150
```

The ON...GOTO statement sends control to one of a list of line numbers, depending on the integer value of an arithmetic expression. The expression between the keywords ON and GOTO is evaluated; if the result is real it is truncated to an integer. If this value is between 1 and the number of line numbers in the list, program execution branches to the line number at the corresponding position in the list. (For example, if the integer value of the expression is 3, execution branches to the third line number in the list.) If the integer value of the expression is 0 or is greater than the length of the list, execution continues with the next statement following the ON...GOTO.

The following program illustrates the use of ON...GOTO:

```
10   INPUT X                              Gets number from keyboard.
20   ON X GOTO 150, 200, 310, 310, 150, 999
                                          Decides where to go, depending on
                                          value of X.
30   PRINT "VALUE OUT OF RANGE, PLEASE RETYPE; "
                                          Control comes here if X = 0 or
                                          X > 6.
40   GOTO 10                              Starts again.
150  PRINT "VALUE IS 1 OR 5"
                                          Control comes here if X = 1 or
                                          X = 5.
160  GOTO 10
200  PRINT "VALUE IS 2"                   Control comes here if X = 2.
210  GOTO 10
310  PRINT "VALUE IS 3 OR 4"
                                          Control comes here if X = 3 or
                                          X = 4.
320  GOTO 10
999  END                                  Control comes here if X = 6.
```

If the integer value of the expression between ON and GOTO is less than 0 or greater than 255, an `ILLEGAL QUANTITY` error occurs and program execution halts.

3.2.2 The IF...THEN Statement

```
IF Z > 255 THEN END
IF H% - 23 < SM - TTL THEN K% = H% - 23 : H% = 0
IF X (I) = 12 THEN GOTO 325
IF A$ >< B$ THEN 300
IF (DELTA > .05) AND NOT (E > .1) GOTO 2150
```

The IF...THEN statement tests for the condition given between the keywords IF and THEN. If the condition is true, the statement or statements following THEN in the same program line are executed. If the condition is false, the remainder of the line following THEN is skipped and execution continues with the next program line in sequence.

When You Can Omit a Keyword: When the statement following THEN is a GOTO, either (but not both) of the keywords THEN and GOTO can be omitted. The following statements are all equivalent:

```
IF X (I) = 12 THEN GOTO 325
IF X (I) = 12 THEN 325
IF X (I) = 12 GOTO 325
```

Notice that when the IF condition is false, program execution continues with the next program line in sequence. No other statements in the IF line are carried out:

```
10  LET J = 1 : K = 2
20  LET A = 10                          A is set to 10 here.
30  PRINT "J HOLDS "; J; " AND K HOLDS "; K
40  IF A > 10 THEN J = 5 : K = 10 : GOTO 100
                                        A is not greater than 10; test fails.
50  PRINT "THE VALUES OF J AND K ARE UNCHANGED."
                                        This message gets printed.
60  GOTO 999
100  PRINT "J NOW HOLDS "; J; " AND K HOLDS "; K
                                        This message is not printed.
999  END
```

When this program is run, the IF test in line 40 fails, the values of J and K are not changed, and execution continues with line 50. If line 20 were changed to

```
20  LET A = 25
```

then the IF test in line 40 would succeed, the values of J and K would be changed, and control would branch to line 100.

Using Numeric Values With IF...THEN: The IF...THEN statement considers a numeric value of 0 to mean false; any nonzero value is taken to mean true. Thus you can write statements such as

```
IF J THEN GOSUB 400
```

which is equivalent to

```
IF J <> 0 THEN GOSUB 400
```

Recall also that Applesoft's relational and logical operators always yield a value of 1 for true and 0 for false. Thus you can combine numeric values with the logical operators: the statement

```
IF NOT J THEN GOTO 500
```

is equivalent to

```
IF J = 0 THEN GOTO 500
```

and

```
IF A AND B THEN END
```

is equivalent to

```
IF (A <> 0) AND (B <> 0) THEN END
```

Numeric values used in this way offer two advantages over the corresponding relational expressions:

- □ They take up less space in memory.
- □ They execute somewhat faster.

See Appendix G for further hints on making your programs more efficient.

Curious Parsing: Applesoft gets confused if the keyword THEN is immediately preceded by a variable name ending in the letter *A*. For example, the statement

```
IF J = BETA THEN 230
```

is interpreted as

```
IF J = BET AT HEN230
```

causing a syntax error. This is because AT and THEN are both reserved words. In the example, the word AT is encountered first, so it is interpreted first. Such is life with Applesoft. You can get around the problem by using parentheses:

```
IF (J = BETA) THEN 230
```

3.3 Loops

A **loop** is a sequence of statements in a program that is executed repeatedly, often with the value of some variable being changed on each pass through the loop. Loops are fundamental to all computer programming: it's practically impossible to write any kind of useful or interesting program that doesn't include at least one loop.

The usual way of writing loops in Applesoft is with the FOR (see Section 3.3.1) and NEXT (see Section 3.3.2) statements. The FOR statement marks the beginning of the loop. It identifies the loop's **index variable** (the variable whose value changes on each pass through the loop) and gives the starting and ending values the index variable is to take on. Sometimes it also specifies the amount by which the value of the index variable is to change on each pass.

The NEXT statement marks the end of the loop and causes the loop to be executed again for the next value of the index variable. When the loop has been executed once for each value of the index variable, as specified in the FOR statement, control passes (falls through) to the statement immediately following the NEXT statement.

Here's an example to show how loops work:

`5 PASS = 0`	Initializes pass count.
`10 FOR X = 3 TO 10`	Executes loop eight times, once for each value of X from 3 to 10.
`20 PASS = PASS + 1`	Counts passes through the loop.
`30 PRINT "PASS #"; PASS`	Displays pass count.
`40 PRINT "INDEX = ";X`	Displays current value of index variable X.
`50 PRINT`	Displays blank line (for neatness).
`60 NEXT X`	Repeats loop for next value of X.
`70 PRINT "LOOP FINISHED"`	Control comes here after last pass through loop.
`80 END`	

The loop begins with the FOR statement in line 10, which specifies that the loop is to be executed once for each value of index variable X from 3 to 10. Lines 20 to 50 form the body of the loop. The NEXT statement in line 60 marks the end of the loop and sends control back to line 20 for the next value of X. After the loop is executed for the last time, with X set to the specified ending value of 10, X is increased to 11. Since this exceeds the ending value, control falls through the NEXT statement to line 70.

When this program is executed, it displays the following results on the screen:

```
PASS #1
INDEX = 3

PASS #2
INDEX = 4

PASS #3
INDEX = 5

PASS #4
INDEX = 6

PASS #5
INDEX = 7

PASS #6
INDEX = 8

PASS #7
INDEX = 9

PASS #8
INDEX = 10

LOOP FINISHED
```

Loop Before You Leap: Exiting from the middle of a FOR/NEXT loop before the index variable reaches the ending value leaves Applesoft expecting a resolution that never comes. This is a dangerous practice that can cause unpredictable results in your program's execution. Don't write loops of the form

```
10  FOR INDEX = LOW TO HIGH
20  LET COUNT = COUNT + 1
30  IF COUNT = LIMIT THEN GOTO 100
40  NEXT INDEX
```

To be on the safe side, it's better to finish the loop this way:

```
30  IF COUNT = LIMIT THEN INDEX = HIGH :
    NEXT INDEX : GOTO 100
```

3.3.1 The FOR Statement

```
FOR Y = 1 TO 10
FOR MASS = 3.5 TO 7 STEP 1.5
FOR YEAR = 1980 TO 1960 STEP -4
FOR V = A + 2 TO 2*B - 3 STEP C / 2
```

The FOR statement marks the beginning of a loop, identifies the loop's index variable, and gives the starting and ending values of the index variable. It may also optionally specify the **step value**, the amount by which the value of the index variable is to change on each pass through the loop. If no step value is given, a value of 1 is understood.

In the example in Section 3.3, no step value was given, so the index variable X was incremented by 1 on each pass through the loop. If line 10 in the example were changed to

```
10  FOR X = 3 TO 10 STEP 2
```

the program would execute a loop for each value of X from 3 to 10 by 2s and would produce the following output on the display screen:

```
PASS #1
INDEX = 3

PASS #2
INDEX = 5

PASS #3
INDEX = 7

PASS #4
INDEX = 9

LOOP FINISHED
```

The loop would be executed four times, with the index variable taking on values of 3, 5, 7, and 9. At the end of the fourth pass, the index variable would exceed the specified ending value (9 plus 2 is 11, which is greater than the ending value of 10), so the loop would end and execution would continue with the statement following the NEXT in line 60.

Applesoft Will Try Anything Once: Notice that the test to see whether the index variable exceeds the ending value is carried out at the *end* of the loop. This means the body of the loop is always executed at least once. Even if the specified starting value is greater than the ending value, as in

```
10  FOR X = 10 TO 3
```

it won't be discovered until after the loop has been executed once (10 plus 1 is 11, which is greater than 3).

It's also possible to specify a negative step value:

```
10  FOR X = 10 TO 3 STEP -2
```

In this case the index variable takes values of 10, 8, 6, and 4. When the step value is negative, the loop ends when the index value becomes less than the ending value (4 plus -2 is 2, which is less than the ending value of 3). Notice that the starting and ending values have been reversed; if the statement read

```
10  FOR X = 3 TO 10 STEP -2
```

the loop would be executed only once (3 plus -2 is 1, which is less than 10).

Stopping an Infinite Loop: A step value of 0 results in an infinite loop. To stop the program and regain control of the computer, press [CONTROL]-[C].

The index variable specified in a FOR statement must be a real variable. Attempting to use an integer variable, such as

```
10  FOR X% = 3 TO 10
```

causes a syntax error at run time. (However, the expressions for the starting, ending, and step values are unrestricted; any or all of these values can be specified by an integer variable.)

3.3.2 The NEXT Statement

```
NEXT
NEXT INDEX
NEXT J,I
```

The NEXT statement marks the end of a loop and causes the loop to be repeated for the next value of the index variable, as specified in the corresponding FOR statement. When the value of the index variable becomes greater than the specified ending value (less than the ending value if the step value is negative), execution proceeds with the statement immediately following the NEXT statement.

Naming the index variable in a NEXT statement is optional; if you omit it, Applesoft automatically repeats the most recently entered loop. If you're using nested loops (see Section 5.3.3), this means the innermost loop containing the NEXT statement is repeated.

> *Helpful Hint:* Leaving out the index variable in NEXT statements makes your programs run slightly faster:
>
> ```
> 10  FOR G = 1 TO 6
> 20  PRINT "WOW, MOM!"
> 30  NEXT                        No index variable necessary.
> ```

3.3.3 Nesting of Loops

FOR/NEXT loops can be nested one inside another to a maximum depth of ten levels. For example,

```
10  FOR A = 1 TO 3              Starts outer loop.
20  FOR B = 1 TO 2              Starts inner loop.
30  PRINT "A = "; A; ", B = "; B
                                Displays values of index variables.
40  NEXT B                      Repeats inner loop.
50  NEXT A                      Outer loop is not repeated until
                                inner loop is finished.
```

The inner loop (lines 20 to 40) is executed twice for each pass through the outer loop; the PRINT statement in line 30 is executed six times in all. This program displays the following on the screen:

```
A = 1, B = 1
A = 1, B = 2
A = 2, B = 1
A = 2, B = 2
A = 3, B = 1
A = 3, B = 2
```

Although this example shows only two levels of nesting, Applesoft allows as many as ten levels (a loop inside a loop inside a loop...ten times). If you nest your loops to a depth greater than ten, your program halts with an `OUT OF MEMORY` error message.

Nested loops must not cross each other—that is, each loop must be completely contained within the body of the next outer loop. Once a loop is started using a particular index variable, the corresponding NEXT must name the same index variable (if it names any at all). In the example above, if lines 40 and 50 were reversed

```
40  NEXT A        Attempts to repeat outer loop
50  NEXT B        before inner loop is finished.
```

the program would halt with an error because of the crossed loops.

> *Combining NEXT Statements:* When two or more NEXT statements occur in a row, you can combine them into a single NEXT statement of the form
>
> ```
> 40  NEXT B,A
> ```
>
> Notice, however, that the index variables must be listed in the reverse order of their corresponding FOR statements, to avoid crossing loops. The statement
>
> ```
> 40  NEXT A,B
> ```
>
> causes the program to end abruptly with the messsage `NEXT WITHOUT FOR ERROR`.

3.4 Subroutines

A **subroutine** is a section of a program that can be executed on request from another part of the program. Applesoft has four statements relating to subroutines:

- GOSUB (see Section 3.4.1) directs control to a particular subroutine.
- RETURN (see Section 3.4.2) sends control back to the statement following the GOSUB that branched to the subroutine.
- ON...GOSUB (see Section 3.4.3) selects one of a number of possible subroutines, depending on the value of an arithmetic expression.
- POP (see Section 3.4.4) removes a return address from the top of the control stack (see the box entitled "How Subroutines Stack Up" later in this section).

To call a subroutine (request its execution), branch to its first line with a GOSUB statement. GOSUB differs from an ordinary GOTO (see Section 3.1) in that it remembers where in the program the subroutine was called from, so that control can return to that point when the subroutine is finished. The same subroutine can be called from many different places in the program; when the subroutine is finished, it sends control back to the statement following the proper **point of call** by executing a RETURN statement.

Here's an example to illustrate the idea:

`10 FOR Z = 1 TO 10`	Executes loop ten times.
`20 LET X = INT (RND (1) * 100)`	Generates a random integer between 0 and 99.
`30 PRINT X " IS ";`	Displays first part of message.
`40 IF X < 50 THEN GOSUB 1000 : GOTO 60`	Branches to subroutine at line 1000 if random number is less than 50; on return, goes to line 60.
`50 GOSUB 2000`	Branches to subroutine at line 2000 if random number is 50 or greater.
`60 PRINT "PASS #"; Z : PRINT`	Counts number of passes through loop.
`70 NEXT Z`	Repeats loop.
`999 END`	Ends program.
`1000 PRINT "LESS THAN 50"`	Prints second part of message for numbers less than 50.
`1010 RETURN`	Returns to statement following point of call.
`2000 PRINT "MORE THAN 49"`	Prints second part of message for numbers greater than 49.
`2010 RETURN`	Returns to statement following point of call.

The loop in lines 10 to 70 generates a random integer between 0 and 99, then calls one of the two subroutines at lines 1000 and 2000, depending on the value of the random number. Each of the subroutines displays an appropriate message, then returns control to the statement following the point of call with a RETURN statement (lines 1010 and 2010). The program then displays a count of the number of passes through the loop and repeats the loop from the beginning. When the loop has been executed ten times, the program ends.

Notice that the RETURN statement returns control to the *statement* following the GOSUB statement, not just to the *line* following it. In line 40 of the example, if the random number generated is less than 50, control is directed to the routine at line 1000. When execution returns from the subroutine, it continues with the statement GOTO 60, branching around line 50.

> ***Don't Use the Back Door:*** Every subroutine should be regarded as a separate, indivisible unit of your program, which should be entered only with a GOSUB and exited only with a RETURN. Careful programmers avoid jumping into or out of the middle of a subroutine with an ordinary GOTO which subverts Applesoft's orderly control stack mechanism. (See "How Subroutines Stack Up," later in this section.)

Subroutine calls can be nested: that is, you can call one subroutine from inside another. Consider the following program:

`10 GOSUB 1000`	Branches to first subroutine.
`20 PRINT "BACK HOME AGAIN"`	This message is displayed last.
`30 END`	Prevents control from accidentally "falling into" a subroutine.
`1000 PRINT "FIRST SUBROUTINE CALLED"`	This message is displayed first.
`1010 GOSUB 2000`	Branches to second subroutine.
`1020 PRINT "BACK AT FIRST SUBROUTINE"`	This message is displayed third.
`1030 RETURN`	Returns to statement following point of call (line 20).
`2000 PRINT "SECOND SUBROUTINE CALLED"`	This message is displayed second.
`2010 RETURN`	Returns to statement following point of call (line 1020).

Line 10 calls the first subroutine, at line 1000. This subroutine displays the first message on the screen, then (line 1010) calls the second subroutine at line 2000. The second subroutine displays its message, then returns control (line 2010) to the statement following the point of call in the first subroutine. The first subroutine then displays another message and returns control (line 1030) to the statement following its point of call. The final message is then displayed (line 20) and the program ends. The lines of the program are executed in the following order:

Line 10
Line 1000
Line 1010
Line 2000
Line 2010
Line 1020
Line 1030
Line 20
Line 30

The program produces the following output on the screen:

```
FIRST SUBROUTINE CALLED
SECOND SUBROUTINE CALLED
BACK AT FIRST SUBROUTINE
BACK HOME AGAIN
```

> *How Subroutines Stack Up:* Applesoft maintains a **control stack** to keep track of the **return addresses**—the points to which control is to return on completion—for all subroutines in progress. Each time a GOSUB is executed, the location of the statement following the GOSUB is **pushed** onto the top of the stack. When a RETURN statement is executed, the top entry is **popped** from the stack and control is directed to that point in the program. This arrangement ensures that control enters and leaves subroutines in LIFO (last-in-first-out) order.

Subroutine calls can be nested up to 25 levels deep: that is, you can GOSUB from a GOSUB from a GOSUB...24 times. Attempting to go more than 25 levels deep results in an `OUT OF MEMORY` error. If this error occurs, you're actually out of stack space, as opposed to program space. Since no rational BASIC program ever uses such complex nesting, this error usually means you've got a subroutine accidentally calling itself.

3.4.1 The GOSUB Statement

```
GOSUB 1000
```

The GOSUB (for go to subroutine) statement is used to branch to a subroutine, saving a return address to which control can return when the subroutine is completed. The location of the statement immediately following GOSUB is pushed onto the control stack (see Section 3.4), and control is sent to the line number specified in the GOSUB statement. GOSUB differs from an ordinary GOTO (see Section 3.1) in that it remembers where in the program the subroutine was called from, so that control can return to that point when the subroutine ends with a RETURN statement.

A GOSUB to a target line that doesn't exist causes a message such as `?UNDEF'D STATEMENT ERROR IN 1350` to be displayed, identifying the line number in which the error occurred, and your program comes to an untimely halt.

3.4.2 The RETURN Statement

```
RETURN
```

The RETURN statement returns control from a subroutine to the statement following its point of call. The top entry is popped off the control stack and control is sent to that return address.

If the control stack is empty when RETURN is executed, your program halts with the message `?RETURN WITHOUT GOSUB`.

3.4.3 The ON...GOSUB Statement

```
ON X GOSUB 150, 200, 310, 310, 150, 999
ON S% - 7 GOSUB 300, 285, 900, 150
```

The ON...GOSUB statement sends control to one of a list of subroutines, depending on the integer value of an arithmetic expression. The expression between the keywords ON and GOSUB is evaluated; if the result is real, it is truncated to an integer. If this value is between 1 and the number of line numbers in the list, program execution branches to the subroutine at the corresponding position in the list. (For example, if the integer value of the expression is 3, execution branches to the subroutine beginning at the third line number in the list.) If the integer value of the expression is 0 or is greater than the length of the list, execution continues with the next statement following the ON...GOSUB.

The following program illustrates the use of ON...GOSUB:

```
10   INPUT X                                  Gets number from keyboard.
20   ON X GOSUB 150, 200, 310, 310, 150, 999
                                              Decides where to go, depending on
                                              value of X.
30   IF X = 0 OR X = 6 THEN PRINT "VALUE OUT OF RANGE,
     PLEASE RETYPE: "                         Displays message if X out of range.
40   GOTO 10                                  Starts again.
150  PRINT "VALUE IS 1 OR 5"
                                              Control comes here if X = 1 or
                                              X = 5.
160  RETURN
200  PRINT "VALUE IS 2"                       Control comes here if X = 2.
210  RETURN
310  PRINT "VALUE IS 3 OR 4"
                                              Control comes here if X = 3 or
                                              X = 4.
320  RETURN
999  END                                      Control comes here if X = 6.
```

Compare this program with the example given for the ON...GOTO statement in Section 3.2.1. The operation of ON...GOSUB is very similar to that of ON...GOTO, except that ON...GOSUB remembers where in the program the subroutine was called from by pushing onto the control stack the location of the next statement following ON...GOSUB. Control can then return to that point with a RETURN statement when the subroutine is finished.

If the integer value of the expression between ON and GOSUB is less than 0 or greater than 255, an `ILLEGAL QUANTITY` error occurs and program execution halts.

3.4.4 The POP Statement

```
POP
```

The POP statement removes (pops) the top return address from the control stack without sending control to that point. This causes the next RETURN statement to send control back to the point of the second most recent subroutine call, instead of the most recent.

Here's an example illustrating the use of POP:

```
10   GOSUB 1000                      Branches to first subroutine.
20   PRINT "BACK HOME AGAIN"         This message is displayed last.
30   END                             Prevents control from accidentally
                                     "falling into" a subroutine.
1000   PRINT "FIRST SUBROUTINE CALLED"
                                     This message is displayed first.
1010   GOSUB 2000                    Branches to second subroutine.
1020   PRINT "BACK AT FIRST SUBROUTINE"
                                     This message is never displayed.
1030   RETURN                        This return is never taken.
2000   PRINT "SECOND SUBROUTINE CALLED"
                                     This message is displayed second.
2005   POP                           Removes return address from stack.
2010   RETURN                        Returns to first subroutine's point of
                                     call (line 20).
```

This program is identical to the one in Section 3.4 illustrating nested subroutine calls, except that a POP statement (line 2005) has been added to the second subroutine. The effect of the POP is to remove the second subroutine's return address (line 1020) from the control stack, causing the RETURN in line 2010 to go back to the statement following the point of call of the first subroutine (line 20) instead. As a result, lines 1020 and 1030 are never executed, and the message `BACK AT FIRST SUBROUTINE` is never displayed. The lines of the program are executed in the following order:

Line 10
Line 1000
Line 1010
Line 2000
Line 2005
Line 2010
Line 20
Line 30

The program produces the following output on the screen:

```
FIRST SUBROUTINE CALLED
SECOND SUBROUTINE CALLED
BACK HOME AGAIN
```

If the control stack is empty when POP is executed, your program halts with a `RETURN WITHOUT GOSUB` error.

Resist Temptation: Although it's sometimes tempting to try to get out of a tight programming situation by using POP, most good programmers avoid it, because it makes program flow really difficult to follow. If you find yourself becoming ensnared in convoluted code, 'tis a far better thing to redesign your program than to resort to the use of POP. Refer to Chapter 8 for a tutorial on program planning.

3.5 Error Handling

Sometimes even the most carefully written program comes to an embarrassing halt at an inopportune moment because of an error. If you've never suffered an "error crash," you're not a programmer. Applesoft's ONERR GOTO (see Section 3.5.1) and RESUME (see Section 3.5.2) statements provide a mechanism for detecting program errors as they occur and dealing with them from within your program. Using these statements, you can make your program display its own error messages or take any other action you consider appropriate, instead of coming to a sudden, screeching stop.

3.5.1 The ONERR GOTO Statement

```
ONERR GOTO 20000
```

The ONERR GOTO statement turns off Applesoft's normal error handling and replaces it with an error-handling subroutine in your program. After this statement is executed, program errors no longer stop the program, but instead transfer control to the error routine beginning at the specified line number.

Before sending control to the error routine, Applesoft stores an **error code** identifying the type of error at a special location in the computer's memory, location 222. The error routine can then look at the contents of this location with the PEEK function (see Section 7.1.1) and decide what action to take, depending on the error. Table 3-1 lists the possible error codes and their meanings. See Appendix E, for further information on the conditions that cause each type of error.

Table 3-1. Error Codes

Code	**Meaning**
0	NEXT without FOR
16	Syntax error
22	RETURN without GOSUB
42	Out of data
53	Illegal quantity
69	Overflow
77	Out of memory
90	Undefined statement
107	Bad subscript
120	Redimensioned array
133	Division by 0
163	Type mismatch
176	String too long
191	Formula too complex
224	Undefined function
254	Bad response to INPUT statement
255	CONTROL-C interrupt attempted

To prevent an error from interrupting the program, the ONERR GOTO statement must be executed before the error occurs. If you're using ONERR GOTO, it's a good idea to make it one of the first lines in your program, as in the following example:

```
10    ONERR GOTO 21500                 Establishes error routine at
                                       line 21500.
.
.
.
21500   LET EC = PEEK (222)   Gets error code.
21510   IF EC <> 255 THEN 21550
                                       Branches if not CONTROL-C.
21520   PRINT "SORRY--PROGRAM CAN'T BE STOPPED WITH
        CONTROL-C"                     If user pressed CONTROL-C,
                                       displays special message...
21530   RESUME                         ...and resumes program
21550   PRINT "UNANTICIPATED ERROR, CODE "; EC
                                       On any other error, displays general
                                       message...
21560   STOP                           ...and halts
```

This program uses its own error-handling routine to prevent the user from interrupting execution by pressing [CONTROL]-[C]. Line 10 turns off Applesoft's normal error handling and substitutes instead the program's own error routine, beginning at line 21500.

If an error later occurs, the first thing the error routine does (line 21500) is get the error code from memory location 222 to find out what type of error occurred. The error code is assigned to variable EC to make it easier to handle. Line 21510 tests for an error code of 255, meaning "[CONTROL]-[C] interrupt attempted" (see Table 3-1). If the error is a [CONTROL]-[C], the message `SORRY--PROGRAM CAN'T BE STOPPED WITH CONTROL-C` is displayed on the screen (line 21520) and control is sent back to the point of the error with the RESUME statement in line 21530.

If the error isn't a [CONTROL]-[C], the IF...THEN test in line 21510 sends control to line 21550. Since the error routine has no special action to take for any of these other errors, and since Applesoft's normal error messages are not being displayed, the error routine just displays a general error message such as `UNANTICIPATED ERROR, CODE 16` (for a syntax error) and stops the program.

▲Warning Once an ONERR GOTO statement has been executed, ordinary error messages are not displayed and the program does not stop if an error is detected. If your program's own error routine doesn't take some appropriate action (such as stop) for every possible error code, the program may hang indefinitely or exhibit other forms of deviant behavior. Make sure your error routine tells the computer what to do in all possible cases of error; see "More PEEKing" for suggestions.

More PEEKing: In the preceding program, the general error message displayed in line 21550 would be more useful if it included the line number where the error occurred as well as the error code itself. Through the magic of the PEEK function (see Section 7.1.1), the following two lines (replacing line 21550 of the original example) do this:

```
21550  EL = PEEK (219) * 256 + PEEK (218)
                                          Gets error line.
21555  PRINT "UNANTICIPATED ERROR, CODE "; EC; ",
       IN LINE "; EL              Displays general error message.
```

For an even nicer way of handling unanticipated errors, see Section 3.5.3 and Appendix F.

The ONERR GOTO statement can be executed only from within a program; you can't use this statement in immediate execution.

3.5.2 The RESUME Statement

```
RESUME
```

The RESUME statement returns control from an error-handling routine to the statement in which the error occurred. It should be used only in error routines, and should never be encountered in the normal flow of control.

▲Warning

If Applesoft encounters a RESUME statement without an error having occurred, the program may stop or hang indefinitely, or other unpredictable, but probably unpleasant, events may happen.

Notice that when an error has occurred, RESUME sends control back to the same statement that caused the error in the first place. If the same error occurs again, the program may hang in an infinite loop. Similarly, if an error occurs within the error-handling routine itself, RESUME causes the program to hang.

Cleaning the Stack: When an error occurs while an ONERR GOTO statement is in effect, Applesoft pushes certain information onto its internal control stack before transferring control to the error routine. When you leave the error routine with a RESUME statement, these control codes are automatically popped off the stack. But if the error routine ends with a GOTO instead of a RESUME, the control codes remain behind on the stack and will probably cause your program to crash unexpectedly. *Always* clean up the stack by using

CALL statement: see Section 7.1.3

```
CALL -3288
```

before leaving an error routine with a GOTO statement.

The RESUME statement should be executed only from within a program. Attempting to use this statement in immediate execution may cause a syntax error, cause the system to hang, or begin executing an existing or even a deleted program.

3.5.3 Restoring Normal Error Handling

You can restore Applesoft's normal error-handling mechanism by using the POKE statement (see Section 7.1.2)

```
POKE 216,0
```

After executing this statement, Applesoft goes back to stopping the program when an error occurs and displaying its usual error messages.

Monitor program: see your Apple's reference manual

One use of this technique is to prevent your program from hanging or falling into the Monitor in case an error occurs in the error-handling routine itself. You can do this by restoring normal error handling with POKE 216,0 at the beginning of your error routine, then reactivating the error routine with ONERR GOTO before returning to the main program. Here's another version of the sample program in Section 3.5.1 that illustrates this technique:

```
10   ONERR GOTO 21500               Establishes error routine at
                                    line 21500,
.
.
.
21500  POKE 216,0                   Restores normal error handling.
21505  LET EC = PEEK (222)          Gets error code.
21510  IF EC <> 255 THEN 21540
                                    If not CONTROL-C, resumes
                                    program under normal error
                                    handling.
21520  PRINT "SORRY--PROGRAM CAN'T BE STOPPED WITH
       CONTROL-C"                   If user pressed CONTROL-C,
                                    displays special message...
21530  ONERR GOTO 21500             ...reactivates this error routine...
21540  RESUME                       ...and resumes program.
```

This program also illustrates another application of POKE 216,0. Notice that if the error is anything other than a CONTROL-C interrupt (code 255), the IF...THEN test in line 21510 sends control directly to the RESUME statement in line 21540, without executing the ONERR GOTO in line 21530.

The effect of this is to re-execute the statement containing the original error, but with Applesoft's normal error handling still in effect. This causes the same error to occur again, but this time Applesoft displays its normal error message and halts the program. Thus CONTROL-C is the only error that gets special handling; all other errors produce the same results as if there were no special error routine.

3.6 Program Termination

The STOP and END statements are used to halt the execution of a program. The only difference between them is that STOP displays a message giving the number of the line at which execution was halted; this information is useful primarily for debugging purposes. END simply stops the program without any message, and is usually used at a program's natural finishing point.

debugging: finding and correcting errors in a program

3.6.1 The STOP Statement

```
STOP
```

The STOP statement halts execution of the program and displays a message giving the number of the program line in which the STOP occurs. For example, the line

```
115 STOP
```

displays the message

```
BREAK IN 115
```

Applesoft returns to its command level, allowing you to enter new lines, examine or change the values of variables, and so on. You can then resume the execution of the program using the CONT command. (See Section 1.3.3.)

3.6.2 The END Statement

```
END
```

The END statement halts execution of the program and returns control to Applesoft's command level. No message is displayed on the screen; program execution just stops quietly.

```
999 END
```

An END statement is purely optional at the end of a program. The program ends by itself, even without an END statement, when it runs out of statements to execute.

Chapter 4

Arrays and Strings

This chapter discusses two important forms of data on which Applesoft programs can operate: arrays and strings. Both topics were treated briefly in Chapter 2, "Variables and Arithmetic," but are covered in more detail here.

- Section 4.1, "Arrays," deals with collections of related information of any type (real, integer, or string), referred to by the same name and distinguished by means of numerical subscripts.
- Section 4.2, "Strings," describes Applesoft's facilities for manipulating strings of characters such as words or names: comparing them, concatenating (chaining) them together, taking them apart, and converting them to and from numeric values.

4.1 Arrays

An **array** is a collection of variables referred to by the same name, usually holding data items that are related to each other in some logical or systematic way. The individual variables in the array are called its **elements**, and are distinguished from one another by means of identifying index numbers called **subscripts**.

An array can be of any type: integer, real, or string. Array names follow the same rules as simple variable names of the same type. To refer to a particular element of an array, write the array name followed by one or more subscripts, separated by commas and enclosed in parentheses. The subscripts refer to the position of the desired element within the array:

`Q (6)`	Element 6 of real array Q.
`FIGURE% (N)`	Element N of integer array FIGURE%.
`NAME$ (J - 3)`	Element J - 3 of string array NAME$.
`COUNT (SUM%, 2)`	Element (SUM%, 2) of real array COUNT.

Figure 4-1 shows a real array named R with five elements, numbered 0 to 4. Element R(0) (pronounced *R-sub-zero*) holds the value 53, R(1) holds 27.35, and so on. If the value of variable S is 2, then the expression R(S) refers to element R(2), whose value is 31.4, and the expression R(S + 2) refers to element R(4), which holds the value 19.

Figure 4-1 A Real Array

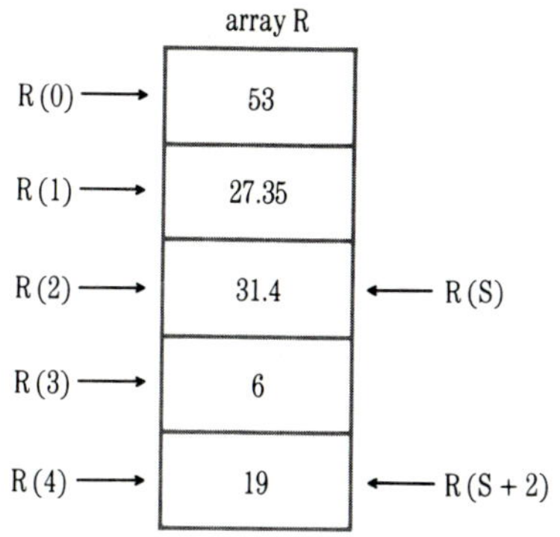

Another example is shown in Figure 4-2, this time a string array named NAME$ with seven elements, numbered 0 to 6. Element NAME$(1) holds the string value "SCOT", NAME$(3) holds the value "BRUCE", NAME$(6) holds "MEG", and so on. If the value of variable C% is 5, then the expression NAME$(C%) refers to element NAME$(5), whose value is "J.D.", and the expression NAME$(C%- 3) refers to element NAME$(2), which holds the value "BITZEL".

Figure 4-2. A String Array

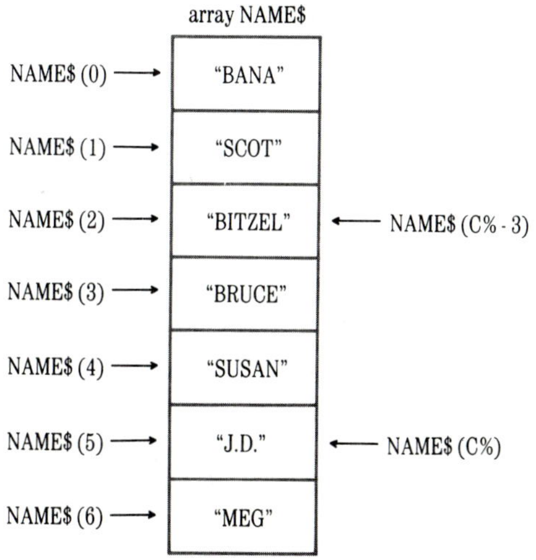

4.1.1 The DIM Statement

```
DIM R (4)
DIM TITLE$ (100)
DIM H5 (J%)
DIM MARK% (3, C / 5, P + 2)
```

The DIM (for dimension) statement defines the size of an array and allocates memory space for its elements. The expressions in parentheses following the array name give the dimensions of the array. There can be from 1 to 88 dimensions.

Once an array has been defined in a DIM statement, any reference to that array with a different number of subscripts, or with a subscript that exceeds the maximum specified for that dimension in the DIM statement, causes the program to halt with a `BAD SUBSCRIPT ERROR` message.

Arrays are limited in size by the amount of available memory. See Section H.2 for detailed information on the amount of space required by each type of array.

> *Subscripts Start From 0:* Since array subscripts in Applesoft begin with 0 (not 1), there is actually one more than the specified number of subscripts in each dimension. For example, the array TITLE$ defined in the second example has 101 (not 100) elements. In the definition
>
> ```
> DIM TEST (12, 3, 5)
> ```
>
> array TEST has 312 elements (13 times 4 times 6), not 180 (12 times 3 times 5) as you might expect.

When Applesoft encounters a reference to an array that has not yet been defined in a DIM statement, it automatically allocates space for 11 subscripts (0 to 10) in each dimension of the array. Later attempting to redefine the same array with a DIM statement causes an error stop with the message `?REDIM'D ARRAY ERROR`. Defining the same array in more than one DIM statement, or executing the same DIM statement twice, produces the same message.

4.1.2 Multidimensional Arrays

The examples shown in Figures 4-1 and 4-2 are both one-dimensional arrays. Actually, arrays in Applesoft can have as many as 88 dimensions, subject to the amount of memory available. Arrays of 88 dimensions aren't terribly useful, but those of 2 and 3 dimensions often are.

Figure 4-3a shows an example of a two-dimensional array named EGGS that has been defined by the DIM statement

```
DIM EGGS (1, 5)
```

Figure 4-3a. A Two-Dimensional Array

array EGGS

	column 0	column 1	column 2	column 3	column 4	column 5
row 0 →	(0,0)	(0,1)	(0,2)	(0,3)	(0,4)	(0,5)
row 1 →	(1,0)	(1,1)	(1,2)	(1,3)	(1,4)	(1,5)

For the newly perplexed, an analogy may be helpful. Think of the array as an empty egg carton. On the outside is written the word EGGS. When you open the egg carton, there are a dozen cup-like indentations where the eggs go—two rows of six cups each—corresponding to the elements of the array. Each of the cups is identified by a row number, 0 or 1, and a column number from 0 to 5 (we're dealing with strange chickens here).

Now suppose you place three eggs in the egg carton, in elements (0,2), (0,5), and (1,3):

```
LET EGGS (0, 2) = "EGG"
LET EGGS (0, 5) = "EGG"
LET EGGS (1, 3) = "EGG"
```

Figure 4-3b shows the result.

Figure 4-3b. A Two-Dimensional Array

array EGGS

	column 0	column 1	column 2	column 3	column 4	column 5
row 0 →			EGG			EGG
row 1 →				EGG		

You might also elect to use your egg carton to hold small change. If you put a nickel in position (0,1), a dime in position (1,1), and a quarter in position (1,4)

```
LET EGGS (0, 1) = 5
LET EGGS (1, 1) = 10
LET EGGS (1, 4) = 25
```

your carton would look like Figure 4-3c.

Figure 4-3c. A Two-Dimensional Array

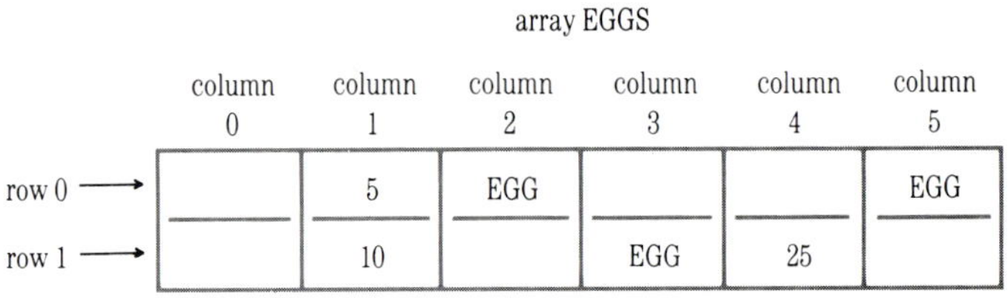

> ***Scrambled Analogy:*** Actually, of course, you can't store eggs in your Applesoft arrays, only numbers and strings—but, after all, analogies aren't always eggsact.

4.2 Strings

A **string** is a sequence of text characters (letters, digits, and punctuation marks). Just as you can write numeric constants such as 27 and 2.236 in your Applesoft programs, you can write string constants by enclosing the characters in the desired string between double quotation marks:

"ON SALE FOR $49.95"
"Truth is impervious to hissing"
"H2SO4"
"???"

> ***Lowercase Okay:*** Even though your version of Applesoft may not understand lowercase letters when you use them in keywords, it allows you to use them in a string constant, as shown in the second example .

A string can contain from 0 to 255 characters; when it contains no characters it is called a **null string**. Two quotation marks with nothing between them denote the null string:

""

A string variable can hold any string as its value. Its name must end with a dollar sign ($). Some legal string variable names are

TITLE$
G2$
D$

Until they are given some other value with an assignment statement, all string variables are preset to the null string.

4.2.1 Comparison of Strings: The ASCII Code

The characters in a string are represented inside the computer in the form of numbers from 0 to 127. The correspondence between these internal character codes and the characters they represent is based on a nationwide computer-industry standard called the American Standard Code for Information Interchange, or ASCII (pronounced *asky*). For instance, ASCII code 65 represents the uppercase letter *A*, 112 represents a lowercase *p*, 52 represents the digit *4*, 43 represents a plus sign (+), and so on. For a complete table of ASCII character codes and the characters they represent, see Appendix C.

Like numbers, strings can be compared with each other using the relational operators. The result of the comparison is based on the ASCII codes of the characters in the strings. Applesoft looks for the first nonidentical characters in the two strings and compares them by ASCII code to decide which is greater. For example, the character *F* (ASCII 70) is considered greater than the character *D* (ASCII 68) but less than the character *H* (ASCII 72). If one string is longer but begins with all the same characters as the other string, the longer string is considered greater. For example,

"A"	is less than	"B"
"AA"	is less than	"AB"
"AB"	is less than	"BA"
"AB"	is less than	"ABC"

Strings and Alphabetical Order: Since letters of the alphabet are represented by consecutive codes in the ASCII table, comparisons between strings of alphabetic letters can be used to place the strings in conventional alphabetical order. For example,

"E"	is less than	"F"
"ED"	is less than	"EDGAR"
"EDGAR"	is less than	"EDWARD"
"EDWARD"	is less than	"EDWARDS"
"EDWARD"	is less than	"FRANK"

There are a few surprises, however: since uppercase letters precede lowercase letters in the ASCII chart,

"Zebra"	is less than	"aardvark"

And since strings are compared strictly character by character,

"48"	is less than	"5"

If you want to compare two strings consisting of digits according to the numbers they represent, use the VAL function. (See Section 4.2.5.)

4.2.2 The LEN Function

The LEN (for length) function counts the number of characters in a string. The argument can be a string constant, a string variable, or a concatenation (see Section 4.2.3) of two or more strings. For example,

`LEN ("APPLE")`	Length of the string "APPLE"; yields 5.
`LEN (SAMPLE$)`	Length of the string contained in variable SAMPLE$.
`LEN (A$ + "****" + B$)`	Length of the concatenation of variable A$, string `"****"`, and variable B$.

Using LEN, you can assign the length of a string to a numeric variable and then use it in further operations:

```
10  LET N% = LEN ("MY HEART SOARS LIKE A
    HAWK.")
20  PRINT "THERE ARE "; N%; " CHARACTERS
    IN THE STRING."
```

When executed, this program displays the following output on the screen:

```
THERE ARE 27 CHARACTERS IN THE STRING.
```

If you use as LEN's argument a concatenation of two or more strings with a combined length of more than 255 (the maximum allowable string length), your program halts with the message `?STRING TOO LONG ERROR`. Instead of writing

```
LEN (A$ + B$ + C$)
```

it's safer to use

```
LEN (A$) + LEN (B$) + LEN (C$)
```

4.2.3 Concatenation of Strings

Concatenation means chaining together. To concatenate two or more strings is to join them together into a new string containing all the characters of the original strings. This operation is represented in Applesoft by a plus sign (+):

`"BORIS" + " AND " + "NATASHA"`	Concatenation of the strings "BORIS", " AND ", and "NATASHA"; yields the string "BORIS AND NATASHA."
`F$ + C$`	Concatenation of the contents of string variables F$ and C$.
`H$ + "RATS!"`	Concatenation of the contents of string variable H$ with the string constant "RATS!"
`H$ + LEFT$(C$, 4)`	Concatenation of the contents of string variable H$ with the leftmost four characters of the contents of string variable C$.

The program

```
10  LET NAME$ = "CHARLIE"
20  LET TITLE$ = "DEAR " + NAME$ + ","
30  PRINT TITLE$
40  PRINT "HAVE WE GOT A SALE!"
```

displays the output

```
DEAR CHARLIE,
HAVE WE GOT A SALE!
```

on the screen. The program

```
10  LET A$ = "GOOD "
20  LET A$ = A$ + "GRIEF!"
30  PRINT A$
```

displays

```
GOOD GRIEF!
```

If the result of a concatenation operation is a string more than 255 characters in length, the program halts with the error message ?STRING TOO LONG ERROR.

You can test how long the result of a concatenation will be beforehand by using the LEN function. For example:

```
10  LET A$ = "HAPPY DAYS"
20  LET L1 = LEN (A$)          How many characters in A$?.
30  LET B$ = " ARE HERE AGAIN"
40  LET L2 = LEN (B$)          How many characters in B$?
50  IF (L1 + L2) < 256 THEN LET A$ = A$ + B$
                               If the combined lengths of A$
                               and B$ are less than 256, combines
                               the two strings into A$.
```

Concatenation Isn't Addition: Don't confuse the concatenation of strings with the addition of numbers, even though both are represented in Applesoft by the same symbol (+). The value of the expression

```
12 + 34
```

is the number 46; the value of the expression

```
"12" + "34"
```

is the string "1234". If you want to add two strings consisting of digits according to the numbers they represent, use the VAL function. (See Section 4.2.5.)

4.2.4 Substring Functions

A **substring** is a string that is part of another string. Applesoft has three built-in functions for extracting substrings from a string:

- LEFT$ extracts a substring from the beginning of a string.
- MID$ extracts a substring from anywhere in a string.
- RIGHT$ extracts a substring from the end of a string.

4.2.4.1 The LEFT$ Function

LEFT$ extracts a specified number of characters from the beginning (left end) of a string. The LEFT$ function takes two arguments, separated by a comma: the string from which the characters are to be taken and the number of characters desired. For example,

`LEFT$ ("THIS IS IT!", 4)`	First 4 characters of the string "THIS IS IT!"; yields "THIS."
`LEFT$ (NAME$, C + 2)`	First C + 2 characters of the contents of string variable NAME$.

If the value you give for the number of characters in the substring is a real number, LEFT$ converts it to the next lower integer. If the value specified is greater than the length of the string, Applesoft returns the entire string; no extra characters are added.

The number of characters requested must be between 1 and 255 or the program halts with the message `?ILLEGAL QUANTITY ERROR`. If you omit the dollar sign ($) from the function name LEFT$, Applesoft treats LEFT as an arithmetic variable name, causing an error stop with the message `?TYPE MISMATCH ERROR`.

4.2.4.2 The MID$ Function

MID$ (for middle) extracts a specified number of characters from a specified position within a string. The MID$ function takes three arguments, separated by commas: the string from which the characters are to be taken, the position within the string of the first character, and the number of characters desired. For example,

`MID$ ("HOW DO I LOVE THEE?", 10, 4)`	4 characters beginning at position 10 in string "HOW DO I LOVE THEE?"; yields "LOVE."
`MID$ (H9$, R + 7, 2 * V)`	2 * V characters beginning at position R + 7 in the contents of string variable H9$,

You can optionally leave out the third argument to MID$. If you don't specify the number of characters you want, or if the number of characters you request is greater than the length of the string, MID$ yields all characters from the designated starting position to the end of the string:

`MID$ ("THERE THEY GO!", 7)`	All characters from position 7 to end of string "THERE THEY GO!"; yields "THEY GO!"
`MID$ (A$, 10)`	All characters from position 10 to end of the contents of string variable A$.
`MID$ ("HI THERE", 4, 20)`	All characters from position 4 to end of string "HI THERE"; yields "THERE."

If the value you give for the starting position or the number of characters in the substring is a real number, MID$ truncates it to the next lower integer. If the designated starting point is greater than the length of the string, or if the number of characters requested is 0, MID$ yields the null string.

The starting position must be between 1 and 255, and the number of characters between 0 and 255, or the program halts with the message `?ILLEGAL QUANTITY ERROR`. If you omit the dollar sign ($) from the function name MID$, Applesoft treats MID as an arithmetic variable name, causing an error stop with the message `?TYPE MISMATCH ERROR`.

4.2.4.3 The RIGHT$ Function

RIGHT$ extracts a specified number of characters from the end (right end) of a string. The RIGHT$ function takes two arguments, separated by a comma: the string from which the characters are to be taken and the number of characters desired. For example,

`RIGHT$ ("GIMME A BREAK", 7)`	Last 7 characters of the string "GIMME A BREAK"; yields "A BREAK."
`RIGHT$ (NAME$, C + 2)`	Last C + 2 characters of the contents of string variable NAME$.

If the value you give for the number of characters in the substring is a real number, RIGHT$ truncates it to the next lower integer. If the value specified is greater than the length of the string, Applesoft returns the entire string; no extra characters are added.

The number of characters requested must be between 1 and 255 or the program halts with the message `?ILLEGAL QUANTITY ERROR`. If you omit the dollar sign ($) from the function name RIGHT$, Applesoft treats RIGHT as an arithmetic variable name, causing an error stop with the message `?TYPE MISMATCH ERROR`.

4.2.5 String Conversion Functions

Strings and numbers are not the same, even when the string looks like a number:

`2 * 123`	Yields 246.
`2 * "123"`	`TYPE MISMATCH ERROR.`
`LEFT$ ("123", 2)`	Yields "12."
`LEFT$ (123, 2)`	`TYPE MISMATCH ERROR.`

This section describes Applesoft's built-in functions for converting between numeric and string values:

- STR$ converts a number to a corresponding string.
- VAL converts a string to a corresponding number.
- CHR$ converts an ASCII code to the corresponding character.
- ASC converts a character to the corresponding ASCII code (see Section 4.2.1).

4.2.5.1 The STR$ Function

The STR$ (for string) function converts a numeric value into a string representing that value. For example,

`STR$ (-100)`	A string representing the number -100; yields "-100."
`STR$ (3.14159)`	A string representing the number 3.14159; yields "3.14159."
`STR$ (MARK)`	A string representing the numeric value of real variable MARK.
`STR$ (COUNT%)`	A string representing the numeric value of integer variable COUNT%.
`STR$ (B^2 - 4*A*C)`	A string representing the numeric value of the expression B ^ 2 - 4*A*C.

The string produced by STR$ is in the same format that Applesoft uses to display or print numbers; see Appendix I for details. For example,

`STR$ (100 000 000)`	Yields "100000000."
`STR$ (1 000 000 000)`	Yields "1E+09."
`STR$ (-.03)`	Yields "-.03."
`STR$ (-.003)`	Yields "-3E-03."

If the numeric value of the argument falls outside the allowable range for real numbers (-9.99999999E+37 to +9.99999999E+37), the program halts with the message `?OVERFLOW ERROR`.

4.2.5.2 The VAL Function

The VAL (for value) function converts a string to the numeric value it represents. For example,

`VAL ("4096")`	Number represented by the string "4096"; yields 4096.
`VAL ("-1.505 E +2")`	Number represented by the string "-1.505 E +2"; yields -150.5.
`VAL (WHOLE$ + "." + FRAC$)`	Number represented by the concatenation of strings WHOLE$, ".", and FRAC$.
`VAL ( RIGHT$ (Q$, 4) )`	Number represented by the last four characters of string Q$.

VAL recognizes the same number formats as can be used in keyboard input. (See Section 5.1.2.) If VAL encounters a non-numeric character in its argument string, it yields the numeric value of everything up to the first non-numeric character, ignoring the rest of the string. (The digits 0 through 9, the signs + and -, the decimal point (.), and the letter *E* for scientific notation are considered numeric characters. Spaces are also allowed, and are simply ignored.) If the first character in the string is non-numeric, VAL yields a value of 0. For example,

`VAL ("12.54 OR SO")`	Yields 12.54.
`VAL ("ABOUT 4.57")`	Yields 0.

If the absolute value of VAL's result is greater than 1E38 or contains more than 38 digits (including trailing zeros), the program halts with the message `?OVERFLOW ERROR`.

4.2.5.3 The CHR$ Function

The CHR$ (for character) function regards its single numeric argument as an ASCII character code and yields a one-character string consisting of the corresponding character.

For example,

`CHR$ (68)`	Character with ASCII code 68; yields the string "D."
`CHR$ (47)`	Character with ASCII code 47; yields the string "/."
`CHR$ (7)`	Character with ASCII code 7; yields a string containing the ASCII bell character (CONTROL-G).
`CHR$ (C1)`	Character whose ASCII code is the value of variable C1.
`CHR$ (L% + 64)`	Character whose ASCII code is the value of expression L% + 64.

If the value of the argument is a real number, CHR$ converts it to the next lower integer. For example,

`CHR$ (81.9)`	Argument is truncated to 81; yields "Q."

An argument less than 0 or greater than 255 causes the program to halt with the message `?ILLEGAL QUANTITY ERROR`.

4.2.5.4 The ASC Function

The ASC (for ASCII) function takes a single string argument and yields the ASCII code corresponding to the first character in the string. For example,

`ASC ("D")`	ASCII code for character D; yields 68.
`ASC ("/")`	ASCII code for character /; yields 47.
`ASC ("e. e. cummings")`	ASCII code for character e; yields 101.
`ASC (B0$)`	ASCII code for the first character in string B0$.
`ASC ( MID$ (NAME$, 5) )`	ASCII code for the fifth character in string NAME$.

If the argument given to ASC is the null string, the program halts with the message `?ILLEGAL QUANTITY ERROR`.

Chapter 5

Input/Output

This chapter is concerned with the ways in which Applesoft programs communicate with the outside world. Here are described Applesoft's facilities for getting information into and out of the computer and for controlling the way information is presented.

- Section 5.1, "Input," deals with the various statements through which Applesoft programs receive information for processing.
- Section 5.2, "Output," describes how programs transfer information to the "outside world": to the display screen, printers, and so forth.

5.1 Input

The input statements discussed in this section enable Applesoft programs to receive information for processing, either from the keyboard or from a peripheral device connected to the computer:

- The IN# statement (see Section 5.1.1) controls the source from which the computer receives its input.
- The INPUT statement (see Section 5.1.2) accepts a line of input from the current input device.
- The GET statement (see Section 5.1.3) reads a single character from the current input device.
- The READ (see Section 5.1.4), DATA (see Section 5.1.4), and RESTORE (see Section 5.1.5) statements are used to read information from within the running program itself.
- A few miscellaneous input facilities (see Section 5.1.6) are available for reading the hand controls and, in the case of the Apple II, Apple II Plus, and Apple IIe, for reading information from a cassette tape recorder.

5.1.1 The IN# Statement

```
IN# 2
IN# X
IN# SLOT - J
```

port or expansion slot: see your Apple's owner's manual and reference manual

The IN# statement specifies the source from which the computer receives subsequent input. The expression following the keyword IN# should evaluate to a number between 0 and 7, designating the appropriate port or expansion slot from which input is to be taken.

When Applesoft is started up, it is set to receive input from the keyboard. Executing an IN# statement with a number from 1 to 7 instructs Applesoft to receive input instead from the peripheral input device (such as a modem) connected to the designated port or slot. Using number 0 reestablishes the keyboard as the current input device. For example, the following program fragment reads a single character from the device connected to port 2, then reestablishes keyboard input:

GET statement: see Section 5.1.3

```
510   IN# 2        Accepts input from port 2.
520   GET A$       Reads one character from port 2.
530   IN# 0        Accepts future input from keyboard.
```

Notice that the character # is part of the keyword IN# and cannot be omitted.

If You Use DOS or ProDOS: If you have DOS or ProDOS active, any IN# or PR# (see Section 5.2.1) statement must be set up as a disk operating system command to prevent the disk operating system from being disconnected. In that case, the example would look like this:

```
510   PRINT CHR$(4);"IN# 2"
520   GET A$
530   PRINT CHR$(4);"IN# 0"
```

See the manual that came with your disk operating system for more details.

▲Warning

If the port designated in an IN# or PR# statement contains a disk controller card, Applesoft attempts to restart the system from the disk contained in drive 1 connected to that port. When you do this on purpose, it's the usual way of restarting the system from within Applesoft; when you do it by mistake, it can be a catastrophe. So be careful!

If no input device is connected to the port designated in an IN# statement, the system hangs. To recover, use CONTROL-RESET. Using a port number between 8 and 255 causes unpredictable and possibly aberrant behavior.

Using a port number less than 0 or greater than 255 in an IN# statement stops the program with an error message.

5.1.2 The INPUT Statement

```
INPUT PRICE
INPUT MNTH%, DAY%, YEAR%
INPUT "WHAT IS YOUR PASSWORD? "; PASSWD$
INPUT ""; X
```

The INPUT statement accepts a line of input (which must be terminated by [RETURN]) from the current input device, specifying values to be assigned to one or more variables. The variables are listed in the INPUT statement, separated by commas.

The INPUT statement can optionally include a message to be displayed or printed on the current output device, prompting the user for the desired input. If present, the prompting message must be given as a string constant immediately following the keyword INPUT and followed by a semicolon to separate it from the list of variable names.

current output device: see Section 5.2.1

The specified prompting string is reproduced exactly as written; if displayed on the screen, it is immediately followed on the same line by the cursor. If the prompting message is omitted from the INPUT statement, a question mark (?) is displayed; the question mark can be suppressed by supplying a null string as the prompting message. For example,

```
10  PRINT "WHAT IS YOUR AGE, PLEASE?"
                                  Displays prompting message on its
                                  own line.
20  INPUT AGE                     Prompts with ? and waits for
                                  response.
30  INPUT "YOUR STREET NAME? "; ST$
                                  Displays prompting message on
                                  same line as cursor and waits for
                                  response.
40  PRINT "PLEASE TYPE YOUR FIRST AND LAST NAMES, ";
    "SEPARATED BY A COMMA:"       Displays prompting message on its
                                  own line.
50  INPUT ""; FN$, LN$            Suppresses ? and waits for two
                                  responses separated by a comma.
```

The INPUT statement in line 20 above displays a question mark to prompt the user for input, followed by the cursor. The INPUT statement in line 30 displays the prompting message `YOUR STREET NAME?` instead of the question mark, again followed by the cursor. The INPUT statement in line 50 displays the cursor only, with no question mark and no prompting message of any kind.

The INPUT statement can be executed only from within a program; you can't use this statement in immediate execution.

5.1.2.1 Multiple Inputs on the Same Line

The INPUT statement can list any number of variables to be read from the same input line. The values the user supplies for these variables must be separated by commas. You can mix string and numeric variables in the same INPUT statement, but the user's responses must each be of the correct type.

If the user presses [RETURN] (or types a colon or [CONTROL]-[@]) without typing enough values for all the variables listed in the INPUT statement, Applesoft displays two question marks to show that it expects further response. If a colon, comma, or [CONTROL]-[@] is the first character of a response, Applesoft interprets the response as 0 or as the null string (depending on the type of variable specified) and the program continues with the next statement.

If the user types more responses than Applesoft expects, or types a colon into the final expected response, Applesoft displays the message `?EXTRA IGNORED` and program execution continues. If the last response is shortened by a [CONTROL]-[@], the program continues but no message is displayed.

> *Be Kind to Users:* Multiple inputs on the same line can be confusing for your users; it's best not to use them except for "quick and dirty" testing purposes while you're debugging your code. Instead of asking for something terribly unfriendly like
>
> ```
> PLEASE TYPE LAST NAME, FIRST NAME, MIDDLE INITIAL:
> ```
>
> use a form such as
>
> ```
> PLEASE TYPE YOUR FIRST NAME:
> ```
>
> followed by
>
> ```
> PLEASE TYPE YOUR MIDDLE INITIAL; JUST PRESS RETURN
> IF YOU HAVE NONE
> ```
>
> and so on. You'll be able to give much clearer instructions, your user will have an easier time giving you what you want, and you'll be better able to detect and deal with errors in the input.

5.1.2.2 General Rules for Input

Users of your program should know the following general rules for input:

- If the user types a colon (:) as part of an input line, the remainder of that input line is ignored. The ASCII null character [CONTROL]-[@] has the same effect.
- An INPUT statement can be interrupted by [CONTROL]-[C] (see Section 1.3.2), but only if it is the first character typed on an input line. In that case, the program halts when [RETURN] is pressed at the end of that line. A [CONTROL]-[C] that is not the first character of the input line is treated as part of the input, the same as is any other character.
- If the user types an input line longer than 255 characters, the whole line is canceled and has to be retyped from the beginning (the Apple beeps from about the 245th character, but no message is displayed). A response of more than 239 but fewer than 255 characters is truncated to 239 characters with no warning message displayed.

5.1.2.3 Rules for String Input

The following rules govern the values the user types for string variables in the INPUT statement:

- The user's response to a string variable can be typed with or without enclosing quotation marks.
- Applesoft ignores all spaces preceding the first nonspace character.
- If the first nonspace character is a quotation mark, the input string is considered to include everything up to (but not including) the next quotation mark, [CONTROL]-[@], or [RETURN]. The string can include commas and colons, but cannot include quotation marks, because these would be interpreted as marking the end of the string. Spaces following the closing quotation mark are ignored, but any other character causes the response to be rejected with the message `?REENTER`.
- If the first nonspace character is not a quotation mark, the input string is considered to include everything up to (but not including) the next comma, colon, [CONTROL]-[@], or [RETURN]. The string can include quotation marks, but cannot include commas or colons, because these would be interpreted as marking the end of the string. Spaces following the last nonspace character are accepted as part of the input string.
- If the first nonspace character is a comma, colon, [CONTROL]-[@], or [RETURN], the response is interpreted as the null string and program execution continues.

- In general, control characters cause problems and should not be used in responding to INPUT statements. The following characters cannot be included in the response:

CONTROL-H	Equivalent to ← or the backspace key.
CONTROL-M	Equivalent to RETURN.
CONTROL-X	Cancels the input line.
CONTROL-@	ASCII null character; causes remainder of input line to be ignored.

- The value supplied for a string variable must be a single string or a constant; it cannot be a string expression involving concatenation, LEFT$, MID$, RIGHT$ or other string operations. Responses such as

```
A$ + B$
LEFT$ (MONTH$, 3)
RIGHT$ (NAME$, L - (FL + 2))
```

are accepted exactly as typed, character for character (up to the first comma), and are not evaluated as string expressions.

5.1.2.4 Rules for Numeric Input

The following rules govern the values a user can supply for numeric variables. If a response is typed that doesn't conform to these rules, Applesoft displays the message `?REENTER`, reissues the prompting message, and waits for another response.

- Spaces are ignored in any position.
- The response is considered to include all nonspace characters up to (but not including) the next comma, colon, CONTROL-@, or RETURN.
- The response can include numeric characters and spaces only. Numeric characters include the digits 0 to 9, the signs + and -, the period (decimal point), and the letter *E* for scientific notation. A response containing a nonnumeric character in any position is invalid.

scientific notation: see Section 5.2.3

- Numeric responses consist of the following elements. Any or all of these elements can be omitted, except that the sign or value of the exponent cannot appear unless preceded by the letter *E*. Even forms such as +E and .E are accepted, and are interpreted as 0. Those that are included must be given in the order listed:

  1. A sign (+ or -)
  2. One or more digits
  3. A decimal point (.)
  4. One or more digits
  5. The letter *E* for scientific notation
  6. A sign (+ or -) for the exponent
  7. One or more digits

- If the first nonspace character is a comma, colon, or [RETURN], the response is interpreted as 0 and program execution continues. A response beginning with [CONTROL]-[@] is invalid.
- The following control characters have special meanings. A response containing any other control character, in any position, is invalid.

[CONTROL]-[H]	Equivalent to [←] or the backspace key
[CONTROL]-[M]	Equivalent to the [RETURN] key
[CONTROL]-[X]	Cancels the input line
[CONTROL]-[@]	ASCII null character; causes remainder of input line to be ignored

- The value supplied for a numeric variable must be a single number; it cannot be a numeric expression involving arithmetic operations or function calls. Responses such as

```
1/2
B^2 - 4 * A * C
SQR (2)
```

are invalid because of the non-numeric characters.

Programming Tip: It's a good idea to use string variables to accept all numeric inputs, using the VAL function (see Section 4.2.5) to convert them to numeric values. This makes it easier to detect and deal with user errors and to display alternate prompting messages.

5.1.2.5 An "Input Anything" Routine

The INPUT statement interprets the colon and the comma (and sometimes the quotation mark) as special symbols and rejects anything typed after them in the input line. Here's what you can use if you anticipate that your user's response may include any of these characters.

The following Applesoft subroutine uses the POKE statement (see Section 7.1.2) to store a special machine-language routine in the computer's memory, one byte at a time, beginning at address 768. The machine-language routine accepts all characters in the input, including colons, commas, and quotation marks, without "censoring" them, and assigns them, character by character, to a string variable for further processing. (The following line numbers are arbitrary; you can locate this subroutine anywhere you like in your program.)

```
62000  REM  SET UP "INPUT ANYTHING" ROUTINE
62010  LET IN$ = "X"             IN$ must be first variable created.
62020  FOR J = 768 TO 790        These are memory addresses where
                                 machine language is to be stored.
62030  READ I                    Gets a byte of machine language.
62040  POKE J, I                 Stores it at next location.
62050  NEXT J                    Goes back for next byte.
62060  DATA 162, 0, 32, 117, 253, 160, 2, 138, 145,
       105, 200, 169, 0, 145, 105, 200, 169, 2, 145,
       105, 6, 57, 213           These are the actual bytes of
                                 machine language.
62070  RETURN                    Returns to statement following
                                 point of call.
```

The DATA statement (see Section 5.1.4) containing the machine language must be reproduced in your program exactly as shown.

The following subroutine uses the CALL statement (see Section 7.1.3) to call the machine-language routine at address 768. (Again, this subroutine can be located anywhere in your Applesoft program, not necessarily at line number 63000.)

```
63000  REM  CALL "INPUT ANYTHING" ROUTINE
63010  CALL 768                  Calls machine-language routine.
63020  IN$ = MID$ (IN$, 1)       IN$ now holds the input that the
                                 machine-language routine accepted.
63030  RETURN                    Returns to statement following
                                 point of call.
```

To accept a line of input from the user, instead of using a statement such as

```
100  INPUT S$
```

substitute this line:

```
100  GOSUB 63000 : LET S$(N) = IN$
```

The variable S$ now contains whatever input the user typed, including the "forbidden" characters; your program can proceed to process the input in whatever way is appropriate.

> *Order of Variables:* For technical reasons having to do with the way variables are stored in memory, the string variable used to pass the user's response between machine language and Applesoft (arbitrarily called IN$ in the example) must be the first variable used or defined in the program. To be safe, you might want to call the "input anything" setup routine from line number 0:
>
> ```
> 0  GOSUB 62000
> ```

5.1.3 The GET Statement

```
GET L$
GET S$(N)
GET C1$, C2$, C3$
```

The GET statement reads a single character from the current input device, without waiting for RETURN to be pressed. Although it can be used to read from any peripheral input device (such as the disk drive or a modem), it is seldom used in actual practice with anything other than the keyboard.

GET accepts one character for each of the string variables listed following the keyword GET. Each single character is read as soon as it is typed, without waiting for the user to press RETURN. The character is not displayed on the screen, and the cursor is not moved in any way.

Here's an example of a program fragment using GET:

semicolon: see Section 5.2.2

```
310  PRINT "PRESS THE 'Y' KEY TO GO ON: ";
                                     Prompts user for response
                                     (semicolon keeps cursor on same
                                     line).
320  GET A$                          Waits for user to press key.
330  IF A$ <> "Y" AND A$ <> "y" THEN 320
                                     Keeps cycling until user presses
                                     correct key.
340  PRINT                           Moves cursor to new line (cancels
                                     effect of semicolon from line 310).
350  PRINT "THANK YOU"               Politeness from machines is always
                                     welcome.
```

The GET statement can be executed only from within a program; you can't use this statement in immediate execution.

If typed in response to a GET, [CONTROL]-[C] is treated like any other character; it does not interrupt program execution.

Following GET With an Operating System Command: A disk operating system command issued immediately after a GET is not recognized. For such commands to be executed properly, you must issue a [RETURN] character immediately after the GET. An easy way to do this is with an empty PRINT statement:

```
PRINT
```

See your disk operating system manual for more information.

Numeric Inputs with GET: The GET statement is neither designed nor intended to obtain values for numeric variables. You can attempt to do so at your own peril, subject to the following limitations:

- A comma or a colon results in the message `?EXTRA IGNORED` and is interpreted as a numeric value of 0.
- A plus sign, minus sign, [CONTROL]-[@], E, space, or period is interpreted as a numeric value of 0.
- Any non-numeric character causes the program to halt with a syntax error.

It's better to use only string variables with the GET statement, using the VAL function (see Section 4.2.5) to convert the response to a numeric value.

5.1.4 The READ and DATA Statements

```
READ PRICE
READ A, B, M%(I), J%, S$(2*J - 1), T$
DATA 12.9, HI HO, 168
DATA 2.236
```

The READ and DATA statements are used to read information from within the Applesoft program itself, rather than from the keyboard or another input device. There can be any number of DATA statements in a program, each containing a list of one or more items of information (numbers or strings) following the keyword DATA and separated by commas. All of the DATA statements in the program are considered to form one long list of items, in sequential order by line numbers; each READ statement reads one or more items from this list.

Each time it executes a READ statement, Applesoft remembers the last item read from the DATA list. The next READ always begins with the next item in the list. There is no way to back up or skip forward in the DATA list, but you can start over from the beginning of the list with the RESTORE statement (see Section 5.1.5).

An attempt to read past the end of the DATA list halts the program with a message such as `?OUT OF DATA ERROR IN 1465` identifying the line number of the READ statement in which the error occurred. Leaving part of the DATA list unread at the end of the program does not cause an error.

The items in a DATA statement are separated by commas and follow the usual rules for numeric and string input, except that a DATA statement cannot contain an unquoted colon (:). The number of items in each DATA statement is limited only by the length of the program line. A DATA statement can appear anywhere in your program; it need not precede the READ statement that uses it. There is no limit to the number of DATA statements in a program.

Here's a sample program showing the use of the READ and DATA statements:

`10 DATA "GO WEST, YOUNG MAN"`	Item containing a comma; OK between quotation marks.
`20 DATA 3.14159, 2, "SAM"`	Mixed types in same DATA statement.
`30 READ A$, B`	Reads GO WEST, YOUNG MAN into string variable A$, and 3.14159 into real variable B; notice that these items come from two different DATA statements.
`40 READ C%, D$, E$`	Reads 2 into integer variable C%, SAM into string variable D$, and THE "WORLD" IS FLAT into string variable E$; begins with next item following previous READ statement.
`50 DATA THE "WORLD" IS FLAT`	Item containing quotation marks; notice that this item follows the READ statement that uses it.
`60 PRINT E$`	Displays `THE "WORLD" IS FLAT`.
`70 PRINT A$`	Displays `GO WEST, YOUNG MAN`.
`80 DATA 98.6, 37, -273.16`	These items never read.
`90 END`	

Null items in a DATA statement are interpreted as 0 or the null string, depending on the type of variable to which they are assigned in a READ statement. A null item is read whenever there are no nonspace characters between

- the keyword DATA and the end of the program line
- the keyword DATA and the first comma
- two consecutive commas
- the last comma and the end of the program line.

Thus the statement

```
DATA,,
```

contains three null items.

An attempt to read a string value in a DATA statement with a numeric variable in a READ statement causes a syntax error. Numeric values can be read into string variables, but must be evaluated with the VAL function (see Section 4.2.5) before they can be used as numbers.

> *Control Characters in DATA Statements:* The characters [CONTROL]-[H], [CONTROL]-[M], [CONTROL]-[X], and [CONTROL]-[@] cannot be embedded in a DATA statement. Any other control character typed into a DATA statement is treated as an ordinary character and becomes part of the input. A [CONTROL]-[C] character in a DATA statement does not interrupt the program.

The READ statement can be executed only from within a program; you can't use this statement in immediate execution.

5.1.5 The RESTORE Statement

```
RESTORE
```

The RESTORE statement restarts the DATA list from the beginning. After RESTORE is executed, the next READ statement reads the first item in the first DATA statement in the program. For example,

`10 DATA "GO WEST, YOUNG MAN"`	
`20 DATA 3.14159, 2, "SAM"`	
`30 READ A$, B`	Reads GO WEST, YOUNG MAN into string variable A$ and 3.14159 into real variable B.
`40 READ C%, D$, E$`	Reads 2 into integer variable C%, SAM into string variable D$, and THE "WORLD" IS FLAT into string variable E$.
`50 DATA THE "WORLD" IS FLAT`	
`60 PRINT E$`	Displays `THE "WORLD" IS FLAT.`
`70 RESTORE`	Restarts list from beginning.
`80 READ Q$`	Reads GO WEST, YOUNG MAN into string variable Q$.
`90 PRINT Q$`	Displays `GO WEST, YOUNG MAN.`
`100 PRINT A$`	Displays `GO WEST, YOUNG MAN` (value of A$ still intact).
`110 END`	
`120 DATA 98.6, 37, -273.16`	These items never read.

There is no way to reposition the DATA list to a specific desired item or line number. The only other Applesoft statement that affects the positioning of the DATA list is RUN (see Section 1.2.4), which also restarts the list from the beginning.

5.1.6 Miscellaneous Input Facilities

This section covers Applesoft's facilities for dealing with the remaining input features of the Apple II: the hand controls and cassette tape input. Refer also to Appendix O.

5.1.6.1 The Hand Controls

If you have a set of hand controls connected to your computer, you can use the PDL function to read their dial settings. The Apple II series of computers can accommodate as many as four hand controls, numbered 0 to 3, connected either through the 9-pin hand control connector on the computer's back panel or, in those models where accessible, the GAME I/O connector inside the case on the main logic board. However, the standard Apple hand control set consists of only two controls, numbered 0 and 1.

The PDL function takes one argument, the number of the hand control to be read, and yields an integer from 0 to 255 representing the current position of the dial on that control. For example,

`10 LET X = PDL (0)`	Reads hand control 0.
`20 LET P% = X * 40 / 256 + 1`	Reduces to a number from 1 to 40.
`30 HTAB (P%)`	Moves cursor to indicated position on current line.
`40 PRINT "<"`	Displays the character <.
`50 LET Y = PDL (1)`	Reads hand control 1.
`60 LET Q% = Y * 40 / 256 + 1`	Reduces to a number from 1 to 40.
`70 HTAB (Q%)`	Moves cursor to indicated position on current line.
`80 PRINT ">"`	Displays the character >.
`90 IF X = 0 AND Y = 0 THEN END`	Ends program when both hand controls read 0.
`100 GOTO 10`	Otherwise repeats the process.

If the argument given to PDL is less than 0 or greater than 255, the program halts with the message `?ILLEGAL QUANTITY ERROR`. If the argument is between 4 and 255, or if no hand control of the designated number is connected, the results are unpredictable.

Consecutive Readings: If your program reads two hand controls in consecutive statements, the reading from the first hand control may affect the reading from the second. To obtain more accurate readings, allow several program lines between calls to PDL or use a short delay loop such as

```
FOR X = 1 TO 10 : NEXT X
```

between PDL calls.

Historical Note: The function name PDL stands for paddle, which in turn is short for game paddle, an older name for the Apple II's hand controls.

The buttons on the hand controls can be read with the function calls

PEEK function: see Section 7.1.1

`PEEK (-16287)`	Yields a value > 127 if button on hand control 0 is being pressed; <= 127 if not.
`PEEK (-16286)`	Yields a value > 127 if button on hand control 1 is being pressed; <= 127 if not.
`PEEK (-16285)`	Yields a value > 127 if button on hand control 2 is being pressed; <= 127 if not.

There is no way to read the button on hand control 3.

The PEEK calls listed are also used to read the apple keys on *some models* of the Apple II keyboard: [open-apple] is equivalent to the button on hand control 0, and [solid-apple] is equivalent to the button on hand control 1.

For More Information: See your Apple computer's reference manual for detailed technical information on the 9-pin hand control connector and/or the internal GAME I/O connector.

5.1.6.2 Cassette Input

Three Applesoft statements, LOAD, RECALL, and SHLOAD, can be used to read information from a cassette tape recorder (Apple II, Apple II Plus, and Apple IIe only). LOAD reads an Applesoft program into memory from tape; RECALL reads the contents of an integer or real array; SHLOAD reads a shape table for use in high-resolution graphics. For details, see Appendix M.

5.2 Output

This section describes the output facilities available in Applesoft:

- Section 5.2.1 covers the PR# statement, which controls the destination to which output is directed.
- Section 5.2.2 contains a detailed discussion of the PRINT statement, Applesoft's primary output statement.
- Section 5.2.3 gives details on the way numbers are formatted when written with the PRINT statement.
- Section 5.2.4 describes Applesoft's wide variety of facilities for controlling the format in which textual information is displayed on the screen.
- Section 5.2.5 touches briefly on various miscellaneous output facilities not covered elsewhere: the Apple II's built-in speaker, annunciator outputs, utility strobe, and cassette tape output.

5.2.1 The PR# Statement

```
PR# 1
PR# X
PR# SLOT - J
```

The PR# statement specifies the destination to which the computer sends subsequent output. The expression following the keyword PR# should evaluate to a number between 0 and 7, designating the port to which output is to be sent.

When Applesoft is started up, it is set to send output to the display screen. Executing a PR# statement with a port number from 1 to 7 instructs Applesoft to send output instead to the peripheral output device (such as a printer or modem) connected to the designated port. A port number of 0 reestablishes the display screen as the current output device. For example, the following program fragment writes a string of characters to the device connected to port 1, then reestablishes screen output:

`610 PR# 1`	Sends output to device in port 1.
`620 PRINT Z$`	Writes contents of string variable Z$ to device in port 1.
`630 PR# 0`	Sends future output to screen.

Notice that the character # is part of the keyword PR# and cannot be omitted.

If You Use DOS or ProDOS: If you have DOS or ProDOS active, any IN# or PR# statement must be set up as a disk operating system command to prevent the disk operating system from being disconnected. The example would look like this:

```
610  PRINT CHR$(4);"PR# 1"
620  PRINT Z$
630  PRINT CHR$(4);"PR# 0"
```

See the manual that came with your disk operating system for more details.

▲Warning

If the port designated in an IN# (see Section 5.1.1) or PR# statement contains a disk controller card, Applesoft attempts to restart the system from the disk contained in drive 1 connected to that port. When you do this on purpose, it's the usual way of restarting the system from within Applesoft; when you do it by mistake, it can be a catastrophe. So be careful!

If no output device is connected to the port designated in a PR# statement, the system hangs. To recover, use CONTROL-RESET.

Using a port number between 8 and 255 in a PR# statement causes unpredictable and possibly aberrant behavior.

If you are using an Apple IIe with the Apple II 80-Column Text Card, or an Apple IIc (which contains the equivalent of that card) deactivate it by typing ESC CONTROL-Q before using PR# to transfer output to another port. Leaving the Text Card active while using a printer or while restarting the system from a disk can produce amusing but confusing fireworks on the screen.

Although the Text Card is installed in the Apple's special auxiliary slot, it appears to the computer as if it were connected to port 3. So to reactivate the Text Card after sending output to another device, type

```
PR# 3
```

You can also return output to the 40-column screen with the Text Card inactive by typing

```
PR# 0
```

However, don't use PR# 0 to redirect output directly from the Text Card to the 40-column screen without first deactivating the Text Card with ESC CONTROL-Q. Under certain circumstances, this may cause text intended for the screen to be written outside the area of memory reserved for it, possibly destroying your Applesoft program or other important information.

Using a port number less than 0 or greater than 255 in a PR# statement stops the program with the message `?ILLEGAL QUANTITY ERROR`.

5.2.2 The PRINT Statement

```
PRINT
PRINT P$, Q, R%
PRINT "DISCRIMINANT = "; B^2 - 4*A*C
PRINT LEFT$ (FN$, 1) + ". " + LN$
PRINT TAB (M); "*"; TAB (M + N); "***";
      TAB (M + N + N); "*"
```

The PRINT statement writes output to the current output device. Expressions representing the values to be written are listed after the keyword PRINT, separated by commas or semicolons.

Any expression can be included in a PRINT statement. Each expression in the list following the keyword PRINT is evaluated. If the value of the expression is a string, the characters of the string are written to the current output device (see Section 5.2.1); if the value is a number, it is written according to the rules discussed in Section 5.2.3, "Number Formats." Calls to the special functions SPC and TAB (see Section 5.2.4) can also be included in a PRINT list; they do not cause anything to be written, but control the positioning of the next item.

When an item in the PRINT list is followed by a semicolon, the cursor (if output is going to the screen) or print head (if to a printer) is left positioned immediately after the last character in the item. The next item written begins in the next available column, with no intervening spaces. A semicolon at the end of a PRINT statement causes the cursor or print head to be left at the end of that line, and prevents a new line from being started.

For example, the statement

```
PRINT 1; 2; 3; 4;
```

produces the output

```
1234
```

and leaves the cursor or print head positioned in the column immediately following the digit 4. The statement

```
PRINT 1/3; 2 * 4; 51
```

produces the output

```
.333333333851
```

If two consecutive items in a PRINT list are not separated by either a comma or a semicolon, a semicolon is understood.

Eliminating Blank Lines: The Apple II's normal display is 40 columns wide. After Applesoft displays the 40th character on a line, it automatically sends the cursor to the beginning of the next line. The next PRINT statement executed starts another new line, causing an unintended blank line to appear on the screen. (Unwanted blank lines are especially annoying in inverse mode.)

For example, the statements

```
10  PRINT "THIS MESSAGE HAS PRECISELY 40
    CHARACTERS"
20  PRINT "SO THERE'S A BLANK LINE ON THE
    SCREEN"
```

display the output

```
THIS MESSAGE HAS PRECISELY 40 CHARACTERS

SO THERE'S A BLANK LINE ON THE SCREEN
```

To eliminate the blank line, add a semicolon to the end of line 10:

```
10  PRINT "THIS MESSAGE HAS PRECISELY 40
    CHARACTERS";
```

Now you get this:

```
THIS MESSAGE HAS PRECISELY 40 CHARACTERS
SO THERE'S A BLANK LINE ON THE SCREEN
```

The second line of this message is now a lie.

A statement such as

```
PRINT A$ + B$
```

causes a halt with the message `?STRING TOO LONG ERROR` if the combined length of the concatenated strings is greater than 255 characters. However, you can print the apparent concatenation regardless of length by using a semicolon:

```
PRINT A$; B$
```

When an item in the PRINT list is followed by a comma, the cursor or print head is advanced to the next available tab position: column 17 or 33 of the current line or column 1 of the next line. The next item written begins at the tab position. A series of consecutive commas advances the cursor or print head a corresponding number of tab positions. A comma at the end of a PRINT statement causes the cursor or print head to be left at the next available tab position, and may prevent a new line from being started. For example, the statement

```
PRINT 1, 2, 3, 4,
```

produces the output

```
1                2                3
4
```

and leaves the cursor or print head positioned in column 17 of the second line, directly under the digit 2. The statement

```
PRINT 1/3, 2 * 4, 51
```

produces the output

```
.333333333      8                51
```

Comma Cautions: If any character appears in columns 24 to 32, or in the case of models II, II Plus, and IIe, if you have the Apple II 80-Column Text Card installed in your computer and running in "active 80" mode, then column 33 is not available as a tab position; a comma after column 17 causes the next item to start at column 1 of the next line.

text window: see Section 5.2.4, Section F.1, and your Apple's reference manual

If the text window is set to fewer than 33 columns wide, commas in a PRINT statement do not function properly and may cause text to be displayed outside the text window.

A PRINT statement that doesn't end with a comma or semicolon always starts a new line after writing its last item and leaves the cursor or print head positioned in column 1 of the new line. The statement

```
PRINT
```

simply starts a new line. If the cursor or print head was already at the beginning of a line, this statement causes a blank line to be displayed or printed.

Here's a sample program using some of the features of PRINT:

```
10  LET A = 5.35 : LET C$ = "FRED" : LET G% = 16
```
Sets up series of variables.

```
20  PRINT "STUFF AND NONSENSE"
```
Displays message and starts new line.

```
30  PRINT
```
Displays a blank line.

```
40  PRINT "A = ";
```
Displays message without starting a new line.

`50  PRINT A`	Displays 5.35 on same line as message from program line 40; starts new line.
`60  PRINT "G% = "; G%`	Displays message and value 16 on same line; starts new line.
`70  PRINT "C$ = ", C$`	Displays message, advances to next tab position, and displays string FRED; starts new line.
`80  PRINT A * G%`	Displays value of expression A * G% (85.6) and starts new line.

When executed, this program produces the following output:

```
STUFF AND NONSENSE


A = 5.35
G% = 16
C$ =                         FRED
85.6
```

Abbreviation for PRINT: You can use a question mark (?) as an abbreviation for the keyword PRINT; if you use it, it appears as `PRINT` in a program listing. If you type

```
100  ? A$
LIST
```

Applesoft displays

```
100  PRINT A$
```

5.2.3 Number Formats

This section describes the formats in which Applesoft displays or prints numeric values. Numbers are not always formatted in the way you might expect; this is particularly true for numbers more than nine digits long or for exceptionally small numbers.

Numeric values in Applesoft must be in the range -1*10 ^ 38 to 1*10 ^ 38. Any number whose absolute value is less than approximately 3*10 ^ -39 is converted to 0. True integer values to be assigned to integer variables (such as A%) must be in the range -32767 to +32767.

A number typed from the keyboard or a numeric constant used in an Applesoft program can have as many as 38 digits. However, only nine digits are significant, and the last digit is rounded off. An Applesoft statement that you type as

```
PRINT 1.23456787654321
```

displays

```
1.23456788
```

on the screen.

Integers are always converted to real form before being used in arithmetic calculations, and the results are converted back to integer form when assigned to an integer variable. Conversion from real to integer form is by truncation to the next lower integer, not by rounding to the nearer integer.

Applesoft displays and prints numbers according to the following rules:

- If the number is negative, it is preceded by a minus sign (-); if it is 0 or positive, no sign is used.
- If the number is an integer with an absolute value from 0 to 999999999, it is formatted as an integer.
- If the number is not an integer and its absolute value is between .01 and 999999999.2, it is formatted with a decimal point in the usual way.
- In all other cases, the number is formatted in scientific notation. (See Table 5-1.)

Table 5-1 shows examples of the formats used for displaying and printing numbers.

Table 5-1. Number Formats

Number	**Output Format**
+1	1
-1	-1
6523	6523
-23.460	-23.46
45.72 * 10 ^ 5	4572000
1 * 10 ^ 20	1E+20
-12.34567896 * 10 ^ 10	-1.2345679E+11
1000000000	1E+09
999999999	999999999

scientific notation: the representation of numbers in terms of powers of 10

The format Applesoft uses for scientific notation is shown in Figure 5-1.

Figure 5-1. Format for Scientific Notation

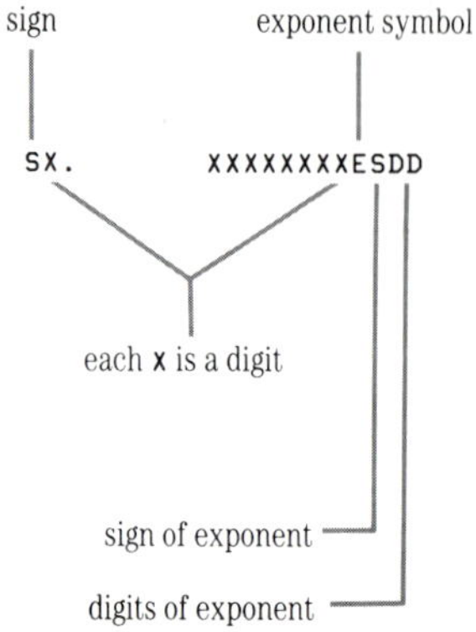

A sign is shown only if the number is negative. There is always exactly one nonzero digit before the decimal point and up to eight digits after it, with trailing zeros suppressed. There are never any leading zeros; the digit before the decimal point is always nonzero. If there is only one digit to print after all trailing zeroes are suppressed, no decimal point is shown. The letter *E* (for exponent) is always followed by a sign and a two-digit exponent. The value of a number represented in this form is the number before the *E* times 10 raised to the power after the *E*. For example,

`PRINT 35 * 345 ^ 14`	Yields 1.18450085E+37.
`PRINT -3.14159 * 567 ^ 5`	Yields -1.84104669E+14.
`PRINT 1 / 999`	Yields 1.001001E-03.
`PRINT -3 / 999`	Yields -3.003003E-03.

5.2.4 Formatting Text on the Screen

This section deals with Applesoft's facilities for controlling the way text is formatted and presented on the display screen. For further information on text formatting, see Section 5.2.2.

- The TEXT and HOME statements are used to clear text and graphics from the screen.
- SPC, TAB, HTAB, VTAB, and POS control the position of the cursor, which determines where characters are displayed on the screen.
- NORMAL, INVERSE, and FLASH control the form in which text characters are presented on the screen.
- The SPEED= command sets the rate at which characters are displayed.

5.2.4.1 The Text Window

The area within which text is displayed and scrolled on the screen is known as the **text window**. Normally, the text window is the full screen. Section F.1 describes how you can create one or more text windows that occupy only part of the screen. See your Apple's reference manual for a more technical discussion.

5.2.4.2 The TEXT Statement

```
TEXT
```

The TEXT statement instructs Applesoft to begin displaying text on the screen; it is customarily used to switch from graphics to text display. The text window is set to the full screen (24 lines, 40 or 80 characters per line depending on your model and switch settings). The Applesoft prompting character ( ]) is displayed in the bottom-left corner of the screen, followed by the cursor.

If the display is already in text mode, the TEXT statement is equivalent to the statement VTAB 24.

5.2.4.3 The HOME Statement

```
HOME
```

HOME clears the currently defined text window and sends the cursor to the top-left corner of the window. If the text window is set to the full screen, the cursor is sent to the beginning of line 1. If the computer is displaying mixed text and graphics (four lines of text at the bottom of the screen), HOME clears the four text lines and sends the cursor to the beginning of line 21.

> *Helpful Hint:* To move the cursor to the top-left corner of the screen without clearing any text, use
>
> ```
> VTAB 1 : HTAB 1
> ```

VTAB and HTAB statements: see Sections 5.2.4.7 and 5.2.4.6

5.2.4.4 The SPC Function

The SPC (for space) function is used in PRINT statements (see Section 5.2.2) to write a specified number of spaces to the current output device. The numeric argument given to the function specifies the number of spaces to be written. If this value is a real number, Applesoft truncates it to the next lower integer.

The SPC function can be called only from within a PRINT statement. SPC differs from TAB (see Section 5.2.4.5) in that it advances the cursor (or print head, if the current output device is a printer) a specified number of columns from its current position, rather than to a specific horizontal position from the beginning of the current line. If the cursor is spaced past the right edge of the screen or text window, it returns to the beginning of the next line and continues spacing. For example, assuming the text window is set to the full screen and the cursor is initially at the left edge, the statements

```
10  PRINT SPC (5); "HELLO"
20  PRINT "THESE"; SPC (10); "ARE"; SPC
    (4); "INTERESTING"; SPC (12);
    "TIMES"
```

display the following on the screen:

```
     HELLO
THESE          ARE    INTERESTING
     TIMES
```

Notice how the output of line 20 wraps around when it reaches the edge of the screen (column 40).

If SPC is the last item in a PRINT statement, Applesoft acts as if the statement ended with a semicolon. The cursor is left positioned the specified number of spaces after the end of the previous item; no new line is started. The next item displayed begins immediately following the last space.

The argument given to SPC must be in the range 0 to 255 or the program halts with the message `?ILLEGAL QUANTITY ERROR`. However, several calls to SPC can be strung together in the form

```
PRINT SPC (255); SPC (255); SPC (255)
```

to provide arbitrarily large numbers of spaces.

Semicolons Optional: Semicolons are optional between SPC items:

```
PRINT "LET"; SPC (10) "ALL" SPC (15);
      "REJOICE"
```

5.2.4.5 The TAB Function

The TAB function is used in PRINT statements (see Section 5.2.2) to advance the cursor to a specified horizontal position measured from the beginning of the current output line. The numeric argument given to the function specifies the position to which the cursor is to be moved. If this value is a real number, Applesoft truncates it to the next lower integer.

The TAB function can be called only from within a PRINT statement. TAB differs from SPC (see Section 5.2.4.2) in that it advances the cursor (or print head, if the current output device is a printer) to a specific horizontal position from the beginning of the current line, rather than a specified number of columns from the current cursor position. If the cursor is advanced past the right edge of the screen or text window, it returns to the beginning of the next line and continues advancing. For example, assuming the text window is set to the full screen and the cursor is initially at the left edge, the statements

```
10  PRINT TAB (15); "THE FLEET'S IN!"
20  PRINT TAB (10); "HELLO"; TAB (30);
      "THERE,"; TAB (45); "SAILOR!"
```

display the following on the screen:

```
               THE FLEET'S IN!
          HELLO               THERE,
SAILOR!
```

Notice how the output of line 20 wraps around when it reaches the edge of the screen (column 40).

> *TAB Moves Forward Only:* Unlike the HTAB statement, which moves the cursor to an absolute horizontal position from the left edge of the screen or the text window, TAB moves the cursor in a forward direction only. If the specified tab position is less than the current cursor position, TAB has no effect; it never moves the cursor to the left on the current line (use HTAB for this purpose).

If TAB is the last item in a PRINT statement, Applesoft acts as if the statement ended with a semicolon. The cursor is left at the specified tab position; no new line is started. The next item displayed begins at the tab position.

The argument given to TAB must be in the range 0 to 255 or the program halts with the message `?ILLEGAL QUANTITY ERROR`. An argument value of 0 moves the cursor to 256 positions from the beginning of the current line.

Semicolons Optional: Semicolons are optional between TAB items:

```
PRINT "DOWN"; TAB (14) "YOU" TAB (27);
      "GO"
```

5.4.2.6 The HTAB Statement

```
HTAB 10
HTAB N
HTAB 41 - LEN (S$)
```

HTAB (for horizontal tab) moves the cursor to a specified horizontal position from the beginning of the current output line. The expression following the keyword HTAB specifies the position to which the cursor is to be moved. If this value is a real number, Applesoft truncates it to the next lower integer.

Unlike the TAB function, which moves the cursor in a forward direction only, the HTAB statement can move the cursor in either direction to a specified horizontal position. For example, in 40-column mode, the program

```
5  HOME
10  HTAB 6 : PRINT "IS THE";
15  FOR Z = 1 TO 500: NEXT Z
20  HTAB 1 : PRINT "THIS";
25  FOR Z = 1 TO 500 : NEXT Z
30  HTAB 13 : PRINT "PROPER ORDER"
```

displays the following on the screen:

```
THIS IS THE PROPER ORDER
```

If you want to use HTAB to display several text items on the same line, you need a semicolon at the end of each PRINT statement to avoid starting a new line.

If there is a text window set, the specified tab position is interpreted relative to the left edge of the window. However, HTAB behaves as though there were 40 columns in each line of the window, regardless of the actual width to which the window has been set; that is, position 1 is considered to be the leftmost column of the current line, position 41 the leftmost column of the next line, position 81 the leftmost column of the line after that, and so on. If the cursor is advanced past the right edge of the screen or text window, it returns to the beginning of the next line and continues advancing.

HTAB can carry the cursor outside the boundaries of the text window, but only long enough to display one character; the cursor then returns to the left edge of the window.

80-Column Text Card Users: If your computer is an Apple II, an Apple II Plus, or an early Apple IIe, HTAB is designed to operate with a 40-column screen only. If you attempt to advance the cursor beyond column 40, it wraps around to the next line, even if you have the Apple II 80-Column Text Card installed and running in "active 80" mode. To tab to a position between columns 41 and 80, use

POKE statement: see Section 7.1.2

```
POKE 1403, XX
```

where XX is the number of the column to which you want to tab. See Section F.1 and the *80-Column Text Card Manual* for more information.

The column number specified to HTAB must be in the range 0 to 255 or the program halts with the message `?ILLEGAL QUANTITY ERROR`. A value of 0 moves the cursor to 256 positions from the beginning of the current line.

A Programming Tip: Many programmers find HTAB to be more convenient to use than TAB, because it is an independent statement and need not be embedded in a PRINT statement. This makes it easier to change, if necessary, during program development.

5.2.4.7 The VTAB Statement

```
VTAB 10
VTAB N
VTAB 25 - H%
```

VTAB (for vertical tab) moves the cursor vertically to a specified line on the screen. The expression following the keyword VTAB specifies the line to which the cursor is to be moved. If the value of this expression is a real number, Applesoft truncates it to the next lower integer.

The top line of the screen is line 1; the bottom line is line 24. VTAB can move the cursor either up or down on the screen, but never to the left or right; it remains at the same horizontal position as before the move. This sample program uses VTAB:

```
10  HOME                          Clears text from screen.
20  VTAB 6                        Moves cursor to line 6.
30  PRINT "LINE 6"                Displays imaginative message.
40  FOR Z = 1 TO 500: NEXT Z
                                  Delays loop so user can see the
                                  order and position of text display.
50  VTAB 18                       Moves cursor to line 18.
```

```
60   PRINT "LINE 18"              Displays another imaginative
                                  message.
70   FOR Z = 1 TO 500: NEXT Z
                                  Another delay loop.
80   VTAB 12                      Moves cursor to line 12.
90   PRINT "THE MIDDLE"           Displays last message.
```

VTAB ignores the setting of the text window, if any. The specified line number is always taken to relate to the entire screen.

The line number specified to VTAB must be in the range 1 to 24 or the program halts with the message `?ILLEGAL QUANTITY ERROR`. If VTAB moves the cursor to a line below the bottom of the text window, all subsequent text is displayed on that same line.

5.2.4.8 The POS Function

The POS (for position) function yields the current horizontal position of the cursor, relative to the left edge of the text window. The value yielded is in the range 0 to 39. A value of 0 represents the left edge of the window.

POS must be followed by an argument in parentheses. What you use for an argument expression doesn't matter, but if Applesoft can't evaluate it as a legal expression, you get an error halt. The argument given to POS is ignored, and has no effect on the operation of the function. However, you can't leave it out—you must include an argument expression of some kind to "keep the parentheses apart."

> *A Difference of Opinion:* Notice that POS numbers columns beginning with 0, whereas TAB and HTAB number them beginning with 1. Thus, assuming the cursor is at the beginning of a line, the statement
>
> ```
> PRINT TAB 10; POS (0)
> ```
>
> prints the value `9`, and
>
> ```
> HTAB 43 : PRINT POS (X)
> ```
>
> prints `2` (since HTAB 43 tabs to the third column of the next display line). Notice in the second case that the value of variable X makes no difference.

5.2.4.9 The INVERSE Statement

```
INVERSE
```

The INVERSE statement causes subsequent text output to be displayed in black-on-white instead of the usual white-on-black (where *white* means the phosphor color of your display, whatever that is). The normal white-on-black display can be restored with the NORMAL statement. (See Section 5.2.4.11.) For example,

`10 INVERSE`	Sets inverse display.
`20 PRINT "BLACK-ON-WHITE"`	Displays `BLACK-ON-WHITE` in black-on-white.
`30 NORMAL`	Restores normal display.
`40 PRINT "WHITE-ON-BLACK"`	Displays `WHITE-ON-BLACK` in white-on-black.

INVERSE affects only subsequent output characters sent to the screen with PRINT statements. It has no effect on characters already on the screen or on keyboard input "echoed" to the screen. Note: lowercase letters can be displayed in inverse video only when the 80-column card is active.

Don't overdo it: INVERSE is most effective when you use it sparingly.

5.2.4.10 The FLASH Statement

```
FLASH
```

The FLASH statement causes subsequent text output to alternate approximately twice a second between black-on-white and the usual white-on-black (where *white* means the phosphor color of your display, whatever that is). The normal white-on-black display can be restored with the NORMAL statement. (See Section 5.2.4.11) For example,

`10 FLASH`	Sets flashing display.
`20 PRINT "FLASHY"`	Displays flashy `FLASHY`.
`30 NORMAL`	Restores normal display.
`40 PRINT "DRAB"`	Displays drab `DRAB`.

FLASH affects only subsequent output characters sent to the screen with PRINT statements. It has no effect on characters already on the screen or on keyboard input "echoed" to the screen.

When FLASH Flops: FLASH doesn't work on characters with ASCII codes (see Section 4.2.1 and Appendix C) above 95, the most important of which are the lowercase letters; instead of making them flash, it turns them into gibberish.

FLASH doesn't work at all if you have an Apple IIc, or an Apple IIe with the Apple II 80-Column Text Card installed and running in "active 80" mode.

FLASH is most effective when used very sparingly. Reserve it for only the most important messages or unusual uses. Cavalier use of FLASH has been known to drive users to delirium.

5.2.4.11 The NORMAL Statement

```
NORMAL
```

The NORMAL statement causes subsequent text output to be displayed in the usual white-on-black (where *white* means the phosphor color of your display, whatever that is). It is usually used to cancel the effects of the INVERSE or FLASH statement. For example,

10	INVERSE	Sets inverse display.
20	PRINT "BLACK-ON-WHITE"	Displays BLACK-ON-WHITE in black-on-white.
30	NORMAL	Restores normal display.
40	PRINT "WHITE-ON-BLACK"	Displays WHITE-ON-BLACK in white-on-black.
50	FLASH	Sets flashing display.
60	PRINT "FLASHY"	Displays flashy FLASHY.
70	NORMAL	Restores normal display.
80	PRINT "DRAB"	Displays drab DRAB.

NORMAL affects only subsequent output characters sent to the screen with PRINT statements. It has no effect on characters already on the screen.

5.2.4.12 The SPEED= Statement

```
SPEED= 255
SPEED= X
SPEED= Z - 6 * F
```

The SPEED= statement sets the rate at which output characters are sent to the display screen or other output device (such as a printer). The slowest rate is 0; the fastest is 255. The normal speed setting (if you don't do anything to change it) is 255. For example,

`10 SPEED= 0`	Sets slowest possible speed.
`20 PRINT "THE TORTOISE"`	Displays `THE TORTOISE` slowly.
`30 SPEED= 255`	Restores normal speed.
`40 PRINT "THE HARE"`	Displays `THE HARE` quickly.

SPEED Is Not a Variable: Notice that the equal sign is part of the keyword SPEED=; it doesn't represent an assignment to a variable named SPEED. A statement such as

```
LET SPEED = X
```

causes a syntax error. The only way to find out the current speed setting is to keep track of it yourself with a variable, as in the following example:

`10 LET X = 250`	Sets initial value for speed.
`20 SPEED= X`	Sets speed to value of X.
`30 PRINT "CURRENT SPEED IS ";X`	Displays current speed.
`40 LET X = X - 25`	Decreases value of X by 25.
`50 IF X >= 0 THEN GOTO 20`	Repeats until X becomes negative.
`60 SPEED= 255 : END`	X is too low; ends the program.

The speed setting is not reset to its normal value by RUN, CLEAR, or [CONTROL]-[RESET].

The speed setting specified to SPEED= must be in the range 0 to 255 or the program halts with the message `?ILLEGAL QUANTITY ERROR`.

SPEED= has no effect on graphics.

5.2.5 Miscellaneous Output Facilities

This section covers Applesoft's facilities for dealing with the remaining output features of the Apple II: the built-in speaker, annunciator outputs, utility strobe, and cassette tape output. Most of these features are controlled by means of PEEK and POKE (see Sections 7.1.1 and 7.1.2); details can be found in Appendix F. The annunciators and utility strobe are seldom used, and are mentioned here just for the sake of completeness.

5.2.5.1 Controlling the Speaker

for technical information on the **built-in speaker:** see your Apple's reference manual

The Apple II has a small, built-in speaker that you can use to add sound to your programs. The easiest way to use it is by sending the ASCII *bell* character (CONTROL-G, ASCII code 7) to the display screen. This causes the computer to emit a short beep.

> *Historical Note:* ASCII code 7 was originally used to ring a small bell on teletype machines, to let the teletype operator know that a message was coming in. On the Apple II it sends a 1-kilohertz tone (1000 cycles per second) to the Apple II's speaker for 1/10 second.

Here's a program to ring the computer's "bell" a number of times specified by the user:

`10 PRINT "ENTER A NUMBER FROM 1 TO 9 (S TO STOP): ";`	Prompts user for input.
`20 GET A$`	Accepts single character from keyboard.
`30 IF A$ = "S" THEN END`	Stops if user typed `S`.
`40 IF VAL (A$) < 1 THEN 20`	If character typed is out of range then tries again.
`50 FOR X = 1 TO VAL (A$)`	Loop requested number of times.
`60 PRINT CHR$ (7)`	Sounds "bell."
`70 NEXT X`	Loops back to 50.
`80 PRINT`	Leaves a blank line.
`90 GOTO 10`	Starts again.

The only other way for Applesoft programs to produce sound from the speaker is with a PEEK or POKE to address -16336. This causes the speaker to emit a single click. By combining such clicks in the appropriate patterns and frequencies, you can produce musical tones and a variety of other sounds. Experiment for yourself!

5.2.5.2 Annunciator Output

The Apple II, Apple II Plus, and Apple IIe have four annunciator outputs, which are pins of the hand control connector on which electrical impulses can be transmitted. The signals on these pins are most commonly used to control devices such as lamps and relays connected to the computer through the hand control connector. The annunciator outputs can be turned on and off with PEEK or POKE to the appropriate addresses; see Section F.4 for details and your Apple's reference manual for further technical information.

5.2.5.3 The Utility Strobe

The Apple II's utility strobe is a pin of the hand control connector that can be triggered to send an electrical impulse lasting one-half microsecond. Like the annunciators, it can be used to control a variety of devices connected to the computer through the hand control connector. The utility strobe can be triggered with a PEEK or POKE to address -16320. See Section F.4 for details and your Apple's reference manual for further technical information.

5.2.5.4 Cassette Output

Two Applesoft statements, SAVE and STORE, can be used to write information to a cassette tape recorder (Apple II, Apple II Plus, and Apple IIe only). SAVE writes the Applesoft program currently in memory to tape; STORE writes the contents of an integer or real array. For details, see Appendix M.

Chapter 6

Graphics

This chapter describes Applesoft's facilities for creating, changing, displaying, and storing both low- and high-resolution graphic designs:

- Section 6.1, "Low-Resolution Graphics," deals with 16-color graphics on a 40-by-48 grid.
- Section 6.2, "High-Resolution Graphics," deals with 6-color graphics on a 280-by-192 grid.
- Section 6.3, "Shape Tables," discusses the use of shape tables for animation sequences.
- Section 6.4, "Graphics in Text Mode," discusses MouseText, a set of graphics you can use in text mode.

6.1 Low-Resolution Graphics

The low-resolution graphics screen consists of 1920 blocks (40 columns by 48 rows) in 16 colors. This section describes the facilities available in Applesoft for using low-resolution graphics:

- The GR statement (see Section 6.1.1) instructs Applesoft to begin displaying low-resolution graphics.
- The COLOR= statement (see Section 6.1.2) controls the colors displayed on the screen.
- The PLOT statement (see Section 6.1.3) plots individual blocks on the screen.
- The HLIN statement (see Section 6.1.4) draws horizontal lines.
- The VLIN statement (see Section 6.1.5) draws vertical lines.
- The SCRN function (see Section 6.1.6) lets you determine what color is currently displayed at a particular position on the graphics screen.

6.1.1 The GR Statement

```
GR
```

The GR (for graphics) statement instructs the computer to display low-resolution graphics. If the screen has been displaying text, it is changed from 40 (or 80) columns by 24 lines of text to 40 columns by 40 rows of graphics, with space for four lines of text at the bottom. (Text display can be restored with the TEXT statement—see Section 5.2.4.) GR clears the screen to black, moves the text cursor to the beginning of the bottom line (line 24), clears any text window that may have been set, and sets the low-resolution display color to 0 (black).

After executing a GR statement, you can convert the display to full-screen graphics (a 40-by-48 grid with no space for text) with the statement

POKE statement: see Section 7.1.2

```
POKE -16302,0
```

This statement changes the bottom four lines of text to eight rows of colored blocks. To clear these rows to black, add

CALL statement: see Section 7.1.3

```
CALL -1998
```

Note that the POKE statement must be executed after GR. If you execute the POKE first, GR resets the screen to mixed graphics and text.

> *Switching From Hi-Resolution Page 2:* If you execute a GR statement while displaying high-resolution page 2 (see Section 6.2.2), GR clears its usual screenful of memory but leaves you looking at page 2 of low-resolution graphics and text. To avoid this problem, always use the TEXT statement before switching from high-resolution page 2 to low resolution.

> *For More Information:* See Section F.3 for more information on the use of the various text and graphics memory pages. See your Apple's reference manual for further technical information on the Apple II's graphics display capabilities.

6.1.2 The COLOR= Statement

```
COLOR= 12
COLOR= C(J)
COLOR= (X - 4) / 16
```

The COLOR= statement sets the display color for plotting low-resolution graphics. There are 16 colors available, represented by numbers from 0 to 15 as shown in Table 6-1. When you enter low-resolution graphics, the GR statement sets the display color to black (0).

Table 6-1. Color Codes for Low-Resolution Graphics

Code	Color
0	Black
1	Magenta
2	Dark blue
3	Violet
4	Dark green
5	Gray 1
6	Medium blue
7	Light blue
8	Brown
9	Orange
10	Gray 2
11	Pink
12	Green
13	Yellow
14	Aqua
15	White

Colors in a Monochrome World: If you're using a monochrome display (black-and-white, or some other single phosphor color), the different colors appear on your screen as various patterns of shading.

The following short program displays each of the 16 available colors in a horizontal bar across the screen:

HLIN statement: see Section 6.1.4

```
10  GR                        Displays low-resolution graphics.
20  FOR X = 0 TO 15           Executes loop for each color.
30  COLOR= X                  Sets next color.
40  HLIN 0, 39 AT X * 2       Draws a bar of this color across the
                              screen, leaving a blank row above it.
50  NEXT X                    Goes back for next color.
```

COLOR Isn't a Variable: Notice that the equal sign is part of the keyword COLOR=; it doesn't represent an assignment to a variable named COLOR. A statement such as

```
LET COLOR = X
```

causes a syntax error. The only way to find out the current display color is to keep track of it yourself with a separate variable, as in the example.

You can specify a color code higher than 15, but the series of color values simply repeats. That is, 16 is equivalent to 0, 18 is equivalent to 2, 35 is equivalent to 3, and so on. However, a color value less than 0 or greater than 255 stops the program with the message `?ILLEGAL QUANTITY ERROR`.

6.1.3 The PLOT Statement

```
PLOT 20, 12
PLOT X - 6, Y + 2
PLOT THETA * 40 / (2*PI), 24 - (SIN(THETA)
     * 23)
```

The PLOT statement places a block of the current low-resolution display color at a specified position on the screen. The first expression following the keyword PLOT specifies the column in which the block is to be plotted (numbered 0 to 39, from left to right); the second expression, separated from the first by a comma, designates the row (numbered 0 to 39 for mixed text and graphics, 0 to 47 for full-screen graphics, from top to bottom). For example, the following program plots a block of pink in column 20, row 2 of the screen:

`10 GR`	Displays low-resolution graphics.
`20 COLOR= 11`	Sets display color to pink.
`30 PLOT 20, 2`	Plots a block of pink in column 20, row 2.

Figure 6-1 shows the system of coordinates used to designate positions on the low-resolution graphics screen. Position 0,0 is the top-left corner and position 39,0 the top-right. When displaying mixed graphics and text, the bottom-left corner is position 0,39 and the bottom-right is 39,39; in full-screen graphics, the bottom-left corner is 0,47 and the bottom-right is 39,47.

Figure 6-1. Screen Coordinates for Low-Resolution Graphics

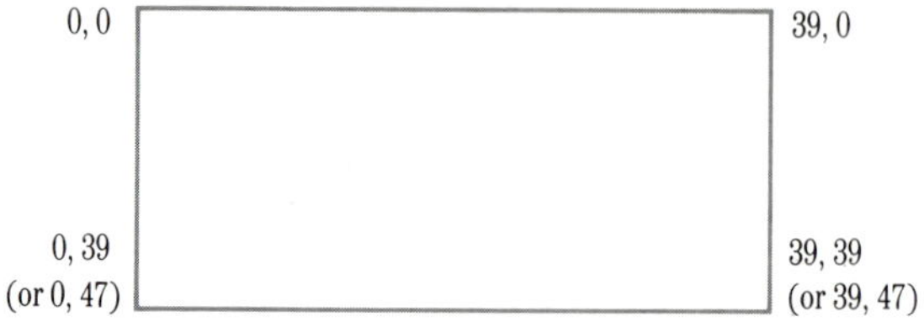

PLOT With Mixed Graphics and Text: If Applesoft is displaying mixed graphics and text and the plotting coordinates designate a row from 40 to 47, a text character instead of a block of color is displayed at the specified coordinates. The particular character displayed depends on the current low-resolution display color. Here's a program to demonstrate this effect:

`10 GR`	Displays mixed low-resolution graphics.
`20 FOR Y = 0 TO 47`	Loops over all screen rows.
`30 FOR X = 0 TO 39`	Loops over all screen columns.
`40 COLOR = X`	Uses color corresponding to column number (colors 0 to 15 repeat after column 15).
`50 PLOT X, Y`	Plots a block at column X, row Y.
`60 NEXT X`	Loops to next column.
`70 NEXT Y`	Loops to next row.

Try changing line 10 to

```
10 TEXT
```

to see the effect on the full screen.

A column coordinate outside the range 0 to 39 or a row coordinate outside the range 0 to 47 causes the program to halt with the message `?ILLEGAL QUANTITY ERROR`.

6.1.4 The HLIN Statement

```
HLIN 5, 20 AT 35
HLIN X, Y AT Z
HLIN Q - 3, J * S8 AT V%
```

The HLIN (for horizontal line) statement draws a horizontal line on the screen in the current low-resolution display color (see Section 6.1.2). The two expressions following the keyword HLIN, separated by a comma, designate the columns in which the line is to begin and end; the expression following the keyword AT specifies the row in which the line is to be drawn. The first end point may be less than, equal to, or greater than the second. For example,

`10 GR`	Displays low-resolution graphics.
`20 COLOR = 4`	Sets color to dark green.
`30 HLIN 10, 30 AT 20`	Draws a horizontal green line in row 20 from column 10 to column 30.

HLIN in Text Instead of Graphics: If you use HLIN while displaying text instead of graphics, or with a row coordinate from 40 to 47 while displaying mixed graphics and text, Applesoft displays a row of characters instead of a bar of color. For example, if line 10 were changed to

```
10 TEXT
```

the result would be a row of dollar signs instead of a bar of dark green. In most cases, when you see patterns like these on your screen it means you forgot to include a GR statement.

A column coordinate outside the range 0 to 39 or a row coordinate outside the range 0 to 47 causes the program to halt with the message `?ILLEGAL QUANTITY ERROR`.

The HLIN statement has no visible effect if you use it while displaying high-resolution graphics.

6.1.5 The VLIN Statement

```
VLIN 5, 20 AT 35
VLIN X, Y AT Z
VLIN Q - 3, J * S8 AT V%
```

The VLIN (for vertical line) statement draws a vertical line on the screen in the current low-resolution display color (see Section 6.1.2). The two expressions following the keyword VLIN, separated by a comma, designate the rows in which the line is to begin and end; the expression following the keyword AT specifies the column in which the line is to be drawn. The first end point may be less than, equal to, or greater than the second. For example,

`10 GR`	Displays low-resolution graphics.
`20 COLOR = 4`	Sets color to dark green.
`30 VLIN 10, 30 AT 20`	Draws a vertical green line in column 20 from row 10 to row 30.

> *VLIN in Text Instead of Graphics:* If you use VLIN while displaying text instead of graphics, or if part of the line being drawn goes beyond row 39 while displaying mixed graphics and text, Applesoft displays text characters instead of blocks of color. For example, if line 10 were changed to
>
> ```
> 10 TEXT
> ```
>
> the result would be a row of flashing `D`'s and a dollar sign instead of a bar of dark green.

A column coordinate outside the range 0 to 39 or a row coordinate outside the range 0 to 47 causes the program to halt with the message `?ILLEGAL QUANTITY ERROR`.

The VLIN statement has no visible effect if you use it while displaying high-resolution graphics.

6.1.6 The SCRN Function

The SCRN (for screen) function reads the color currently displayed at a designated position on the low-resolution graphics screen. This function takes two arguments, the first specifying the column and the second the row of the desired position. It yields a number from 0 to 15 representing the color displayed at that position. For example, the expression

```
SCRN (5, 9)
```

yields the code (see Table 6-1) for the color displayed at column 5, row 9.

The SCRN function is not intended for use with high-resolution graphics.

> *For Experts Only—Strange Extensions:* Although the ordinary limits for coordinates on the low-resolution graphics screen are 39 and 47, SCRN actually accepts values up to 47 for both arguments. But if the column parameter is greater than the usual limit of 39, odd things happen. The code yielded by SCRN gives the color for the block whose column is the designated column minus 40, and whose row is the designated row plus 16.
>
> If the row-plus-16 number is in the range 40 through 47, and if mixed graphics and text are being displayed, then the code yielded is not a color code, but is related to the text character at that position in the text area below the graphics (see "For Experts Only—Reading the Text Screen," below).
>
> If the row-plus-16 number is in the range 48 to 63, SCRN yields a meaningless result.

> *For Experts Only—Reading the Text Screen:* When text is being displayed, SCRN yields numbers in the range 0 to 15 whose value is either the high-order four bits (if the row number is odd) or the low-order four bits (if the row number is even) of the character in column C + 1 and row (R + 1) / 2, where C and R are the column and row numbers given as arguments to SCRN. Thus the following expression yields the character at position X, Y:

```
CHR$ ( SCRN (X - 1, 2 * (Y - 1) + 1) * 16
      + SCRN (X - 1, 2 * (Y - 1)) )
```

6.2 High-Resolution Graphics

There are two separate regions in the Apple II's memory, designated page 1 and page 2, that can be used for displaying high-resolution graphics. Each consists of 53,760 points (280 columns by 192 rows) in six colors. This section describes the facilities available in Applesoft for using high-resolution graphics:

- The HGR statement (see Section 6.2.1) instructs Applesoft to begin displaying page 1 of high-resolution graphics.
- The HGR2 statement (see Section 6.2.2) instructs Applesoft to begin displaying page 2 of high-resolution graphics.
- The HCOLOR= statement (see Section 6.2.3) controls the colors displayed on the high-resolution screen.
- The HPLOT statement (see Section 6.2.4) plots individual points and lines on the high-resolution screen.

Section 6.2.5 tells how to protect your programs and high-resolution graphics from overwriting each other in the computer's memory.

6.2.1 The HGR Statement

```
HGR
```

The HGR (for high-resolution graphics) statement instructs Applesoft to display page 1 of high-resolution graphics. If the screen has been displaying text, it is changed from 40 (or 80) columns by 24 lines of text to 280 columns by 160 rows of high-resolution graphics, with space for four lines of text at the bottom. The graphics area of the screen is cleared to black; the high-resolution display color is not affected. HGR doesn't affect the contents of the text screen, the setting of the text window, or the location of the text cursor; the cursor is not visible unless it is in one of the bottom four lines of the screen.

After executing an HGR statement, you can convert the display to full-screen graphics (a 280-by-192 grid with no space for text) with the statement

```
POKE -16302, 0
```

This statement changes the bottom four lines of text to high-resolution graphics. To return to mixed graphics and text, use

```
POKE -16301, 0
```

Notice that the first POKE statement must be executed after HGR. If you execute the POKE first, HGR resets the screen to mixed graphics and text.

The TEXT statement returns to text display with the text window set to the full screen and the cursor at the bottom of the screen. To turn off high-resolution graphics and return to text display with the text window and cursor intact, use the statement

```
POKE -16303, 0
```

▲Warning If you use the reserved word HGR as the first three characters of a variable name, the HGR statement may be executed before a syntax error is detected. For example, executing the statement

```
HGRIP = 4
```

unexpectedly turns on high-resolution graphics and may destroy part of your program.

For More Information: If you intend to use HGR with an Applesoft program longer than about 6000 (decimal) bytes, see Section 6.2.5 on how to protect your program and graphics from overwriting each other.

See Section F.3 for more information on the use of the various text and graphics memory pages, and Section H.1 for the memory locations occupied by the high-resolution graphics pages. See your computer's reference manual for further technical information on the Apple II's graphics display capabilities.

6.2.2 The HGR2 Statement

```
HGR2
```

The HGR2 (for high-resolution graphics, page 2) statement instructs Applesoft to display page 2 of high-resolution graphics. If the screen has been displaying text, it is changed from 40 (or 80) columns by 24 lines of text to 280 columns by 192 rows of high-resolution graphics. The screen is cleared to black; the high-resolution display color is not affected. HGR2 doesn't affect the contents of the text screen, the setting of the text window, or the location of the text cursor.

The TEXT statement (see Section 5.2.4) returns to text display with the text window set to the full screen and the cursor at the bottom of the screen. To turn off high-resolution graphics and return to text display with the text window and cursor intact, use the statements

`POKE -16300, 0`	Switches from page 2 to page 1
`POKE -16303, 0`	Switches from graphics to text

Avoid Mixing Graphics and Text With HGR2: After executing an HGR2 statement, you can convert the display to mixed graphics and text (a 280-by-160 grid with four lines of text at the bottom) with the statement

```
POKE -16301, 0
```

However, when you use this statement while displaying high-resolution page 2, the four lines of text are taken from text page 2 instead of the usual page 1. Since Applesoft uses the same memory locations allocated to text page 2 for program storage, you end up displaying garbage in the bottom four lines of your screen. For this reason, most programmers avoid mixing graphics and text when using high-resolution page 2.

▲Warning If you use the reserved word HGR2 as the first four characters of a variable name, the HGR2 statement may be executed before a syntax error is detected. For example, executing the statement

```
HGR2PIECES = 4
```

unexpectedly turns on high-resolution graphics and may destroy part of your program.

For More Information: If you intend to use HGR2 with an Applesoft program longer than about 14000 (decimal) bytes, see Section 6.2.5 on how to protect your program and graphics from overwriting each other.

See Section F.3 for more information on the use of the various text and graphics memory pages, and Section H.1 for the memory locations occupied by the high-resolution graphics pages. See your computer's reference manual for further technical information on the Apple II's graphics display capabilities.

6.2.3 The HCOLOR= Statement

```
HCOLOR= 6
HCOLOR= C(J)
HCOLOR= (X - 4) / 8
```

The HCOLOR= (for high-resolution color) statement sets the display color for plotting high-resolution graphics. There are six colors available, represented by numbers from 0 to 7, as shown in Table 6-2.

Table 6-2. Color Codes for High-Resolution Graphics

Code	**Color**
0	Black 1
1	Green
2	Violet
3	White 1
4	Black 2
5	Orange
6	Blue
7	White 2

> *Color in a Monochrome World:* If you're using a monochrome display (black-and-white, or some other single phosphor color), the different colors appear on your screen as various patterns of shading.

The high-resolution display color is not affected by HGR, HGR2, or RUN. Until your program executes an HCOLOR= statement, the display color for high-resolution graphics is indeterminate.

> *HCOLOR Isn't a Variable:* Notice that the equal sign is part of the keyword HCOLOR=; it doesn't represent an assignment to a variable named HCOLOR. A statement such as
>
> ```
> LET HCOLOR = X
> ```
>
> causes a syntax error. The only way to find out the current display color is to keep track of it yourself with a separate variable.

Curious Behavior: As you wander deeper into the recesses of the Apple II's graphics system, you'll begin to notice that the colors in high-resolution graphics don't always act as you might expect. For example, carefully drawn vertical lines may refuse to be visible, a white line crossing a field of green may leave jagged blocks of orange in its wake, or a point plotted with HCOLOR= 3 (white 1) may look blue if its column coordinate is even, green if the column coordinate is odd, and white only if a point is plotted in the next column as well. These strange phenomena are a result of the way the Apple II's high-resolution graphics features interact with the color circuitry in your television set. See your computer's reference manual for further explanation.

If you specify a color code higher than 7, your program halts with the message `?ILLEGAL QUANTITY ERROR`.

6.2.4 The HPLOT Statement

```
HPLOT 140, 80
HPLOT X - 16, Y + 12 TO X + 16, Y - 12
HPLOT 70,40 TO 210,40 TO 210,120 TO 70,120
      TO 70,40
HPLOT TO THETA * 280 / (2*PI), 96 -
      (SIN(THETA) * 95)
```

The HPLOT (for high-resolution plot) statement plots points and lines on the high-resolution graphics screen in the current high-resolution display color. The first expression in each pair specifies a column (numbered 0 to 279, from left to right); the second expression, separated from the first by a comma, designates a row (numbered 0 to 159 for mixed text and graphics, 0 to 191 for full-screen graphics, from top to bottom). For example, the following program plots a white point at column 100, row 50 of the screen:

`10 HGR`	Displays high-resolution graphics.
`20 HCOLOR= 3`	Sets display color to white 1.
`30 HPLOT 100, 50`	Plots a point at column 100, row 50.

▲Warning Be sure to precede HPLOT by either HGR or HGR2 or you will write over lots of memory, including your program and variables.

Figure 6-2 shows the system of coordinates used to designate positions on the high-resolution graphics screen. Position 0,0 is the top-left corner and position 279,0 the top-right. When displaying mixed graphics and text, the bottom-left corner is position 0,159 and the bottom-right is 279,159; in full-screen graphics, the bottom-left corner is 0,191 and the bottom-right is 279,191.

Figure 6-2. Screen Coordinates for High-Resolution Graphics

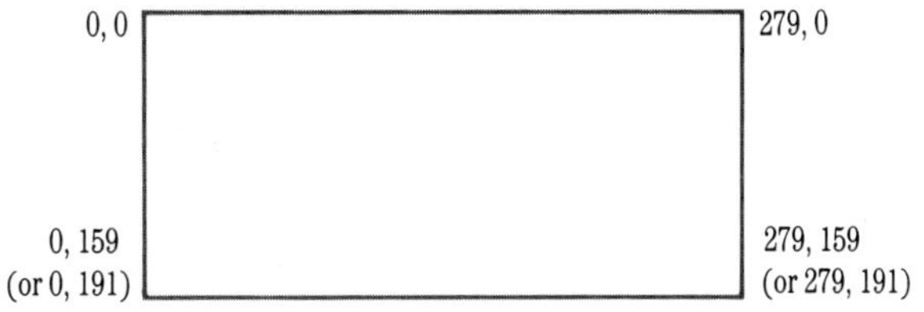

To draw a line with HPLOT, specify the starting and ending points, separated by the keyword TO. The next example draws a white line across the screen:

```
10  HGR                              Displays high-resolution graphics.
20  HCOLOR= 3                        Sets display color to white 1.
30  HPLOT 0, 50 TO 279, 50           Draws a line across row 50.
```

You can draw a series of connected lines in the same HPLOT statement by using a series of TO clauses. Each line begins where the last one ended. The following program, for example, draws a rectangle, as illustrated by the solid lines in Figure 6-3:

```
10  HGR                              Displays high-resolution graphics.
20  HCOLOR= 3                        Sets display color to white 1.
30  HPLOT 70,40 TO 210,40 TO 210,120 TO 70,
      120 TO 70,40                   Draws a rectangle.
```

Figure 6-3. Drawing a Rectangle With HPLOT

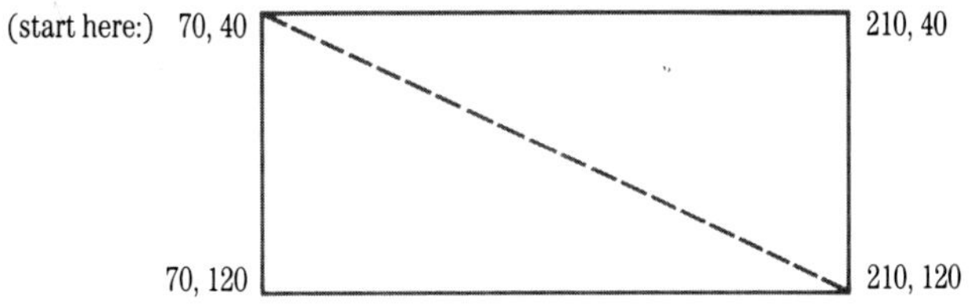

You can extend the series of lines almost indefinitely within the same HPLOT statement, subject only to the limit of 239 characters in a program line.

You can also continue from wherever the last HPLOT statement ended, by writing the keyword TO immediately after the word HPLOT. For example, adding the line

```
40  HPLOT TO 210, 120
```

to the previous program causes it to draw in the diagonal of the rectangle, represented by the dashed line in Figure 6-3. Applesoft assumes that the starting point (which ordinarily would have appeared between the words HPLOT and TO) is the last point plotted.

The color of the new line drawn by HPLOT TO is the same as that of the last point plotted. Even if you insert a new HCOLOR= statement between lines 30 and 40, the line drawn by the HPLOT TO in program line 40 appears in the same color as those drawn in line 30.

To change the color of the line, use a whole new HPLOT:

```
35  HCOLOR= 6                        Changes color to blue.
40  HPLOT 70, 40 TO 210, 120
                                     Continues drawing from last point.
```

HPLOT With Mixed Graphics and Text: If the screen is displaying mixed text and graphics, an attempt to plot a point whose row coordinate is in the range 160 to 191 has no visible effect. However, if you draw a line either beginning or ending in rows 160 to 191, Applesoft displays as much of the line as it can. If you later switch to full-screen graphics with POKE -16302,0 the hidden portion of the line appears.

If the column coordinate given to HPLOT is outside the range 0 to 279, or the row coordinate outside the range 0 to 191, the program halts with the message `?ILLEGAL QUANTITY ERROR`.

6.2.5 Protecting High-Resolution Graphics

Apple II memory allocation: see Section H.1

The two high-resolution graphics pages lie pretty much in the center of things: page 1 resides at memory addresses 8192 to 16383 (hexadecimal $2000 to $3FFF) and page 2 at addresses 16384 to 24575 (hexadecimal $4000 to $5FFF). Because Applesoft program storage begins at location 2048 (hexadecimal $800) and works its way up, it's easy for your program and graphics to get in each other's way. For example, if you're using the HGR statement (see Section 6.2.1) to display page 1 of high-resolution graphics, you have only 6144 bytes of program and variable space (8192 minus 2048) before your program overwrites the graphics area. This section tells how to prevent them from colliding.

One way to protect your program and graphics from each other is to use the HIMEM: statement (see Section 7.2.1) to set the upper limit of program memory at 8192. This is a reasonable method to use for short programs; but Applesoft tends to use a lot of memory, and longer programs would soon run out of space.

Another method that allows the program a bit more breathing room is to use the second page of graphics instead of the first (HGR2 instead of HGR). This has the benefit of starting the graphics at a higher memory location, so you can set HIMEM: to 16384 instead of 8192, allowing 14336 bytes (16384 minus 2048) for your program and variable space. The disadvantage of this method is that you lose the four lines of text at the bottom of the screen, which are available with HGR but not with HGR2.

A third method, probably the best for long programs with lots of variables, is to use the wizardry of the POKE statement to change the start, instead of the end, of Applesoft's program storage space. The following statements start program and variable storage above graphics page 1, beginning at address 16384 (hexadecimal $4000):

```
POKE 103, 1
POKE 104, 64
POKE 16384, 0
```

These statements start program and variable storage above high-resolution page 2, beginning at address 24576 (hexadecimal $6000):

```
POKE 103, 1
POKE 104, 96
POKE 24576, 0
```

No matter where you start program space in memory, your next command should be

```
NEW
```

to clear out any old variables and system control information so you can start a fresh program beginning at the new location. (If your computer is equipped with one or more disk drives, you can accomplish the same thing by loading a new program from a disk with the RUN command.)

6.3 Shape Tables

Applesoft has a number of special facilities that allow you to manipulate shape tables defining shapes on the high-resolution graphics screen. Because shape tables have the advantages of both flexible design and very fast execution, they are ideal for applications such as on-screen animation. This section contains detailed information on creating and manipulating shape tables.

For Hackers Only: Since the advent of the Apple II series of computers, a number of excellent graphics software packages have appeared on the market. Available at most computer stores, these packages take the hard-core technical work (binary arithmetic and machine-language manipulation) out of designing and using shape tables. The information in this section is intended for those programmers who enjoy "twiddling the bits" themselves.

To use this section effectively, you'll need to know about bits and bytes and the rudiments of hexadecimal arithmetic. This information is available in any basic text on computer science; see the bibliography in the owner's manual that came with your computer. All computer memory addresses in this section are in hexadecimal; all other numbers, unless otherwise noted, are in decimal.

6.3.1 Creating a Shape Table

An Applesoft shape definition consists of a sequence of plotting vectors that are stored in a series of consecutive bytes in the computer's memory. One or more such shape definitions, with their indexes (see Section 6.3.1.4), make up a **shape table**.

6.3.1.1 Plotting Vectors

plotting vector: a code representing a single step in drawing a shape on the screen

Each byte in a shape definition has three sections. Each section can contain a **plotting vector**, specifying whether or not to plot a point at the current screen position and in what direction to move (up, down, left, or right) before processing the next vector. Thus each byte can represent up to three plotting vectors.

Figure 6-4 shows how the three sections are arranged within each of the bytes that make up a shape definition. In each plotting vector, bit P specifies whether to plot a point before moving, and the pair of bits designated DD specify the direction in which to move before processing the next vector.

Figure 6-4. Plotting Vectors in a Byte

section:	C		B			A		
bit number:	7	6	5	4	3	2	1	0
specifies:	D	D	P	D	D	P	D	D

if DD = 00 move up
= 01 move right
= 10 move down
= 11 move left

if P = 0 don't plot
= 1 plot a point

Notice that the last section in each byte (the two high-order bits, labeled C in the figure) does not include a P bit. The value of P in such a section is always assumed to be 0 (don't plot); thus section C can only specify a move without plotting.

6.3.1.2 How Plotting Vectors Are Interpreted

The DRAW and XDRAW statements (see Section 6.3.2) read through each byte in the shape definition, from the first byte in the definition to the last. Within each byte, the sections are processed from right to left: section A, then B, then C. When a byte is encountered that contains all zeros, the shape definition is complete.

At any section in the byte, if all the remaining sections contain only zeros, then those sections are ignored. Thus a byte can't end with a move in section C of 00 (move up without plotting) because that section, containing only zeros, is ignored. Similarly, if section C is 00 (ignored), then section B cannot be a move of 000 (move up without plotting), since that is also ignored. And a vector of 000 in section A ends your shape definition unless there is a 1 bit somewhere in section B or section C.

6.3.1.3 Coding a Shape Table

Suppose you want to draw a shape like that shown in Figure 6-5a. To convert the shape into an Applesoft shape definition, follow these steps:

1. Draw the shape on graph paper, one dot per square.
2. Decide where to start drawing the shape and draw a path through each point in the shape, using only 90-degree angles on the turns, as in Figure 6-5b.
3. Redraw the shape as a series of plotting vectors, each vector moving one place up, down, left, or right, and distinguish those vectors that plot a point before moving. This step is illustrated in Figure 6-5c; vectors that plot before moving are marked in the figure with a dot at the beginning of the direction arrow.
4. "Unwrap" the vectors and write them out in sequential order, as in Figure 6-5d.

Figure 6-5. Plotting a Shape

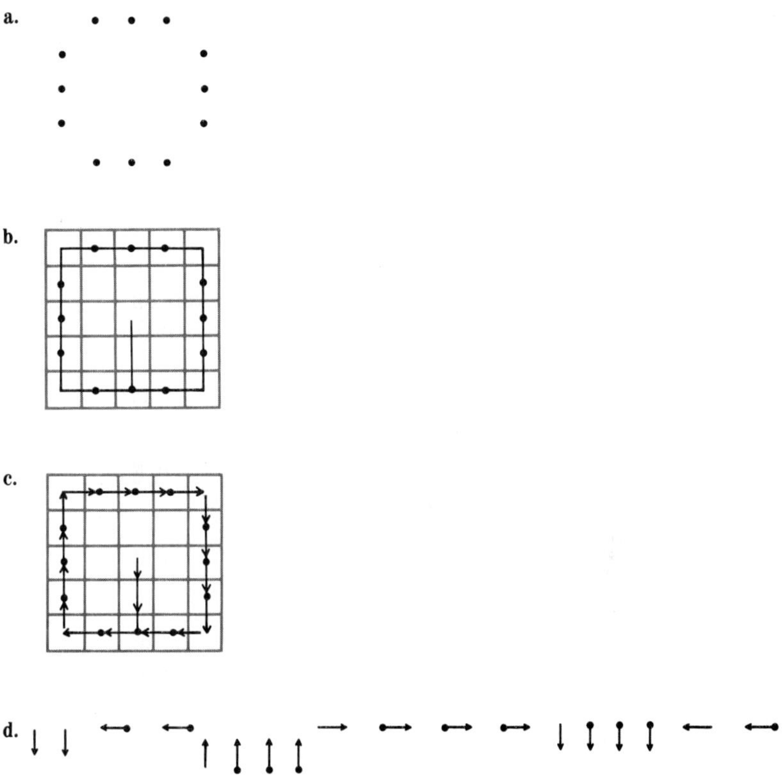

Now you're ready to code the plotting vectors as a shape definition table. Figure 6-6 gives the binary codes corresponding to each possible vector. For each vector in the shape, determine the proper bit code and place it in the next available section in the table, as shown in Figure 6-7. If the code won't fit (for instance, the vector in section C can't plot a point) or is a 00 (or 000) at the end of a byte, then just fill that section with zeros.

Figure 6-6. Codes for Plotting Vectors

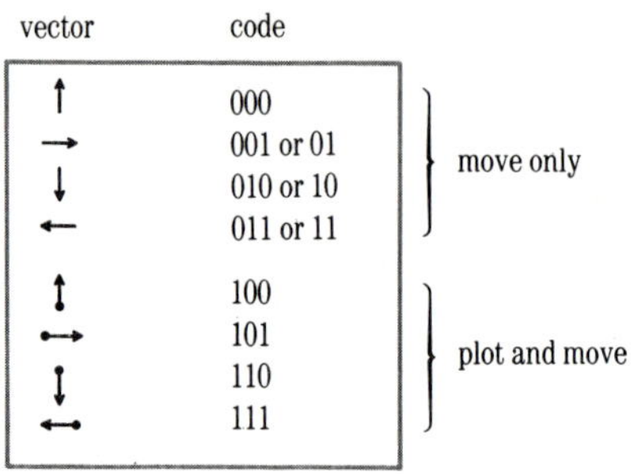

Figure 6-7. Shape Definition Table

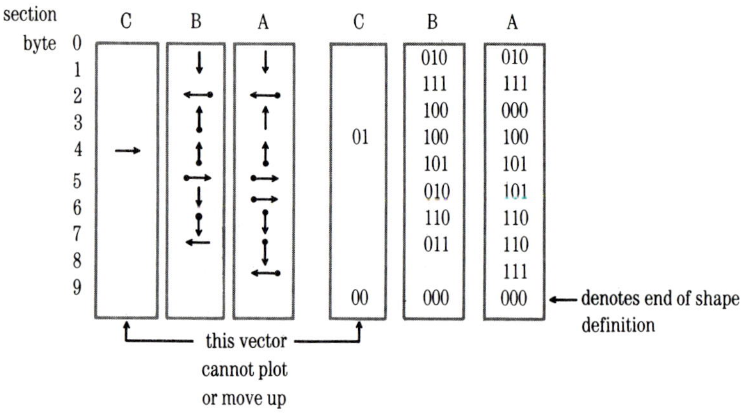

The final step is to convert the binary codes representing the plotting vectors into hexadecimal form so you can type them into the computer.

Table 6-3. Hexadecimal Byte Codes

Binary	**Hex**
0000	0
0001	1
0010	2
0011	3
0100	4
0101	5
0110	6
0111	7
1000	8
1001	9
1010	A
1011	B
1100	C
1101	D
1110	E
1111	F

As shown in Table 6-3, each hexadecimal code corresponds to a group of four bits; so each row of eight bits in your definition table is represented by two such codes (called *hexadecimal digits*). This step is illustrated in Figure 6-8. The final shape definition for the shape in Figure 6-5 is

```
12 3F 20 64 2D 15 36 1E 07 00
```

Figure 6-8. Converting the Shape Definition to Hexadecimal

section	C B A			bytes recoded in hex	
byte 0	0001	0010	=	12	
1	0011	1111	=	3F	
2	0010	0000	=	20	
3	0110	0100	=	64	
4	0010	1101	=	2D	
5	0001	0101	=	15	
6	0011	0110	=	36	
7	0001	1110	=	1E	
8	0000	0111	=	07	
9	0000	0000	=	00	← denotes end of shape definition
hex:	digit 1	digit 2			

6.3.1.4 The Shape Table Index

There is still a little more information you need to provide before you have a complete shape table: the table must have an index. This is simply a list indicating where in memory the computer can find a particular shape. The computer needs the index so that it can find the shape later, when your Applesoft program tries to draw the shape on the screen.

The form of a complete shape table, including the index, is shown in Figure 6-9. The shape table's starting location, whose address is called S in the figure, contains the number of shape definitions in the table (between 00 and FF) in hexadecimal. The next byte (address S + 1) is unused; it is followed by a sequence of two-byte pairs giving the locations of the shapes in the table. (Notice that the shape locations are given with the bytes reversed—low-order byte first—and that the locations are specified relative to address S, the start of the table itself, and not in absolute memory addresses.) For simplicity, the shape definitions themselves are usually placed immediately after the index.

Figure 6-9. Form of a Complete Shape Table

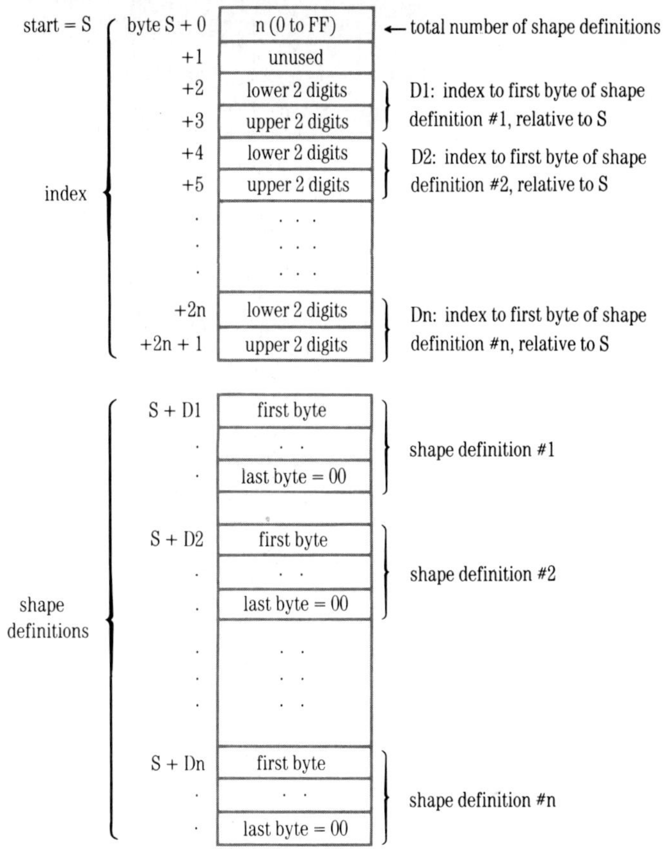

Figure 6-10 shows the complete shape table for our example. Since there's only one shape in the table, location S contains the value 1. Bytes S + 2 and S + 3 are needed to specify the shape's location; the shape definition itself can start in the next available byte, S + 4. So index byte S + 2 contains the value 04 and index byte S + 3 contains the value 00. Next come the bytes of the shape definition, as derived in Figure 6-8. The table ends with the 0 byte marking the end of the shape definition.

Figure 6-10. A Complete Shape Table

start (store address in E8 and E9) ↓

	byte	value	
byte	0	01	← number of shapes
	1	00	
	2	04	index to shape definition #1, relative to start
	3	00	
first byte →	4	12	shape definition #1
	5	3F	
	6	20	
	7	64	
	8	2D	
	9	15	
	A	36	
	B	1E	
	C	07	
last byte →	D	00	

6.3.1.5 Loading a Shape Table Into Memory

Now that you've figured out how to code your shape in the form of a shape table, you have to get it into the computer's memory so Applesoft can draw it on the screen. You also have to tell Applesoft where in memory to look for the shape table.

First you must choose a starting address. This address must be less than the highest memory address available in your system, and must not be located in the high-resolution graphics page that you'll be using to display the shapes (locations 2000 through 3FFF for page 1, 4000 through 5FFF for page 2). For this example, we'll use hexadecimal address 1DFC, which is just below high-resolution page 1.

▲Warning Be sure you don't place your shape table in an area that conflicts with your program or variable space, or with vital internal information used by the system. See "Protecting Your Shape Table," in this section, for information on how to keep your program and shape table out of each other's way; see Appendix H for the memory locations of important system information.

While you're in the process of creating the shape table, you'll probably want to type the table into memory directly from the keyboard using the Monitor program. Then you can draw the shape on the screen with an immediate-execution DRAW statement (see Section 6.3.2.1), see if it looks the way you want it, and go back and change it if it doesn't. See your computer's reference manual for information on the use of the **Monitor program**.

Once your shape table looks correct, you'll want to be able to use it from within a program. Your program can store the table in memory by using POKE (see Section 7.1.2). To do this, you have to convert the starting address of the table, and each byte of the table itself, from hexadecimal to decimal, then store the decimal values in memory one at a time.

The shape table we've been developing consists of the following hexadecimal bytes:

01 00 04 00 12 3F 20 64 2D 15 36 1E 07 00

The equivalent decimal values are the following:

1 0 4 0 18 63 32 100 45 21 54 30 7 0

The starting address we've chosen for the table, hexadecimal 1DFC, is equivalent to 7676 decimal. So the following statements in a program store the shape table in memory:

```
10   FOR X = 7676 TO 7689         Memory locations where shape
                                  tables will go.
20   READ A                       Reads byte of table.
30   POKE X, A                    Stores at next location.
40   NEXT X                       Goes back for next byte.
50   DATA 1,0,4,0,18,63,32,100,45,21,54,30,7,0
                                  Contents of table.
```

Another way for a program to store a shape table in memory is to load it from a disk or tape cassette. Details are given in Section 6.3.1.6.

Now that you have your shape table in memory, you have to tell Applesoft where to find it. Applesoft looks for the table's starting address in hexadecimal locations E8 (low-order byte) and E9 (high-order byte), so you have to arrange somehow to store the correct starting address in these locations.

If you've been using the Monitor program to type the shape table into memory from the keyboard, you can type its address into locations E8 and E9 the same way. From within a program, you can do it with two more POKE statements. The hexadecimal addresses E8 and E9 are equivalent to decimal 232 and 233; the two bytes of the table's starting address, 1D and FC, are equivalent to 29 and 252. So the following POKE statements will do the trick:

```
50  POKE 232, 252 : POKE 233, 29
```

Your shape table is now stored correctly in the computer's memory, ready to be drawn on the screen from within your program with a DRAW statement.

A Reminder: Remember to store the two bytes of the starting address in reverse order, with the low-order byte before the high-order byte. This convention is always followed when storing memory addresses in the Apple II's memory.

When you use SHLOAD (see Section 6.3.2.5) to load a shape table from a tape cassette, the starting address is set up for you automatically in the proper locations.

ProDOS Users Take Note: ProDOS deals with memory in 256-byte chunks. Thus in the first example cited, you set HIMEM: to 7680, which is exactly 30 times 256.

▲Warning If you locate your shape table above the high-resolution graphics page and your system is equipped with one or more disk drives, be careful not to run into the memory space occupied by the disk operating system. Check the disk operating system manual for the exact starting memory location.

Protecting Your Shape Table: In choosing a location in memory for your shape table, it's important to keep it out of the way of your Applesoft program, so the two don't overwrite each other. One way to do this is simply to use HIMEM: (see Section 7.2.1) to set the upper limit of program memory to the starting address of the table. In the example, HIMEM: is set to 7676. This too is done automatically when you use SHLOAD to get the table from a tape cassette.

Unfortunately, this method leaves very little room for your program and variables—in the example, only 5628 bytes (7676 minus 2048). You can buy a little more space for your program by setting HIMEM: to the beginning of the graphics page you're using (8192 for page 1, 16384 for page 2), as suggested in Section 6.2.5. You can then locate the shape table above the graphics page: that is, above location 16384 if you're using page 1, 24576 if you're using page 2.

Perhaps the best method is to locate the program and variables above the graphics page, again as described in Section 6.2.5. This leaves room for the shape table below the start of the graphics page. If you're using graphics page 1, that's 6144 bytes (8192 minus 2048)—enough room for a very extensive shape table!

6.3.1.6 Saving and Loading a Shape Table

To save your shape table on a disk, you need to know two things:

- □ The starting address of the table (1DFC in the example)
- □ The length of the table in bytes (14 in the example—hexadecimal 000E—including the "stop" byte).

Next, you must choose a filename under which to store your shape table on the disk. We'll use SHAPE1 for this example.

To save the table on a disk in immediate execution, put the disk in the disk drive and issue the following command:

```
BSAVE SHAPE1, A$1DFC, L$000E
```

binary file: a file containing "raw" information not expressed in text form

This command says "store a binary file named SHAPE1 on the disk, containing the current contents of memory starting at hexadecimal address 1DFC, and 000E (hexadecimal) bytes long."

If You're Not Using Drive 1: If you're using a disk drive other than the main startup drive, the BSAVE command should also include port and drive parameters specifying which disk drive to use; see your disk operating system manual for details.

To issue the same command from within an Applesoft program, use the statement

```
PRINT CHR$ (4); "BSAVE SHAPE1, A$1DFC,
      L$000E"
```

Again, see your disk operating system manual for details.

To load the table back into memory from the disk, you can use the command

```
BLOAD SHAPE1
```

in immediate execution, or the statement

```
PRINT CHR$ (4); "BLOAD SHAPE1"
```

from within a program. Notice that you don't have to include the starting address and the table length; this information is picked up automatically from within the disk file itself. However, the starting address is not stored automatically in the special addresses where Applesoft looks for them, so you (or your program) have to do that for yourself:

```
POKE 232, 252 : POKE 233, 29
```

To save your shape table on a tape cassette (Apple II, Apple II Plus, and Apple IIe only) you need to know three things:

- □ The starting address of the table (1DFC in the example);
- □ The last address of the table (1E09 in the example);
- □ The difference between the first two items (hexadecimal 000D, decimal 14).

Item 3, the difference between the last address and the first address of the table, must be stored in locations 0 (low-order byte) and 1 (high-order byte). From the Monitor, type

```
0:0D 00
```

and press RETURN. Now you must write to the cassette first the table length from locations 0 to 1, then the shape table itself:

```
0.1W 1DFC.1E09W
```

Don't press RETURN until you have put a cassette in your tape recorder, rewound it, and started it recording.

To load the shape table back from the tape, use the SHLOAD statement (see Section 6.3.2.5).

6.3.2 Using Shape Tables

The commands in this section are used to draw and manipulate on the screen shapes defined by a shape table in memory:

- DRAW and XDRAW draw shapes from a shape table onto the high-resolution screen.
- SCALE= controls the scale at which shapes are drawn on the screen.
- ROT= controls the rotation of shapes on the screen.
- SHLOAD loads a shape table into memory from a tape cassette (Apple II, Apple II Plus, and Apple IIe only).

As a preview of what the commands in this section can do, here's a sample Applesoft program for you to try. The program first stores in memory the shape table developed in Section 6.3.1, using the POKE statement (see Section 6.3.1.5). Then it uses the statements described in this section to produce a somewhat surprising effect on the screen. See if you can guess what the program will display, then type it, switch to 40-column display, and run it:

```
10  FOR X = 7676 TO 7689        Memory locations where shape table
                                will go.
20  READ A                      Reads byte of table.
30  POKE X, A                   Stores at next location.
40  NEXT X                      Goes back for next byte.
50  DATA 1,0,4,0,18,63,32,100,45,21,54,30,7,0
                                Contents of table.
60  POKE 232, 252: POKE 233, 29
100  HGR2
110  HCOLOR= 3
120  FOR R = 1 TO 50
130  ROT= R
140  SCALE= R
150  XDRAW 1 AT 140, 96
160  NEXT R
170  GOTO 120
```

When you get tired of watching the show, interrupt the program by pressing CONTROL-C to regain control of the system.

6.3.2.1 The DRAW Statement

```
DRAW 5
DRAW 1 AT 140, 96
DRAW SHAPE AT XCENTER + XOFFSET, YCENTER
     + YOFFSET
```

The DRAW statement draws a shape from a shape table (see Section 6.3.1) on the high-resolution graphics screen at a specified location. The expression following the keyword DRAW gives the index number of the desired shape in the shape table currently in memory. The location at which the shape is to be drawn is specified by a pair of expressions following the keyword AT, separated by a comma. The first expression gives the horizontal screen position of the shape's starting point; the second gives the vertical position.

The designated shape is drawn in the current display color, scale, and rotation, as specified in the most recently executed HCOLOR=, SCALE=, and ROT= statements.

▲Warning You must specify the color, scale, and rotation of the shape before DRAW is executed. If any of these have not been specified, the results are random: odd dots may appear, bizarre shapes may be drawn, and memory may be overwritten.

Assuming that a shape table is already loaded into memory (see Section 6.3.1.5), the following program draws the first shape in the table at column 50, row 100:

`10 HGR`	Displays high-resolution graphics.
`20 HCOLOR= 3`	Sets color to white 1.
`30 ROT= 0`	Orients shape as originally defined.
`40 SCALE= 5`	Enlarges shape five times.
`50 DRAW 1 AT 50, 100`	Draws shape 1 at column 50, row 100.

If you omit the keyword AT and the screen coordinates 50 DRAW 1, Applesoft puts the shape on the screen starting at the last point plotted by the most recently executed HPLOT, DRAW, or XDRAW statement. (The shape drawn on the screen may not actually begin at the last point previously plotted. If the first plotting vector in the shape doesn't actually plot a point, there is an offset between the first visible point in the shape and the last point plotted.) If no such statement has been executed, the results are unpredictable.

If the shape number specified is less than 0 or greater than the actual number of shapes in the shape table, the program halts with the message `?ILLEGAL QUANTITY ERROR.`

▲Warning If you execute DRAW without first loading a shape table into memory, the system may hang (use CONTROL-RESET to recover), or Applesoft may draw random shapes anywhere in the high-resolution graphics area of memory (locations 8192 to 24575 decimal), whether or not HGR or HGR2 has previously been executed. This can have disastrous consequences if your program is longer than about 6000 bytes.

6.3.2.2 The XDRAW Statement

```
XDRAW 5
XDRAW 1 AT 140, 80
XDRAW SHAPE AT XCENTER + XOFFSET, YCENTER
      + YOFFSET
```

The XDRAW statement works exactly the same as DRAW, except that the color used to draw the shape is the complement of the color already existing at each point plotted. The following pairs of colors are complements:

- black and white
- violet and green
- blue and orange

XDRAW is most commonly used to erase a previously drawn shape. The following program, which assumes that a shape table has already been loaded into memory (see Section 6.3.1.5), illustrates the point by drawing and then erasing the same shape, leaving the screen blank:

```
10  HGR2                        Displays full-screen high-resolution
                                graphics.
20  HCOLOR= 3                   Sets color to white 1.
30  ROT= 0                      Orients shape as originally defined.
40  SCALE= 5                    Enlarges shape five times.
50  DRAW 1 AT 50, 100           Draws shape at column 50, row 100.
60  FOR Z = 1 TO 500 : NEXT Z
                                Stalls for a short time.
70  XDRAW 1 AT 50, 100          Erases the shape.
```

Animation With DRAW and XDRAW: If you use DRAW and XDRAW alternately in a loop, you can do animation:

`10 HGR2`	Displays full-screen high-resolution graphics.
`20 HCOLOR= 3`	Sets color to white 1.
`30 ROT= 0`	Orients shape as originally defined.
`40 SCALE= 5`	Enlarges shape five times.
`50 FOR X = 1 TO 200`	Loops 200 times.
`60 DRAW 1 AT 50 + X, 100`	Draws shape in a different column each time.
`70 XDRAW 1 AT 50 + X, 100`	Erases shape.
`80 NEXT X`	Repeats loop.

If the shape number specified is less than 0 or greater than the actual number of shapes in the shape table, the program halts with the message `?ILLEGAL QUANTITY ERROR.`

▲Warning If you execute XDRAW without first loading a shape table into memory, the system may hang (use CONTROL-RESET to recover), or Applesoft may draw random shapes anywhere in the high-resolution graphics area of memory (locations 8192 to 24575 decimal), whether or not HGR or HGR2 has previously been executed. This can have disastrous consequences if your program is longer than about 6000 bytes.

6.3.2.3 The SCALE= Statement

```
SCALE= 10
SCALE= Z / 4
```

The SCALE= statement sets the scale factor (relative size) for the high-resolution graphics shape to be drawn by DRAW or XDRAW. The expression following the keyword SCALE= specifies the scale factor, which can range from 1 (reproduces the shape exactly as originally defined) up to a maximum of 255 (draws the shape 255 times the size originally defined).

Assuming that a shape table is already loaded into memory (see Section 6.3.1.5), the following program draws the first shape in the table at three different positions on the screen and in three different sizes:

`10 HGR2`	Displays full-screen high-resolution graphics.
`20 HCOLOR= 3`	Sets color to white 1.
`30 ROT= 0`	Orients shape as defined.
`40 SCALE= 1`	Uses original size.
`50 DRAW 1 AT 100, 100`	Draws shape at column 100, row 100.
`60 SCALE= 2`	Scales to twice original size.
`70 DRAW 1 AT 150, 100`	Draws at column 150, row 100.
`80 SCALE= 3`	Scales to three times size.
`90 DRAW 1 AT 200, 100`	Draws at column 200, row 100.

A scale setting of 0 is considered equivalent to the maximum setting (255). If the scale setting specified is less than 0 or greater than 255, the program halts with the message `?ILLEGAL QUANTITY ERROR`.

Scale factors are useful only up to a certain point. Large scale settings produce some rather outlandish results on the screen.

> ***SCALE Isn't a Variable:*** Notice that the equal sign is part of the keyword SCALE=; it doesn't represent an assignment to a variable named SCALE. A statement such as
>
> ```
> LET SCALE = X
> ```
>
> has no effect on the scale setting. The only way to find out the current scale setting is to keep track of it yourself with a separate variable.

6.3.2.4 The ROT= Statement

```
ROT= 16
ROT= 32 + 2 * R
```

The ROT= (for rotation) statement sets the angular rotation for the high-resolution graphics shape to be drawn by DRAW or XDRAW. The expression following the keyword ROT= specifies the rotation in units of 5.625 degrees (1/64 of a circle). ROT= 0 orients the shape exactly as defined in the shape table, ROT= 16 rotates the shape 90 degrees clockwise, ROT= 32 rotates it 180 degrees, and so on. The process repeats starting at ROT= 64.

Assuming that a shape table is already loaded into memory (see Section 6.3.1.5), the following program draws the first shape in the table, five times its original size, at two different positions on the screen, once oriented as originally defined and once rotated by 45 degrees:

`10 HGR2`	Displays full-screen high-resolution graphics.
`20 HCOLOR= 3`	Sets color to white 1.
`30 SCALE= 5`	Scales shape to five times original size.
`40 ROT= 0`	Orients shape as originally defined.
`50 DRAW 1 AT 150, 100`	Draws shape at column 50, row 100.
`60 ROT= 8`	Rotates shape 45 degrees.
`70 DRAW 1 AT 100, 100`	Draws shape at column 100, row 100.

The amount of rotation obtainable is somewhat dependent on the current scale setting. For SCALE= 1, Applesoft recognizes only four rotation values (0, 16, 32, 48); for SCALE= 2, it recognizes eight rotation values (0, 8, 16,...); for SCALE= 3, it recognizes twelve rotation values; and so on. For scale settings of 16 or more, the full range of rotation values is available. For unrecognized rotation values, Applesoft usually orients the shape with the next smaller rotation that it recognizes.

ROT Isn't a Variable: Notice that the equal sign is part of the keyword ROT=; it doesn't represent an assignment to a variable named ROT. A statement such as

```
LET ROT = X
```

causes a syntax error. The only way to find out the current rotation setting is to keep track of it yourself with a separate variable.

If the rotation setting specified is less than 0 or greater than 255, the program halts with the message `?ILLEGAL QUANTITY ERROR`.

6.3.2.5 The SHLOAD Statement

```
SHLOAD
```

II, II Plus, IIe

The SHLOAD (for shape load) statement loads a shape table from a tape cassette. The shape table is loaded just below the upper limit of available program and variable space (HIMEM:); HIMEM: is then set to just below the shape table to protect it.

To use SHLOAD in immediate execution, turn on your tape recorder with the proper tape inserted and cued up to the proper place. Then type

```
SHLOAD
```

and press RETURN. You should hear one beep when the shape table's length has been read successfully, and another when the table itself has been read.

You can also use SHLOAD from within a program (with appropriate prompting messages) to allow users to load their own shape tables:

`100 PRINT "CUE UP YOUR SHAPE TAPE AND PRESS THE PLAY BUTTON."`	
`110 PRINT "THEN PRESS THE RETURN KEY TO LOAD THE SHAPE TABLE."`	Prompts user with instructions.
`120 GET STALL$`	Waits for keypress.
`130 SHLOAD`	Loads shape table from tape.
`140 PRINT "TABLE LOADED--PLEASE SHUT OFF YOUR RECORDER."`	Tells user table is loaded.

If you load a second shape table replacing the first one, you or your program should reset HIMEM: to avoid wasting memory. See Section 6.3.1.5 for more information on shape tables and memory usage.

More Ways to Hang Your System: If you try to use SHLOAD without a tape recorder connected, turned on, and set to play, the system hangs indefinitely. Use CONTROL-RESET to regain control.

If a variable name begins with the reserved word SHLOAD, as in SHLOADER = 59, SHLOAD may be executed before a syntax error is detected. In such a case, the system patiently waits (forever, if necessary) for a shape table to be loaded from a tape cassette. Again, use CONTROL-RESET to recover.

For More Information: For information on saving a shape table on tape, see Section 6.3.1.6. See Appendix M for a list of all statements dealing with tape cassettes.

6.4 Graphics in Text Mode (MouseText)

It *is* possible to put graphics on the screen without first using GR or HGR. You must have either an Apple IIc, or an enhanced Apple IIe with an 80-column card.

If you have the required equipment, try entering this program, which displays 32 uppercase characters in inverse mode:

```
10  D$=CHR$(4)
20  PRINT D$;"PR#3 : REM Turn on 80-column video
30  PRINT
40  INVERSE
50  PRINT "ABCDEFGHIJKLMNOPQRSTUVWXYZ[|]_\"
60  NORMAL
70  END
```

Run the program and observe the screen. Then, add two new lines:

```
45  PRINT CHR$(27)
55  PRINT CHR$(24)
```

Line 45 turns on MouseText, a set of graphics that you can use in your programs. Line 55 turns it off. These characters are an alternate representation of certain inverse uppercase characters. They can be used both in 40-column and 80-column displays.

Note that some of the MouseText characters are meant to be used in tandem—for example, the ones represented by F and G in your program listing produce a running figure. Another pair, x and y, produces a file folder.

Figure 6-11. MouseText Characters

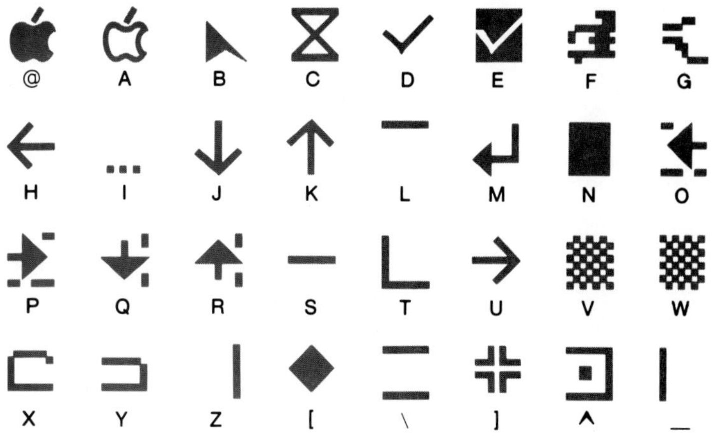

Chapter 7

Utility Statements

The features covered in this chapter are concerned with low-level control of the programming environment.

- Section 7.1, "System Utilities," discusses facilities for direct access to specific locations in the computer's memory from within an Applesoft program.
- Section 7.2, "Memory Management," describes the ways in which Applesoft programs can control the limits of program space.
- Section 7.3, "Debugging," tells how to trace the execution of a running program for debugging purposes.

7.1 System Utilities

This section describes statements and functions that give Applesoft programs direct access to the Apple II's memory:

- PEEK (see Section 7.1.1) examines the contents of a memory location.
- POKE (see Section 7.1.2) alters the contents of a memory location.
- CALL (see Section 7.1.3) and USR (see Section 7.1.4) allow Applesoft programs to execute machine-language subroutines stored in the computer's memory.
- WAIT (see Section 7.1.5) suspends program execution until a specified signal is received from a peripheral device.

7.1.1 The PEEK Function

The PEEK function directly examines the contents of a specified location in memory. The argument given to PEEK is the decimal address of the desired memory location. PEEK yields the contents of the specified location, which will be an integer from 0 to 255. For example, the following program displays the contents of addresses 100 through 120:

```
10  FOR ADDR = 100 TO 120           Loops through desired addresses.
20  PRINT "LOCATION "; ADDR; " HOLDS THE VALUE ";
    PEEK (ADDR)                     Displays contents of location.
30  NEXT ADDR                       Goes back for next address.
```

Certain locations in the memory of the Apple II hold special system information or produce special effects whenever their contents are read. One important use of PEEK is manipulating these special locations. See Appendix F for details.

The following program yields the borders of the current text window:

```
10  HOME
20  PRINT "THE CURRENT TEXT WINDOW" : PRINT
30  PRINT " - BEGINS AT COLUMN " PEEK (32)
40  PRINT " AND IS " PEEK (33) "COLUMNS WIDE. ":PRINT
50  PRINT " - ITS TOP EDGE IS ROW " PEEK (34)
60  PRINT " AND ITS BOTTOM IS ROW " PEEK (35)
```

If PEEK is given a negative argument value, it adds 65536 (2 to the 16th power) to obtain an equivalent positive address. For example,

This	Is Equivalent To
`PEEK (-16384)`	`PEEK (49152)`
`PEEK (-1)`	`PEEK (65535)`
`PEEK (-32768)`	`PEEK (32768)`
`PEEK (-65500)`	`PEEK (36)`

If the argument is not in the range -65535 to +65535, the program halts with the message `?ILLEGAL QUANTITY ERROR`.

7.1.2 The POKE Statement

```
POKE 34, 8
POKE -16302, 0
POKE ADDR, (2*D1 + 3*D2) / (U - V)
```

The POKE statement stores a specified value into a location in the computer's random-access memory. The first expression following the keyword POKE gives the decimal address of the memory location; the second expression, separated from the first by a comma, gives the value to be stored in that location. For example,

```
POKE 34, 8
```

stores value 8 in location 34.

▲Warning Be certain that the address in which you are storing doesn't contain part of your program or some vital system information that you don't want to change. An ill-advised POKE can hang the system, drop you into the Monitor, or alter the operation of the system or of your program in unpredictable and possibly disastrous ways. In the event of catastrophe, use CONTROL-RESET to regain control of the system. See Appendix H for the locations of vital system pointers that shouldn't be tampered with.

Certain locations in the memory of the Apple II hold special system information or produce special effects whenever a value is stored in them. One important use of POKE is manipulating these special locations. For example, POKEs to memory locations 32 through 35 are used to set the borders of text windows. See Appendix F for details.

If POKE is given a negative target address, it adds 65536 (2 to the 16th power) to obtain an equivalent positive address. For example,

This	Is Equivalent To
`POKE -16384, 0`	`POKE 49152, 0`
`POKE -32768, 112`	`POKE 32768, 112`
`POKE -65502, 8`	`POKE 34, 8`

If the target address is not in the range -65535 to +65535, or if the specified value is not in the range 0 to 255, the program halts with the message `?ILLEGAL QUANTITY ERROR.`

7.1.3 The CALL Statement

```
CALL 54915
CALL -936
CALL ROUTINE (J)
```

The CALL statement executes a machine-language subroutine from within an Applesoft program. The decimal address of the desired subroutine follows the keyword CALL. Control is transferred to the subroutine at the designated address; when the subroutine is finished, execution continues with the statement following the CALL. For example,

```
CALL 64668
```

executes the machine-language subroutine beginning at address 64668.

▲Warning Make sure the address you give in the CALL statement is the beginning of a valid machine-language subroutine! A misdirected CALL can have unpredictable and probably unpleasant consequences, such as hanging the system or dropping you into the Monitor. If this happens to you, use CONTROL-RESET to regain control of the system.

The Apple II's built-in firmware contains a number of useful subroutines accessible with the CALL statement. See Appendix F for details.

You can also use CALL to execute machine-language subroutines of your own, which you have stored in memory with the POKE statement (see Section 7.1.2), typed from the keyboard via the Monitor, or loaded into the computer from a disk or tape.

If CALL is given a negative target address, it adds 65536 (2 to the 16th power) to obtain an equivalent positive address. For example,

This	Is Equivalent To
`CALL -936`	`CALL 64600`
`CALL -868`	`CALL 64668`
`CALL -1998`	`CALL 63538`

If the target address is not in the range -65535 to +65535, the program halts with the message `?ILLEGAL QUANTITY ERROR`.

7.1.4 The USR Function

The USR (for user-supplied routine) function executes a machine-language function routine stored in the computer's memory by you, the user. Such a routine typically performs some high-speed computation that cannot be done efficiently, or cannot be expressed at all, in Applesoft. The argument supplied to the USR function is passed unchanged to the machine-language routine, and the result yielded by the routine is passed back as the value of the USR call.

> *Not for Everyone:* This feature is intended for expert programmers only, and requires a knowledge of machine-language programming. Readers with fewer than sixteen fingers are advised to skip this section.

The function routine to be executed with USR can be stored in the computer's memory with the POKE statement, typed from the keyboard via the Monitor, or loaded into the computer from a disk or tape. When USR is called, the value supplied as an argument is placed in the floating-point accumulator in the computer's memory (hexadecimal locations $9D to $A3); control is then transferred via a machine-language JSR (jump to subroutine) instruction to hexadecimal address $0A (decimal 10).

Locations $0A to $0C (decimal 10 to 12) must contain a machine-language JMP (jump) instruction to the beginning of the machine-language routine. The routine should leave its result in the floating-point accumulator and return control to Applesoft with an RTS (return from subroutine) instruction. The contents of the floating-point accumulator are then passed back to your Applesoft program as the value yielded by USR.

Here is a trivial example showing the use of the USR function. The machine-language routine shown here simply takes the argument value it receives and multiplies it by 8:

`] CALL -151`	Leaves Applesoft; enters Monitor.
`* 0A:4C 00 03`	Sets up machine-language jump to hexadecimal address $300.
`* 0300:18 A5 9D 69 03 85 9D 60`	Enters short machine-language routine to multiply contents of floating-point accumulator by 8.
* CONTROL-C	Returns to Applesoft.
`] PRINT USR (3)`	Executes routine with argument value 3.
`24`	Result displayed on screen.

At hexadecimal address $0A, there is a JMP (opdcode 4C) to hexadecimal address $300. (As usual in 6502 machine language, the low-order byte of the address, 00, precedes the high-order byte, 03.) Beginning at address $300 is a machine-language routine to multiply the value in the floating-point accumulator by 8. Back in Applesoft, when the function call USR (3) is executed, the argument value 3 is placed in the floating-point accumulator and control is passed to the machine-language routine via the JMP at location $0A. The machine-language routine gets the value in the floating-point accumulator, multiplies it by 8, puts the result (24) back into the floating-point accumulator, and returns control to Applesoft with an RTS instruction (opcode 60). The value 24 is then passed back as the result of the USR call.

To obtain a two-byte integer from the value in the floating-point accumulator, your machine-language routine should do a JSR to address $E01C. Upon return, the integer value is in locations $A0 (high-order byte) and $A1 (low-order byte).

To convert an integer result to its floating-point equivalent, so that the function can return that value, place the two-byte integer in registers A (high-order byte) and Y (low-order byte). Then do a JSR to address $E2F2. Upon return, the floating-point value is in the floating-point accumulator.

7.1.5 The WAIT Statement

```
WAIT 49347, 15
WAIT 49401, 240, 192
WAIT ADDR%, M1%, M2%
```

mask: a pattern of bits for use in bit-level logical operations

> ***For Experts Only:*** This feature is intended for expert programmers only, and requires an understanding of bit-masking operations. If you think a mask is something you wear on Halloween, you can safely afford to skip this section. You won't miss a thing.

The WAIT statement suspends program execution until a specified bit pattern appears at a specified memory location. It is typically used to cause a program to pause until a status signal is received from a peripheral device. For example, a printer running out of paper might cause a program to WAIT until it receives a signal from the printer that it has paper.

The first expression following the keyword WAIT designates the address of the memory location to be tested. The second expression represents a one-byte mask specifying which bits of the designated location are of interest: a 1 bit in the mask means that the corresponding bit of the memory location is to be tested; a 0 bit means it is to be ignored. The optional third expression is another one-byte mask specifying the bit value to be tested for in each position of the memory location: a 1 bit in the mask tests for a 0 bit in the corresponding position of the memory location, and vice-versa (!). If the second mask is omitted, all bit positions specified by the first mask are tested for a 1 bit. For example,

`WAIT ADDR, 255`	Waits for a 1 bit anywhere in location ADDR.
`WAIT ADDR, 255, 255`	Waits for a 0 bit anywhere in location ADDR.
`WAIT ADDR, 1`	Waits for low-order bit of location ADDR to become 1.
`WAIT ADDR, 128, 128`	Waits for high-order bit of location ADDR to become 0.
`WAIT ADDR, 3, 2`	Waits for low-order bit of location ADDR to become 1 or second low-order bit to become 0.

When WAIT is executed, the contents of the location specified by the first expression are exclusive-ORed with the mask represented by the third expression (if any); the result is then ANDed with the mask represented by the second expression. If the result is nonzero (that is, if any of the bits of interest are in the specified state), then program execution proceeds; if the result is 0 (none of the bits of interest are in the specified state), then the test is repeated. Thus program execution is suspended until one of the specified bits is set to the specified state by an outside agency (presumably a signal from a peripheral device).

▲Warning If the specified bit pattern never appears, program execution hangs forever. Make sure that the memory location you're testing is receiving information that will eventually test true. The only way to interrupt a WAIT is with CONTROL-RESET.

If WAIT is given a negative target address, it adds 65536 (2 to the 16th power) to obtain an equivalent positive address. For example,

This	Is Equivalent To
`WAIT -16189, 15`	`WAIT 49347, 15`

If the target address is not in the range -65535 to +65535, or if either of the masks is not in the range 0 to 255, the program halts with the message `?ILLEGAL QUANTITY ERROR`.

7.2 Memory Management

The features discussed in this section are used to control the way Applesoft allocates memory space for your program:

- The HIMEM: statement (see Section 7.2.1) sets the upper limit of available program memory.
- The LOMEM: statement (see Section 7.2.2) sets the lower limit of available program memory.
- The FRE function (see Section 7.2.3) determines the amount of remaining memory space available to the program.

7.2.1 The HIMEM: Statement

```
HIMEM: 8192
```

The HIMEM: statement sets the highest memory address available to an Applesoft program for storage of program lines and variables. The upper limit of available program memory is set to the value of the expression following the keyword HIMEM:. The area above this address is available for use by the disk operating system, high-resolution graphics, or machine-language programs.

Notice that the colon is part of the keyword HIMEM: and is required.

Applesoft automatically sets HIMEM: to the address of the highest writable memory (RAM) address available on your computer. On systems equipped with disk drives, loading the disk operating system automatically resets HIMEM: to a lower value in order to protect the area of memory occupied by the disk operating system itself. See your disk operating system manual for further information.

You can change the setting of HIMEM: only by

- executing the HIMEM: statement
- typing CONTROL-B to the Monitor program
- restarting the system
- loading a machine-language program.

▲Warning Resetting HIMEM: above its current value is an extremely dangerous practice that can result in writing over the disk operating system or other vital system information. Wise programmers carefully investigate reserved memory areas before writing to them.

A common use of HIMEM: is protecting your program and high-resolution graphics from overwriting each other. See Section 6.2.5 for details.

Helpful Hint for Disk Operating System Users: The current value of HIMEM: is stored in decimal memory locations 115 and 116; to obtain that value, use the expression

```
PEEK (116) * 256 + PEEK (115)
```

If HIMEM: is given a negative address, it adds 65536 (2 to the 16th power) to obtain an equivalent positive address. For example,

This	Is Equivalent To
`HIMEM: -57344`	`HIMEM: 8192`

If the specified address is not in the range -65535 to +65535, the program halts with the message `?ILLEGAL QUANTITY ERROR`.

If the specified address is lower than the current setting of LOMEM:, or doesn't allow enough room for the program already in memory, the program halts with the message `?OUT OF MEMORY ERROR`.

7.2.2 The LOMEM: Statement

```
LOMEM: 24576
```

The LOMEM: statement sets the lowest memory address available to an Applesoft program for storage of variables. The lower limit of available program memory is set to the value of the expression following the keyword LOMEM:. The area below this address is available for high-resolution graphics or machine-language programs. LOMEM: also resets all variables to their initial values and wipes out all functions defined with DEF FN (see Section 2.4.3).

Notice that the colon is part of the keyword LOMEM: and is required.

Applesoft ordinarily begins to store variables at the end of the program in memory. Each time you add, delete, or change a program line, Applesoft resets LOMEM: to a location just above the final line of the program. Executing the NEW command (see Section 1.2.1) or typing CONTROL-B to the Monitor resets LOMEM: to its initial value.

The value of LOMEM: can only be increased from its current setting. An attempt to set LOMEM: to a lower value than the one already in effect halts the program with the message `?OUT OF MEMORY ERROR`.

▲Warning Changing LOMEM: during the course of a program is a most dangerous practice that can cause portions of the program or of Applesoft's internal control information to become unavailable, which in turn causes the program to act in outlandish ways (if at all).

Helpful Hint: The current value of LOMEM: is stored in decimal memory locations 105 and 106; to obtain that value, use the expression

```
PEEK (106) * 256 + PEEK (105)
```

If LOMEM: is given a negative address, it adds 65536 (2 to the 16th power) to obtain an equivalent positive address. For example,

This	Is Equivalent To
`LOMEM: -49152`	`LOMEM: 16384`

If the specified address is not in the range -65535 to +65535, the program halts with the message `?ILLEGAL QUANTITY ERROR`.

If the specified address is higher than the current setting of HIMEM:, or lower than the address of the highest memory location occupied by the current operating system (plus any currently stored program), the program halts with the message `?OUT OF MEMORY ERROR`.

7.2.3 The FRE Function

The FRE function yields the number of bytes of unused writable (RAM) memory available to the running program. For example,

```
LET AVAIL = FRE(0)
```

sets AVAIL to the amount of available memory remaining.

Notice that the name of the function is FRE, not FREE.

FRE requires an argument in parentheses. The argument given to FRE is ignored, and has no effect on the operation of the function. However, you can't leave it out—you must include an argument expression of some kind to "keep the parentheses apart." What you use for an argument expression doesn't matter, but if Applesoft can't evaluate it as a legal expression, you get an error halt.

If the number of free bytes exceeds 32767, FRE yields a negative result; adding 65536 gives you the actual number of free bytes:

```
IF FRE(0) < 0 THEN AVAIL = FRE(0) + 65536
```

If you have set HIMEM: beyond the highest RAM address in your Apple II, FRE may yield a value higher than the computer's actual memory capacity. The reliability of such a value is to be taken lightly.

> ***How Applesoft Manages Free Space:*** The amount of free space reported by FRE is the number of bytes remaining below the string storage space and above the numeric array and string pointer array space (see Section H.2). When Applesoft changes the contents of a string variable during the course of a program (say from "CAT" to "DOG"), the characters in the old string ("CAT") are not erased from memory; Applesoft simply allocates some fresh space to hold the new string ("DOG"). As a result, characters left over from unused strings take up "dead space" and slowly fill memory from HIMEM: down to the top of the array space.
>
> Applesoft automatically clears out these leftover characters when the bottom of string space "collides" with the top of array space. But if you're using any of the free space for machine-language programs or for high-resolution graphics, they may be overwritten.

Light Housecleaning: The automatic "housecleaning" just described takes time (anywhere from a fraction of a second to over two minutes, depending on the number of string variables your program is using). Furthermore, such housecleaning occurs at unpredictable moments—whenever your string and array spaces happen to collide. If it happens while Applesoft is in the middle of displaying a message on the screen, for instance, it can cause unfortunate confusion for your program's user, who is left waiting for the computer to finish displaying a half-delivered message.

The FRE function provides a tool for warning the user that the computer will be busy for a while. The address of the current beginning of string space is kept in locations 111 and 112 of the computer's memory; the end of array space is kept in locations 109 and 110. Whenever Applesoft needs to allocate more memory, it compares the contents of these locations; if they differ by less than 1, Applesoft does its automatic housecleaning.

Since Applesoft checks these locations, so can you. When the difference between them starts getting close to 0, it's time to display some kind of "don't worry" message and force housecleaning. Using a statement of the form

```
IF (PEEK(112)*256 + PEEK(111)) -
   (PEEK(110)*256 + PEEK(109)) > 2
   THEN PRINT "PLEASE STAND BY..."
   : Q = FRE (0)
```

periodically within your program forces housecleaning to occur and prevents such confusion.

Since the housecleaning can take as long as several minutes each time it occurs, don't do it too often. It's best to use FRE (0) when you need a pause anyway—such as after you write information onto a disk, or while the user is reading information on the display screen.

7.3 Debugging Facilities

This section details two Applesoft commands used as debugging aids: TRACE and NOTRACE. They're useful when a program isn't behaving as intended and you need to find out why.

7.3.1 The TRACE Command

```
TRACE
```

TRACE causes Applesoft to display the line number of each statement it executes. Each line number displayed is preceded on the screen by a number sign (#). For example, the program

```
10  TRACE
20  I = I + 1 : I = I + 1
30  J = J + 1 : J = J + 1
40  GOTO 20
```

displays the output

```
#20 #20 #30 #30 #40 #20 #20 #30 #30 #40
#20 #20 #30 #30 #40 #20 #20 #30 #30 #40
#20 #20 #30 #30 #40 #20 #20 #30 #30 #40
#20 #20 #30 #30 #40 #20 #20 #30 #30 #40
#20 #20 #30 #30 #40 #20 #20 #30 #30 #40
. . .
```

until you press [CONTROL]-[C].

As the example shows, TRACE can be used from within a program as well as in immediate execution. A more realistic use in debugging would be to test for some error condition and turn on tracing only if the error condition holds:

```
IF X > Y THEN TRACE
```

Be sure to remove the TRACE statements from your program after you've found and exterminated the bug!

> ***Tracing and Display Formatting:*** When the program being traced contains display-formatting statements—VTAB, HTAB, TAB, semicolons, commas (see Section 5.2.4)—line numbers displayed by TRACE may appear in a confused fashion or may be overwritten entirely.

Once tracing has been started, it can be canceled only by

- □ executing the NOTRACE statement
- □ restarting the system
- □ typing [CONTROL]-[B] to the Monitor program.

7.3.2 The NOTRACE Command

```
NOTRACE
```

The NOTRACE command cancels the effects of TRACE. After this command is executed, line numbers are no longer displayed on the screen as Applesoft executes them.

Chapter 8

Programming: Bringing It All Together

Good programs don't just happen. Programs that are efficient, economical, and easy to debug and to modify are the result of careful planning. This chapter presents a method to facilitate such planning, using as its example a program to calculate postage fees for United States mail. A copy of this program is included on the *ProDOS BASIC Programming Examples* disk; a complete listing can be found in Appendix N.

- Section 8.1, "Planning the Program," shows how to develop a list of program specifications and how to convert the list into a kind of program outline.
- Section 8.2, "Writing the Code," shows how to refine the outline developed in Section 8.1 into a final Applesoft program.

8.1 Planning the Program

Although you can afford to be "quick and dirty" for casual or one-time-only applications, you'll need to do some preliminary planning for more serious ones. In general, the more planning you do the more efficient and bug-free your finished program will be.

To demonstrate some of the principles of program planning, this chapter develops a program to calculate postage rates on certain classes of mail sent in the United States.

8.1.1 Program Specification

Program planning begins with deciding what your program is to do or what problem you want it to solve. You might want to design a space-war game, a tax planner, or a data base management system. It doesn't matter how simple or how complex the task—whatever it is, you have to decide in detail what the program is supposed to do.

To make writing the program easier, it's a good idea to begin with a list of program specifications. This list specifies what information the program needs, what the program should and should not do, how the results are to be presented, and so forth.

8.1.1.1 What the Program Needs

It's fairly simple to determine what information a postage rates program needs. Since the goal is to determine how much it costs to mail an item, and since cost is a function of mail class and weight, the program needs someone or something to tell it what weight item is being mailed in what class. To keep things simple, the program gets this information from the program user:

- □ The user tells the program the class of mail.
- □ The user also tells the program the weight of the item, since postage rates are based both on class and weight.

When the program has the weight and class of mail (for instance, three ounces of first class), it needs to determine the postage based on some scale. It must either calculate the postage with a formula or look up the rate in a table stored in the computer's memory. Since all computers are inherently stupid and must be told everything, you have to include formulas or tables with which your computer can work:

- □ The program includes formulas and/or tables of postage rates for various weights and classes of mail.
- □ The program includes information on the maximum allowable weight.

This last specification is a matter of postal regulations; first class mail above 12 ounces is called priority mail and is charged at a different rate; 70 pounds is the maximum weight for priority mail; and so forth. Program planning, then, calls for information often outside the programmer's immediate purview. That's why God created libraries and telephones—so that programmers can obtain information they don't already have.

8.1.1.2 What the Program Will and Won't Do

Deciding on the limits of a program is often as important as determining what the program is supposed to accomplish. United States mail has four classes, several types within certain classes, optional extras like insurance and various forms of registry, and so forth. To make designing and writing the program simpler, we'll assume that our postage is never below first class, and further that we never insure or register mail (what fools these mortals...). We'll also assume that packages sent by overnight delivery (express mail) never weigh more than nine pounds and always travel in the same postal zone:

- □ The program is limited to express, first class, and priority mail (one zone only).
- □ The heaviest express mail package is nine pounds; first class and priority mail can be of any weight, up to Post Office limits.

> ***By the Way:*** There is no guarantee that this program agrees with current postal regulations!

8.1.1.3 Validating the Data

Now that the program has information both from the user and from its own internal resources (charts of rates and so on), it must check the validity and consistency of the information.

First for validity: Does the information the user typed make sense in terms of what the program expected? If the program needs a digit for the weight of a letter, what should it do if it gets a word? In designing any program, it's important to remember:

- Most humans do not possess genetic information about what to type into computers.
- Most humans make mistakes.

The program, then, must display clear instructions telling the user what to enter (kind of information needed) and what form to use (letters, digits, words):

- The program displays a list of classes of mail on the screen, with instructions for the user about what to type.
- After it gets the class of mail, the program solicits the weight from the user with proper instructions.
- There is a mechanism for accepting valid information and rejecting invalid information (that is, there are error-handling provisions).

Naturally, if the program rejects invalid information, it must try again to get valid information from the user:

- If information is rejected as invalid, the program continues to solicit information until it gets what it needs.

Now to consistency: Although a user might plausibly ask the cost of sending a five-pound package via first class mail, only the program knows (by checking its table of limits) that five pounds is too heavy for first class. It must notify the user that some other action is called for:

- If information is rejected as inconsistent, the program notifies the user with appropriate recommendations for further action.

8.1.1.4 Displaying the Results

The specifications must also include the form in which the results are to be given to the user. In this case we'll keep it simple:

- □ The final calculated postage charge is displayed on the display screen with appropriate labeling.

Finally, the specifications must tell what the program does when its job is completed. Here, it repeats the whole process until the user types in some kind of "I'm done" signal:

- □ The program continues to solicit information to calculate new postage charges until the user enters an "end" signal.

8.1.1.5 Final Specifications

Reordering the list of specifications into a more logical form, we obtain this final list:

- □ The program displays a list of classes of mail on the screen, with instructions for the user about what to type.
- □ The program is limited to express, first class, and priority mail (one zone only).
- □ The user tells the program the class of mail.
- □ After it gets the class of mail, the program solicits the weight from the user with proper instructions.
- □ The user tells the program the weight of the item.
- □ The program includes information on the maximum allowable weight.
- □ The heaviest express mail package is nine pounds; first class and priority mail can be of any weight, up to Post Office limits.
- □ There is a mechanism for accepting valid information and rejecting invalid information.
- □ If information is rejected as invalid, the program continues to solicit information until it gets what it needs.
- □ If information is rejected as inconsistent, the program notifies the user with appropriate recommendations for further action.
- □ The program includes formulas and/or tables of postage rates for various weights and classes of mail.
- □ The final calculated postage charge is displayed on the screen with appropriate labeling.
- □ The program continues to solicit information to calculate new postage charges until the user enters an "end" signal.

Reviewing the list, you can see that the program's actions fall into a natural chronological order:

1. Computer displays prompting messages.
2. User responds.
3. Program checks validity of responses.
4. If any information is invalid, program solicits new information.
5. Program checks consistency of responses.
6. If any information is inconsistent, program solicits clarified information.
7. Program processes validated information.
8. Program displays results and goes back to step 1.

You'll find that most interactive programs—programs that carry on a "dialogue" with a human sitting at the computer—involve most of these categories in roughly the same order.

8.1.2 Program Layout

Before rushing to put fingers to keyboard, it's best to take your planning at least one step further. Now is the time for program layout. Here you plan the form for each section of the program as described in both the specification list and the chronological order list.

The program layout technique presented here is called *stepwise refinement*. What this means is laying out broad sections of the program, then going back and refining each section step by step.

8.1.2.1 The Initial Layout

Here is an initial layout of the Postage Rate program in the broadest terms:

Repeat

Display menu

Accept class

Accept weight

Compute charge

Display results

until *done*

The layout says that there are five general sections to the program (*Display menu, Accept class, Accept weight, Compute charge,* and *Display results*), and that the program is to repeat this sequence of steps in order until somehow told to stop.

Each section can now be treated as an independent module, to be designed and coded separately. The smaller the chunks of program you work with and the more independent each chunk is, the less chance for error and the easier the program is to debug.

8.1.2.2 Refining the Layout

Now that we have the program laid out in skeletal form, we can begin to put some flesh on the bones. Here is the first refinement, in which each of the broad steps in the initial layout is spelled out in more detail:

Repeat

  Display menu:
    List choices

  Accept class:
    Instruct user how to choose
    Repeat
      Get postage class from user
    until *valid menu item*

  Accept weight:
    Repeat
      Instruct user how to type
      Get weight from user
    until *consistent*

  Compute charge:
    Calculate from formula or look up in table

  Display result:
    Format result with dollar sign, trailing zeros
    Label and display result
    Wait for signal from user before proceeding

until *user signals end*

At this point, many programmers would take outline in hand and attack the keyboard. But a couple of the modules need further refinement: both the *Accept weight* and the *Compute charge* modules need to do specialized processing depending on the class of mail specified by the user. The new information in the *Compute charge* module comes from examining postage rate charts. First class mail is fairly regular, so a formula can be used to compute the charge. Express mail follows no regular pattern, so it's easier to create a table of charges. Priority mail requires a combination of both formula and table. The final program layout looks like this:

Repeat

  Display menu:
    List choices

  Accept class:
    Instruct user how to choose
    Repeat
      Get postage class from user
    until *valid menu item*

  Accept weight:
    Repeat
      Instruct user how to type
      Get weight from user:
        Check validity of response
        Express?
          If *item more than 9 pounds*
            then *suggest alternative*
        First class?
          If *item more than 12 ounces*
            then *suggest alternative*
        Priority?
          If *item less than 12 ounces*
            then *suggest alternative*
          If *item more than 70 pounds*
            then *suggest alternative*
    until *valid* and *consistent*

Compute charge:
Express?
Look up charge in table
First class?
Calculate charge from formula
Priority?
If *item less than 10 pounds*
then *look up charge in table*
otherwise *calculate charge from formula*

Display result:
Format result with dollar sign, trailing zeros
Label and display result
Wait for signal from user before proceeding

until *user signals end*

8.2 Writing the Code

Now that you've refined the program layout to a sufficient level of detail, you're finally ready to start writing code. The layout is only a guide; it isn't the last word. As you write and test the actual program, you may find you need to make changes in your original design. That's perfectly all right; use the design to keep you on track.

What follows in this section represents one way to turn the outline into a working program. It isn't the only way; a hundred programmers would produce a hundred different programs for the same task. It does, however, work. Because it's been developed in an orderly, methodical way, it's also logically organized and easy for a person to follow. This is an important consideration, because it makes the program easy to debug and easy to modify. (Almost all serious programs need to be modified at some time or other, often by someone other than the original programmer.)

> ***Note to Purists:*** Any resemblance between the following program and true top-down structured code is purely coincidental.

8.2.1 Preliminaries

Your program should begin with a block of REM statements identifying the program and describing what it does. Most programmers add their own name and the date of the program's current version:

`10 REM POSTAGE RATES`	Name of program.
`20 :`	Colon leaves line empty.
`30 REM DETERMINES POSTAGE FEES`	What program does.
`40 REM FOR EXPRESS, 1ST CLASS,`	
`50 REM AND PRIORITY MAIL`	Empty line inserted by embedding CONTROL-J (line feed) at end of REM statement in line 50.
`60 REM V3 10/05/83`	Number and date of this version.
`70 REM BY JOHN SCRIBBLEMONGER & SCOT KAMINS`	Programmers' credit line.

8.2.2 Display the Menu

Now you can refer to your outline and base your code directly on it. Notice the REM statements introducing the different sections. All comments shown in the second column could also be included as REM statements:

`100 REM MENU OF POSTAGE CLASSES`	CONTROL-J here.
`110 HOME`	Begins with a clear screen.
`120 TITLE$ = "POSTAGE RATES"`	
`130 PRINT`	
`140 HTAB 21 - LEN (TITLE$) / 2`	Formula to center title.
`150 PRINT TITLE$`	
`160 VTAB 6`	
`170 PRINT "1. EXPRESS"`	
`180 PRINT "2. FIRST CLASS"`	
`190 PRINT "3. PRIORITY"`	
`200 PRINT`	
`210 PRINT "4. END THE PROGRAM"`	The escape hatch.

8.2.3 What's the Postage Class?

This section finds out what mail class the user wants. Note that CONTROL-J, the line feed character, sets off the REM statements for easier reading (line 300):

`300 REM`	CONTROL-J here.
`    GET CLASS OF MAIL`	CONTROL-J here.
`310 VTAB 14`	
`320 PRINT "Press the number of your choice: ";`	Semicolon keeps response on same line.
`330 GET C$`	Only one keypress needed—cuts down on error possibilities; note use of string variable to get number—avoids type mismatch errors.
`335 REM`	CONTROL-J here.
`    VARIOUS CHECKS`	Another CONTROL-J (last time this is noted).
`340 IF C$ = "4" THEN END`	Ends program if user types a 4.
`350 IF VAL (C$) > 0 AND VAL (C$) < 4 THEN 380`	Skips next two lines if valid choice typed.
`360 PRINT CHR$(7); CHR$(7);`	Beeps twice to get attention.
`370 GOTO 330`	Response was invalid; tries again.
`380 PRINT C$`	Since choice accepted via GET, it isn't displayed on the screen; displays it back to user.
`390 C = VAL (C$)`	Needs this value later to determine what section of program to branch to for proper processing.

8.2.4 What Does It Weigh?

Now the program asks the user for the weight of the letter or package. The program makes sure that the user follows the instructions and types a number for the weight and a symbol (O or P) for ounces or pounds. Notice that the program accepts both the numeric weight of the item and the ounce/pound designation in the same string (line 530).

```
500 REM
    GET WEIGHT OF ITEM
515 VTAB 16
510 PRINT "Please enter the WEIGHT - a number plus
    an O (for ounces) or a P  (for pounds) - and
    press the RETURN key: ";
```

Prompting message to tell user what information to type and how to type it.

```
520 CALL -868
```

Clears to end of line; useful to erase any errors that might be typed.

```
530 INPUT "";W$
```

Empty string suppresses question mark.

```
540 W1$ = RIGHT$ (W$, 1)
```

Rightmost letter should be either O or P; use it later to see if weight is consistent with postal regulations.

```
550 W = VAL (W$)
```

How many ounces or pounds?

```
555 REM
    WAS ENTERED WEIGHT VALID?
560 IF W > 0 AND (W1$ = "O" OR W1$ = "P") THEN 710
```

If a weight was typed, and if last character was either O for ounces or P for pounds, then proceeds.

```
570 PRINT CHR$ (7); CHR$ (7);
```

Beeps twice to get attention.

If the program has progressed this far, then everything typed by the user is valid from the computer's point of view. However, the user's choices still may not be consistent with postal regulations or the program's limitations. First class letters must weigh less than 12 ounces, the program can't handle express mail above a certain weight, and so on. This section of code uses the value of variable C (set in line 390) to direct control to the proper subroutine to check for consistency.

```
700 REM
    CHECK CONSISTENCY
710 ON C GOSUB 10000, 11000, 12000
```

Branches to appropriate subroutine to see if weight typed is within postal rules or program limitations for mail class chosen.

```
720 IF NOT EFLAG THEN 910
```

If no inconsistency detected in subroutine then proceed with processing.

```
730 GOSUB 60000 : REM KEYSTALL
```

Waits for user to acknowledge message.

```
740 KEYSTALL = 0
```

Clears error flag set in subroutine.

```
750 CLEAR
```

Resets all variables, clears arrays, and so on.

```
760 GOTO 100
```

Restarts program loop.

8.2.5 Compute the Charge

Now that everything checks out all right, the program can proceed to calculate the postage. The calculation is different for each of the three classes of postage, so there are three separate calculating routines. Again, what routine the program goes to depends on the value of C, the number representing the postal class chosen by the user.

```
900 REM
    FIND APPROPRIATE CODE FOR PROCESSING
```

Everything is valid and consistent; now program can solve for the postage rate!

```
910 ON C GOSUB 1000, 2000, 3000
```

Branches to proper calculating routine.

```
920 GOSUB 61000 : REM FORMATTER
```

Formats result for display.

```
930 PRINT
```

8.2.6 Display the Results

It's finally time to display the results!

```
935 REM
    DISPLAY RESULTS
940 PRINT "POSTAGE NEEDED: $ "; T$
                                        Finally, the postage due!
950 GOSUB 60000 : REM KEYSTALL
                                        Doesn't go on until user is ready.
960 CLEAR                               Prepares for restart...
970 GOTO 100                            ...and does it.
```

8.2.7 Calculating Routines

The following three subroutines do the actual rate calculations, based on formulas, tables, or both. The rates for express mail are fairly straightforward; they are based on a table created in the express mail consistency-checking routine at line 10000. First class rates couldn't be simpler; a little arithmetic is all that's needed. Priority mail is another story, however; when you get to it, you'll find an explanation.

```
999 REM
    SUBROUTINES BEGIN HERE
1000 REM
     EXPRESS MAIL CALCULATION
1010 W = INT (W + .99)                 Weight must be increased to
                                       compensate for fractions; postal
                                       rates read "NOT MORE THAN
                                       x POUNDS."
1020 T = R (W)                         Rate array filled in express mail
                                       consistency-checking routine
                                       (line 10000).
1030 RETURN                            Ends routine.
2000 REM
     FIRST CLASS CALCULATION
```

```
2010 T = .20 + INT (W + .99 - 1) * .17
```

First class rate is 20 cents first ounce plus 17 cents for each additional ounce or portion thereof (January 1984 rates).

```
2020 RETURN
```

Ends routine.

Although there is something approaching a pattern to priority mail charges, the pattern is obscure at best. This is especially true for the first ten pounds. Pounds 1 through 5 are charged by the half-pound; pounds 6 through 10 are full-pound charges. It's simpler and quicker to use a table for these charges (lines 3030 to 3140) than to figure out a formula.

Weights over five pounds follow a more regular pattern than the first five; they are all charged in full-pound increments. Furthermore, each five pounds costs $2.38. Unfortunately, the cost for pound 6 is different from the cost for pound 7, and so on. What it boils down to is that five-pound lots can be charged at the same rate (line 3170), and anything that isn't a multiple of 5 must be looked up in a table (lines 3180 to 3220).

If all this strains credulity, refer to United States Mail Service poster 103, November 1981.

```
3000 REM
     PRIORITY MAIL CALCULATION
3010 W = INT (W + .99)
```

Compensates for partial ounces or pounds.

```
3020 IF W > 10 THEN 3160
```

Goes to line 3160 for weights greater than ten pounds (ounce weights converted to pounds in consistency subroutine starting at line 12000).

```
3025 REM
     PRIORITY RATES TO 10 POUNDS
3030 IF W <= 1 THEN T = 2.24
3040 IF W > 1 AND W <= 1.5 THEN T = 2.30
```

Rates in half-pound increments.

```
3050 IF W > 1.5 AND W <= 2 THEN T = 2.54
3060 IF W > 2 AND W <= 2.5 THEN T = 2.78
3070 IF W > 2.5 AND W <= 3 THEN T = 3.01
3072 IF W > 3 AND W <= 3.5 THEN T = 3.25
3078 IF W > 3.5 AND W <= 4 THEN T = 3.49
3080 IF W > 4 AND W <= 4.5 THEN T = 3.73
3090 IF W > 4.5 AND W <= 5 THEN T = 3.97
```

```
3100 IF W > 5 AND W <= 6 THEN T = 4.44
                                   Rates by the pound now!
3110 IF W > 6 AND W <= 7 THEN T = 4.92
3120 IF W > 7 AND W <= 8 THEN T = 5.39
3130 IF W > 8 AND W <= 9 THEN T = 5.87
3140 IF W > 9 THEN T = 6.35
3150 GOTO 3240                     Branches to RETURN statement.
3160 REM
     PRIORITY RATES FOR OVER 10 POUNDS
3170 T1 = INT (W / 5 - 1) * 2.38 + 3.97
                                   First five pounds cost $3.97; each
                                   added five pounds cost $2.38.
3180 W1 = W - INT (W / 5) * 5
                                   How many odd pounds are there
                                   (pounds that are not multiples of 5
                                   and must be charged at a special
                                   rate)?
3190 IF W1 = 1 THEN T2 = .47
3200 IF W1 = 2 THEN T2 = .95
3210 IF W1 = 3 THEN T2 = 1.42
3220 IF W1 = 4 THEN T2 = 1.90
3230 T = T1 + T2                   Adds the five-pound-multiples rate
                                   to the odd-pounds rate.
3240 RETURN                        Ends routine.
```

8.2.8 Consistency-Checking Routines

The next three routines make sure that first class letters aren't too heavy, that the requested rate can be calculated by the program and, in general, that the program can deliver what the user wants. The express mail routine begins by loading its rates into a table. (It gets the rates from a DATA list; DATA lists are excellent places to store information you might need in a program.) Then it checks to see if it has a rate for the package being sent. First class just makes sure that the package weighs 12 ounces or less; that's the maximum weight for a first-class item. Priority mail also has an easy job; it just makes sure the package weighs more than 12 ounces but not more than 70 pounds.

```
10000 REM
      EXPRESS MAIL CONSISTENCY CHECK
10010 DATA 9.35, 9.35, 9.55, 9.90, 10.30, 10.65,
      11.00, 11.40, 11.75, 0
                                   Express mail rates; 0 at end is "last
                                   item" flag.
```

`10020 X = 0`	Sets up counter to check how many rates are read from DATA list.
`10030 X = X + 1`	Increments counter.
`10040 READ R (X)`	Puts price into proper array element.
`10050 IF R (X) = 0 THEN 10070`	Price of 0 marks end of list.
`10060 GOTO 10030`	Gets next price.
`10070 X = X - 1`	X includes count of "last item" flag from 10050; subtracts it from count since it's a "dummy" item.
`10080 IF W1$ = "P" THEN 10100`	Next line is for ounces only.
`10090 W = W / 16`	Converts ounces to pounds.
`10100 IF W <= X THEN 10140`	If weight in pounds is covered by the rate chart, then goes ahead.
`10110 PRINT`	
`10120 PRINT CHR$ (7); CHR$ (7); "TOO HEAVY FOR MY TABLES - PLEASE CALL THE POST OFFICE"`	Sorry; can't help you.
`10130 EFLAG = 1`	Sets flag indicating inconsistent weight/type; will be checked at line 720.
`10140 RETURN`	Ends routine.
`11000 REM FIRST CLASS CONSISTENCY CHECK`	
`11010 IF W1$ = "O" AND W < 12.01 THEN 11060`	OK if not more than 12 ounces.
`11020 PRINT`	
`11030 PRINT CHR$ (7); CHR$(7); "TOO HEAVY FOR FIRST CLASS"`	Sorry—inconsistent!
`11040 PRINT "TRY PRIORITY MAIL"`	Suggests alternative.
`11050 EFLAG = 1`	Sets flag indicating inconsistent weight/type; will be checked at line 720.
`11060 RETURN`	Ends routine.
`12000 REM PRIORITY MAIL CONSISTENCY CHECK`	
`12010 IF W1$ = "P" THEN 12090`	If in pounds, then skips down.

`12020 IF W > 12 THEN 12080`	Skips down if weight is between 12 and 16 ounces.
`12030 PRINT`	
`12040 PRINT CHR$ (7); CHR$ (7); "TOO LIGHT FOR FOR PRIORITY MAIL - "`	Too light!
`12050 PRINT "TRY FIRST CLASS"`	Suggests alternative.
`12060 EFLAG = 1`	Sets flag indicating inconsistent weight/type; will be checked at line 720.
`12070 GOTO 12150`	Branches to end of routine.
`12080 W = W / 16`	Converts ounces to pounds.
`12090 IF W <= 70 THEN 12150`	Final check: is item on the charts?
`12100 PRINT`	
`12110 PRINT CHR$ (7); CHR$ (7); "TOO HEAVY FOR FOR PRIORITY MAIL -"`	Off the charts.
`12120 PRINT "TRY ONE OF THE AIR EXPRESS COMPANIES`	Too big for the Post Office!
`12130 EFLAG = 1`	Sets flag indicating inconsistent weight/type; will be checked at line 720.
`12150 RETURN`	Ends routine.

To Be Truly Friendly: A truly friendly program would automatically convert too-heavy first class mail to priority mail and too-light priority mail to first class, would present a list of air freight companies (with phone numbers, of course) for mail too heavy for the Post Office, and so on. We'll leave it to you to add such niceties.

8.2.9 The Keystall Routine

The keystall routine interrupts execution of the program and waits for the user to press a key before going on. The GET statement in line 60040 actually does the waiting; when the user presses a key, the program continues. What key the user presses doesn't matter—the program doesn't care what value is assigned to A$.

`59999 REM UTILITY ROUTINES`	Routines useful for various tasks but ancillary to rest of program.
`60000 REM KEYSTALL`	Routine to interrupt program until user presses a key.
`60010 VTAB 24`	Moves cursor to screen bottom.

```
60020 INVERSE                      Sets text to appear black-on-white.
60030 PRINT "PRESS RETURN TO GO ON...";
60040 GET A$                       Waits for keypress.
60050 NORMAL                       Restores ordinary white-on-black.
60060 RETURN                       Ends routine.
```

8.2.10 The Formatting Routine

After the postage charge is calculated, the program branches to this final subroutine. Here the final result is checked to see how it will look when it is displayed. Does it have a decimal point? Applesoft suppresses trailing zeros after a decimal point, but people are used to seeing them when dealing with dollars and cents. The formatting subroutine adds trailing zeros as needed.

```
61000 REM
      MONEY FORMATTER              Adds zeros after the decimal point
                                   where needed.
61010 T$ = STR$ (T)                Turns the calculated postage fee
                                   into a string.
61020 IF T = INT (T) THEN T$ = T$ + ".00"
                                   If charge is in whole dollars, adds a
                                   decimal point and two zeros.
61030 IF ASC (RIGHT$ (T$,2)) = 46 THEN T$ = T$ + "0"
                                   If second character from the right is
                                   a decimal point (ASCII code 46)
                                   then number has only one digit to
                                   right of decimal—so adds a "0" to
                                   the string.
61040 RETURN                       Ends the routine.
```

8.3 Final Advice to the New Programmer

The program planning methods discussed and demonstrated in this chapter won't necessarily work for everyone. Different people have different programming styles, and some people won't be comfortable with the (perhaps) coldly logical model presented here. What's important is to find a style that works for you. Programming is a logical art; it shouldn't be a confining one. Be as creative as your own internals will let you be, remembering that poets also plan.

Keep in mind as you learn to program, please, when a bug is as hard to find as cheap gas, that deep down at the bit level—down where the computer deals with the only things it really understands—there are only zeros and ones.

Appendix A

Summary of Applesoft Statements and Functions

This appendix lists abbreviated descriptions of all Applesoft statements and functions. Each description is preceded by a syntactic definition and at least one example; see Appendix B for definitions of syntactic terms used here. References in square brackets at the end of each description give the section or appendix of this manual where more detailed information about the feature can be found.

ABS

Syntax: `ABS (`aexpr`)`
Example: `ABS (-2.77)`

Yields the absolute value (value without regard to sign) of the argument. The example yields 2.77. [2.4.1.1]

ASC

Syntax: `ASC (`sexpr`)`
Example: `ASC ("QUEST")`

Yields the ASCII code for the first character in the argument. The example yields 81 (ASCII code for Q). [4.2.5.4, C]

Assignment Statement

Syntax: `[LET]` avar = aexpr
`[LET]` svar = sexpr
Examples: `LET A = 23.567`
`A$ = "HUMBUG"`

Assigns the value of the expression following = to the variable preceding it. LET is optional. [2.2]

ATN

Syntax: `ATN (`aexpr`)`
Example: `ATN (.8771)`

Yields the arc tangent, in radians, of the argument. The example yields .720001187 (radians). [2.4.1.8]

CALL

Syntax: `CALL` aexpr
Example: `CALL -922`

Executes a machine-language subroutine at the specified decimal memory address. The example issues a line feed. [7.1.3, F]

CHR$

Syntax: `CHR$ (`aexpr`)`
Example: `CHR$ (65)`

Yields the character corresponding to the ASCII code given as an argument. The example yields the letter *A*. [4.2.5.3]

CLEAR

Syntax: `CLEAR`
Example: `CLEAR`

Resets all variables and internal control information to their initial state. Program code is unaffected. [1.2.2]

COLOR=

Syntax: `COLOR=` aexpr
Example: `COLOR= 12`

Sets the display color for plotting low-resolution graphics. The example sets the display color to green. [6.1.2]

CONT

Syntax: `CONT`
Example: `CONT`

Resumes program execution after it has been halted by STOP, END, CONTROL-C, or (sometimes) CONTROL-RESET. [1.3.3]

COS

Syntax: `COS (aexpr)`
Example: `COS (2)`

Yields the cosine of the argument, which must be expressed in radians. The example yields -.416146836. [2.4.1.6]

DATA

Syntax: `DATA` [literal | string | real | integer] [{, [literal | string | real | integer] }]
Example:

```
DATA JOHN SMITH, "CODE 32",
      23.45, -6
```

Creates a list of items for use by READ statements. In the example, the first item is the string "JOHN SMITH", the second is the string "CODE 32", the third is the real number 23.45, and the fourth is the integer -6. [5.1.4]

DEF FN

Syntax: `DEF FN` name (name) = aexpr
Example: `DEF FN CUBE (X) = X * X * X`

Defines a new function for use in the program. The example defines a function that yields the cube of its argument. [2.4.3]

DEL

Syntax: `DEL` linenum , linenum
Example: `DEL 23, 56`

Deletes a range of consecutive lines from the program. The example deletes lines 23 to 56, inclusive. [1.1.5]

DIM

Syntax: `DIM` name[%|$] subscript
[{, name[%|$] subscript}]

Example: `DIM MARK (50,3), NAME$ (50)`

Defines and allocates space for one or more arrays. The example defines a two-dimensional real array MARK, whose first subscript varies from 0 to 50 and whose second varies from 0 to 3, and a string array NAME$ with one subscript that varies from 0 to 50. [4.1.1]

DRAW

Syntax: `DRAW` aexpr [`AT` aexpr, aexpr]

Examples:

```
DRAW 4 AT 50,100
DRAW 4
```

Draws a shape at a specified point on the high-resolution graphics screen from the shape table currently in memory. The first example draws shape number 4, beginning in column 50, row 100, using the current color, scale, and rotation settings; the second example draws shape 4 at the last point plotted by HPLOT, DRAW, or XDRAW. [6.3.2.1]

END

Syntax: `END`

Example: `END`

Terminates the execution of the program and returns control to the user. No message is displayed. [3.6.2]

EXP

Syntax: `EXP (`aexpr`)`

Example: `EXP (2)`

Yields the mathematical exponential of its argument (the constant $e = 2.7182818$ raised to the power specified by the argument). The example yields e squared, or 7.3890561. [2.4.1.9]

FLASH

Syntax: `FLASH`
Example: `FLASH`

Causes all text displayed on the screen with subsequent PRINT statements to flash between white-on-black and black-on-white. May not work properly for lowercase letters (and other characters with ASCII codes above 95) if the 80-Column Text Card is installed and running in "active-80" mode. [5.2.4.10]

FN

Syntax: `FN` name `(`aexpr`)`
Example: `FN CUBE (6)`

Applies a designated function to the value of the argument expression. Assuming the definition for the function CUBE given under DEF FN, the example yields the value 216. [2.4.3]

FOR

Syntax: `FOR` name = aexpr `TO` aexpr [`STEP` aexpr]
Examples:

```
FOR J = 1 TO 10
FOR MARK = 0 TO 100 STEP 5
FOR NUMBER = 20 TO -20 STEP -2
```

Marks the beginning of a loop, identifies the index variable, and gives the variable's starting and ending values and (optionally) the amount by which it is to change (step) on each pass through the loop. The first example begins a loop whose index variable J takes on all values from 1 to 10, stepping by 1; the second begins a loop whose index variable MARK takes on values from 0 to 100, stepping by 5; the third begins a loop whose index variable NUMBER takes on values from 20 to -20, stepping by -2. [3.3.1]

FRE

Syntax: `FRE (expr)`
Example: `FRE (0)`

Yields the amount of remaining memory, in bytes, available to the program. Also forces "garbage collection" of dead strings. The argument is ignored, but must be a valid Applesoft expression. [7.2.3]

GET

Syntax: `GET` var
Example: `GET ANSWER$`

Accepts a single character from the keyboard without displaying it on the screen and without requiring that the RETURN key be pressed. Program execution is suspended until the user presses a key. In the example, the character typed is assigned to the variable ANSWER$. [5.1.3]

GOSUB

Syntax: `GOSUB` linenum
Example: `GOSUB 250`

Executes a subroutine beginning at the designated line number (250 in the example). [3.4.1]

GOTO

Syntax: `GOTO` linenum
Example: `GOTO 400`

Sends control unconditionally to the designated line number (400 in the example). [3.1]

GR

Syntax: `GR`
Example: `GR`

Converts the display to 40 rows of low-resolution graphics with four lines of text at the bottom. The screen is cleared to black, the cursor is moved to the beginning of the last line, and the low-resolution display color is set to black. [6.1.1]

HCOLOR=

Syntax: `HCOLOR=` aexpr
Example: `HCOLOR= 1`

Sets the display color for plotting high-resolution graphics. The example sets the display color to green. [6.2.3]

HGR

Syntax: `HGR`
Example: `HGR`

Converts the display to 160 rows of high-resolution graphics with four lines for text at the bottom. The screen is cleared to black and page 1 of high-resolution graphics is displayed. The contents of the text display, the location of the cursor, and the high-resolution display color are unaffected. [6.2.1]

HGR2

Syntax: `HGR2`
Example: `HGR2`

Converts the display to full-screen (192 rows) high-resolution graphics with no text. The screen is cleared to black and page 2 of high-resolution graphics is displayed. The contents of the text display, the location of the cursor, and the high-resolution display color are unaffected. [6.2.2]

HIMEM:

Syntax: `HIMEM:` aexpr
Example: `HIMEM: 32767`

Sets the address of the highest memory location available to the Applesoft program, including its variables. The example sets the end of program and variable storage to 32767. Used to protect an area of memory for data, high-resolution graphics, or machine-language code. [7.2.1]

HLIN

Syntax: `HLIN` aexpr1, aexpr2 `AT` aexpr3
Example: `HLIN 10, 20 AT 30`

Draws a horizontal line in low-resolution graphics, using the current low-resolution display color. The example draws a line across row 30 from column 10 to column 20. [6.1.4]

HOME

Syntax: `HOME`
Example: `HOME`

Clears all text from the text window and moves the cursor to the top-left corner of the window. [5.2.4.3]

HPLOT

Syntax: `HPLOT` aexpr, aexpr [{`TO` aexpr, aexpr}]
`HPLOT TO` aexpr, aexpr [{`TO` aexpr, aexpr}]

Examples:

```
HPLOT 75, 20
HPLOT 48, 115 TO 79, 84 TO 110,
     115
HPLOT TO 270, 10
```

Plots a point or line on the high-resolution graphics screen in the current high-resolution display color. The first example plots a single point at column 75, row 20; the second example draws lines from column 48, row 115 to column 79, row 84 to column 110, row 115; the third draws a line to column 270, row 10 from the last point plotted with HPLOT, using the color of the last point plotted (not necessarily the current display color). [6.2.4]

HTAB

Syntax: `HTAB` aexpr

Example: `HTAB 23`

Positions the cursor to a specified column of the text display. The example moves the cursor to column 23. If you have the Apple II 80-Column Text Card, see the manual accompanying that product for further information on using HTAB. [5.2.4.6]

IF...THEN

Syntax:

`IF` expr `THEN` statement [{`:` statement}]

`IF` expr `THEN` [`GOTO`] linenum

`IF` expr [`THEN`] `GOTO` linenum

Examples:

```
IF AGE < 18 THEN A = 0 : B = 1
   : C = 2
IF ANSWER$ = "YES" THEN GOTO
   100
IF N > MAX THEN GOTO 25
IF N > MAX THEN 25
IF N > MAX GOTO 25
```

Executes or skips one or more statements, depending on the truth of a stated condition. The first example sets A to 0, B to 1, and C to 2 if the value of AGE is less than 18; the second branches to line 100 if the value of ANSWER$ is the string "YES"; the last three all branch to line 25 if the value of N is greater than that of MAX. In all cases, if the stated condition is false, execution continues with the next program line. [3.2.2]

IN#

Syntax: `IN#` aexpr
Example: `IN# 2`

Specifies the source for subsequent input. The example causes subsequent input to be read from the device at port 2. [5.1.1]

INPUT

Syntax: `INPUT` [string] var [{, var}]
Examples:

```
INPUT A%
INPUT "TYPE AGE, THEN A COMMA,
        THEN NAME "; AGE, NAME$
```

Reads a line of input from the current input device. The first example reads a value into variable A%; the second displays a prompting message and then reads values into variables AGE and NAME$. [5.1.2]

INT

Syntax: `INT (`aexpr`)`
Examples:

```
INT (98.6)
INT (-273, 16)
```

Yields the integer part of the argument value. The examples yield 98 and -274, respectively. [2.4.1.3]

INVERSE

Syntax: `INVERSE`
Example: `INVERSE`

Causes all text displayed on the screen with subsequent PRINT statements to appear in black-on-white instead of the usual white-on-black. May not work properly for lowercase letters (and other characters with ASCII codes above 95) if the 80-Column Text Card is installed and running in "active-80" mode. [5.2.4.9]

LEFT$

Syntax: `LEFT$ (`sexpr, aexpr`)`
Example: `LEFT$ ("APPLESOFT", 5)`

Yields a specified number of characters from the beginning of a string. The example yields the string "APPLE". [4.2.4.1]

LEN

Syntax: `LEN (`sexpr`)`
Example: `LEN ("NEVER A DULL MOMENT")`

Yields the length of a string in characters. The example yields 19. [4.2.2]

LET

See "Assignment Statement."

LIST

Syntax: `LIST` [linenum1] [-linenum2]
`LIST` [linenum1] [, linenum2]

Examples:

```
LIST
LIST 150
LIST 200-300
LIST 200, 300
```

Displays all or part of the program on the screen, or writes it to the current output device. The first example lists the entire program; the second lists line 150 only; the last two list lines 200 to 300, inclusive. [1.2.3]

LOAD

Syntax: `LOAD` [name]

Examples: `LOAD`

`LOAD DEMO`

Reads a program into memory from a disk or tape. The first example reads a program from a tape cassette; the second reads from a disk file named DEMO (casette tape cannot be used with Apple IIc). If you have one or more disk drives, see your disk operating system manual for further information. [1.2.6, M]

LOG

Syntax: `LOG (`aexpr`)`

Example: `LOG (2)`

Yields the natural logarithm of the argument. The example yields .693147181. [2.4.1.10]

LOMEM:

Syntax: `LOMEM:` aexpr

Example: `LOMEM: 24576`

Sets the address of the lowest memory location available to the program for variable storage. The example sets the beginning of variable storage to 24576. [7.2.2]

MID$

Syntax: `MID$ (`sexpr, aexpr [, aexpr]`)`

Examples: `MID$ ("AN APPLE A DAY", 4, 5)`

`MID$ ("AN APPLE A DAY", 4)`

Yields a specified number of characters beginning at a specified position in a given string. The first example yields the string APPLE"; the second yields the string "APPLE A DAY". [4.2.4.2]

NEW

Syntax: `NEW`
Example: `NEW`

Clears the current program from memory and resets all variables and internal control information to their initial states. [1.2.1]

NEXT

Syntax: `NEXT` [avar [{, avar}]]
Examples:

```
NEXT
NEXT INDEX
NEXT J, I
```

Marks the end of a loop and causes the loop to be repeated for the next value of the index variable, as specified in the corresponding FOR statement. The first example ends the most recently entered loop; the second ends the loop whose index variable is INDEX; the third ends the pair of nested loops whose index variables are J and I. [3.3.2]

NORMAL

Syntax: `NORMAL`
Example: `NORMAL`

Causes all text displayed on the screen with subsequent PRINT statements to appear in the usual white-on-black; cancels the effects of INVERSE or FLASH. [5.2.4.11]

NOTRACE

Syntax: `NOTRACE`
Example: `NOTRACE`

Stops the display of line numbers for each statement executed; cancels the effects of TRACE. [7.3.2]

ON...GOSUB

Syntax: `ON` aexpr `GOSUB` linenum [{, linenum}]

Example:

```
ON ID GOSUB 100, 200, 23, 4005,
   500
```

Chooses a subroutine to execute depending on the value of an expression. The example transfers control to the subroutine beginning at line 100, 200, 23, 4005, or 500, depending on whether the value of ID is 1, 2, 3, 4, or 5; if ID has none of these values, execution continues with the next statement. [3.4.3]

ON...GOTO

Syntax: `ON` aexpr `GOTO` linenum [{, linenum}]

Example:

```
ON ID GOTO 100, 200, 23, 4005,
   500
```

Chooses a line number to branch to depending on the value of an expression. The example transfers control to line 100, 200, 23, 4005, or 500, depending on whether the value of ID is 1, 2, 3, 4, or 5; if ID has none of these values, execution continues with the next statement. [3.2.1]

ONERR GOTO

Syntax: `ONERR GOTO` linenum

Example: `ONERR GOTO 500`

Replaces Applesoft's normal error-handling mechanism with a subroutine beginning at a specified line number. The example establishes an error-handling subroutine beginning at line 500. [3.5.1, E]

PDL

Syntax: `PDL (`aexpr`)`

Example: `PDL (1)`

Reads the current dial setting on a designated hand control. The example reads the dial on hand control 1. [5.1.6.1, F.4]

PEEK

Syntax: `PEEK (aexpr)`
Example: `PEEK (37)`

Yields the contents of a specified location in memory. The example yields the contents of location 37, which contains the current vertical position of the text cursor on the display screen. [7.1.1, F.1]

PLOT

Syntax: `PLOT aexpr, aexpr`
Example: `PLOT 10, 20`

Plots a single block of the current display color at a specified position on the low-resolution graphics screen. The example plots a block at column 10, row 20. [6.1.3]

POKE

Syntax: `POKE aexpr, aexpr`
Example: `POKE -16302, 0`

Stores a value in a specified location in memory. The example stores the value 0 at location 49234 (65536 - 16302), causing the display to switch from mixed graphics and text to full-screen graphics. [7.1.2, F]

POP

Syntax: `POP`
Example: `POP`

Removes the most recent return address from the control stack, causing the next RETURN statement to send control to the statement following the second most recently executed GOSUB. [3.4.4]

POS

Syntax: `POS (expr)`
Example: `POS (0)`

Yields the current horizontal position of the cursor on the text display. The argument is ignored, but must be a valid Applesoft expression. [5.2.4.8]

PR#

Syntax: `PR#` aexpr
Example: `PR# 1`

Specifies the destination for subsequent output. The example causes subsequent output to be sent to the device at port 1. [5.2.1]

PRINT

Syntax: `PRINT` [{ expr [,|;] }]
Examples: `PRINT`
`PRINT A$, "X = "; X`

Writes a line of output to the current output device. The first example writes a blank line; the second writes the value of variable A$, followed at the next available tab position by the string "X = ", followed immediately by the value of variable X. [5.2.2]

READ

Syntax: `READ` var [{ , var }]
Example: `READ A, B%, C$`

Reads values from DATA statements in the body of the program. The example reads values into variables A, B%, and C$. [5.1.4]

RECALL

Syntax: `RECALL` name[%]
Example: `RECALL MX`

II, II Plus, IIe

Reads values into an array from a tape cassette. The example reads values into array MX [M]

REM

Syntax: `REM` {character}
Example: `REM THIS A REMARK`

Includes remarks in the body of a program for the benefit of a human reader. [1.1.7]

RESTORE

Syntax: `RESTORE`
Example: `RESTORE`

Causes the next READ statement executed to beginning reading at the first item of the first DATA statement in the program. [5.1.5]

RESUME

Syntax: `RESUME`
Example: `RESUME`

At the end of an error-handling routine (see ONERR GOTO), causes resumption of the program at the beginning of the statement in which the error occurred. [3.5.2]

RETURN

Syntax: `RETURN`
Example: `RETURN`

The last statement in a subroutine returns control from a subroutine to the statement following the GOSUB that called the subroutine. [3.4.2]

RIGHT$

Syntax: `RIGHT$` (sexpr, aexpr)
Example: `RIGHT$ ("APPLESOFT", 4)`

Yields a specified number of characters from the end of a string. The example yields the string "SOFT". [4.2.4.3]

RND

Syntax: `RND` (aexpr)
Example: `RND (1)`

Yields a random number between 0 and 1. Zero and negative argument values yield repeatable sequences of random numbers. [2.4.2]

ROT=

Syntax: `ROT=` aexpr
Example: `ROT= 16`

Sets the angular rotation for high-resolution shapes to be drawn with DRAW or XDRAW. The example causes the shape to be rotated 90 degrees clockwise. [6.3.2.4]

RUN

Syntax: `RUN` [linenum | name]
Examples:

```
RUN
RUN 500
RUN DEMO
```

Executes an Applesoft program. The first example executes the program currently in memory from the beginning; the second executes the program in memory, starting at line 500; the third loads and executes a program from a disk file named DEMO. [1.2.4]

SAVE

Syntax: `SAVE` [name]
Examples: `SAVE`
`SAVE DEMO`

II, II Plus, IIe

Writes the Applesoft program currently in memory to a disk or tape. The first example writes the program to a tape cassette; the second writes it to a disk file named DEMO. [1.2.5, M]

SCALE=

Syntax: `SCALE=` aexpr
Example: `SCALE= 10`

Sets the scale factor for high-resolution shapes to be drawn with DRAW or XDRAW. The example causes the shape to be drawn ten times bigger than the definition given in the shape table. [6.3.2.3]

SCRN

Syntax: `SCRN (`aexpr, aexpr`)`
Example: `SCRN (10, 20)`

Yields the code for the color currently displayed at a designated position on the low-resolution graphics screen. The example yields the code for the color at column 10, row 20. [6.1.6]

SGN

Syntax: `SGN (`aexpr`)`
Example: `SGN (-144)`

Yields a value of -1, 0, or +1, depending on the sign of the argument. The example yields -1. [2.4.1.2]

SHLOAD

Syntax: `SHLOAD`
Example: `SHLOAD`

II, II Plus, IIe | Loads a shape table into memory from a tape cassette. [6.3.2.5, M]

SIN

Syntax: `SIN (aexpr)`
Example: `SIN (2)`

Yields the sine of the argument, which must be expressed in radians. The example yields .909297427. [2.4.1.5]

SPC

Syntax: `SPC (aexpr)`
Example: `SPC (8)`

Introduces a specified number of spaces into the line being written by a PRINT statement. The example writes eight spaces. [5.2.4.4]

SPEED=

Syntax: `SPEED= aexpr`
Example: `SPEED= 50`

Sets the rate at which text characters are to be sent to the display screen or other input/output device. The slowest rate is 0; the fastest is 255. [5.2.4.12]

SQR

Syntax: `SQR (aexpr)`
Example: `SQR(2)`

Yields the positive square root of the argument; the example yields 1.41421356. [2.4.1.4]

STOP

Syntax: `STOP`
Example: `STOP`

Terminates the execution of the program and returns control to the user. A message is displayed identifying the program line in which the STOP statement appears. [3.6.1]

STORE

Syntax: `STORE` name[`%`]
Example: `STORE MX`

II, II Plus, IIe

Stores values from an array onto a tape cassette. The example stores the contents of array MX. [M]

STR$

Syntax: `STR$ (`aexpr`)`
Example: `STR$ (12.45)`

Yields a string representing the numeric value of the argument. The example yields the string "12.45". [4.2.5.1, I]

TAB

Syntax: `TAB (`aexpr`)`
Example: `TAB (23)`

Positions the text cursor at a specified position on the output line during execution of a PRINT statement. The example moves the cursor to column 23. [5.2.4.5]

TAN

Syntax: `TAN (aexpr)`

Example: `TAN (2)`

Yields the tangent of the argument, which must be expressed in radians. The example yields -2.18503987. [2.4.1.7]

TEXT

Syntax: `TEXT`

Example: `TEXT`

Converts the display to 24 lines of text, with the cursor positioned at the beginning of the bottom line. [5.2.4]

TRACE

Syntax: `TRACE`

Example: `TRACE`

Causes the line number of each statement to be displayed on the screen as it is executed. [7.3.1]

USR

Syntax: `USR (aexpr)`

Example: `USR (3)`

Executes a machine-language subroutine supplied by the user, passing it a specified argument. The subroutine is entered via a JMP (jump) instruction stored at addresses $0A through $0C hexadecimal. The example passes the argument value 3. [7.1.4]

VAL

Syntax: `VAL (`sexpr`)`
Example: `VAL ("-3.7E4")`

Yields the numeric value represented by the string supplied as an argument. The example yields -37000. [4.2.5.2]

VLIN

Syntax: `VLIN` aexpr`,` aexpr `AT` aexpr
Example: `VLIN 10, 20 AT 30`

Draws a vertical line in low-resolution graphics, using the current low-resolution display color. The example draws a line down column 30 from row 10 to row 20. [6.1.5]

VTAB

Syntax: `VTAB` aexpr
Example: `VTAB 15`

Positions the cursor to a specified row of the text display. The example moves the cursor to row 15. [5.2.4.7]

WAIT

Syntax: `WAIT` aexpr`,` aexpr [`,` aexpr]
Examples: `WAIT 49347, 15`
`WAIT 49347, 15, 12`

Suspends program execution until a specified bit pattern appears at a specified memory location. Used to wait for a status signal from a peripheral device. The second and (optional) third arguments are masks: the second specifies which bits of the designated location are of interest, the third specifies the values to be tested for in those bits. The first example suspends execution until a 1 bit appears in any of the four low-order bit positions of location 49347; the second waits for a 1 bit in position 0 or 1 or a 0 bit in position 2 or 3. [7.1.5]

XDRAW

Syntax: `XDRAW` aexpr [`AT` aexpr`,` aexpr]

Examples:

```
XDRAW 4 AT 50, 100
XDRAW 4
```

Draws a shape from the shape table currently in memory at a specified point on the high-resolution graphics screen. Each point in the shape is plotted using the complement of the color currently displayed at that point. Typically used to erase a shape already drawn. The first example erases shape number 4, beginning in column 50, row 100, using the current scale and rotation settings; the second example erases shape 4 at the last point plotted by HPLOT, DRAW, or XDRAW. [6.3.2.2]

Appendix B

Syntax Definitions

This appendix describes the syntax definitions given in Appendix A. The following symbols are used in the syntax definitions:

:=	means "is defined as"
|	separates alternative definitions (alternative definitions for the same term may also be given separately)
[ ]	enclose elements that can be omitted
{ }	enclose elements that can be repeated one or more times

aexpr (arithmetic expression)

:= real | integer | avar | fcall
:= unop aexpr
:= aexpr alop aexpr
:= sexpr relop sexpr
:= (aexpr)

Parentheses cannot be nested more than 36 levels deep.

alop (arithmetic or logical operator)

:= aop | relop | lop

aop (arithmetic operator)

:= + | - | * | / | ^

avar (arithmetic variable)

:= realvar | intvar

character

:= letter | digit | spchar | quote | space

digit

:= 0 | 1 | 2 | 3 | 4 | 5 | 6 | 7 | 8 | 9

expr (expression)

:= aexpr | sexpr

fcall (function call)

:= name (expr [{, expr}])

integer

:= [+ | -] {digit}

Integers must be between -32767 and +32767 to be valid.

intvar (integer variable)

:= name% [subscript]

letter

:= uppercase | lowercase

line

:= linenum [{statement:}] statement RETURN

linenum (line number)

:= digit [{digit}]

Line numbers must be in the range 0 to 63999.

literal

:= [{character}]

lop (logical operator)

:= AND | OR

Notice that NOT is not included here.

lowercase

:= a | b | c | d | e | f | g | h | i | j | k |
l | m | n | o | p | q | r | s | t | u | v |
w | x | y | z

name

:= uppercase [{uppercase | digit}]

A name can be of any length. When distinguishing one name from another, Applesoft ignores any characters after the first two. However, even the ignored portion of a name must not contain a special character or any of Applesoft's reserved words.

quote

:= "

real

:= [+ | -] {digit} [. {digit}] [E [+ | -] [digit [digit]]]
:= [+ | -] [{digit}] . [{digit}] [E [+ | -] [digit [digit]]]

The letter *E* in a real number stands for "times 10 raised to the power after the *E*." Valid reals must be between -1E38 and +1E38.

Applesoft recognizes the following as reals and evaluates them as 0:

.   +.   -.   .E   +.E   -.E

.E+   .E-   +.E+   +.E-   -.E+   -.E-

In addition, the following are recognized as reals and evaluated as 0 when used as numeric responses to INPUT or as numeric elements of DATA:

[SPACE]   +   -   E   +E   -E

E+   E-   +E+   +E-   -E+   -E-

The GET statement evaluates all of the single-character reals listed as 0.

realvar (real variable)

:=   name [subscript]

relop (relational operator)

:=   =|<|>|<=|=<|>=|=>|<>|><

schar (string character)

:=   letter | digit | spchar | space

Notice that the quote character (") is not included here.

sexpr (string expression)

:=   string | svar
:=   sexpr sop sexpr
:=   (sexpr)

Parentheses cannot be nested more than 36 levels deep.

sop (string operator)

:=   +

space

:=   [SPACE]

spchar (special character)

:=   +|-|*|/|^|=|<|>|(|)|,|.|:|;|
%|$|#|?|&|'|@|!|[|]|{|}|\|
|:|_||~|

Control characters (characters typed while holding down the [CONTROL] key) and the null character are also considered special characters. Notice that the quote character (") and [SPACE] are not included here.

statement

See Appendix A for syntactic definitions of all Applesoft statements.

string

:= "[{schar}]"
:= "[{schar}]

The second form of string can appear only at the end of a line.

subscript

:= (aexpr [{, aexpr}])

The maximum number of dimensions (aexpr's) is 89, although in practice this is limited by the extent of memory available.

svar (string variable)

:= name$ [subscript]

unop (unary operator)

:= + | - | NOT

uppercase

:= A | B | C | D | E | F | G | H | I | J | K |
L | M | N | O | P | Q | R | S | T | U | V |
W | X | Y | Z

var (variable)

:= avar | svar

Appendix C

ASCII Character Codes

This appendix contains a chart of the ASCII (American Standard Code for Information Interchange) character codes. The first 32 codes represent control characters; to type these characters from the Apple computer keyboard, press CONTROL and hold it down while pressing the designated character. (Some of these characters also have single-key representations, as noted.) The abbreviations given for these codes in the column labeled *Char* represent standard control functions originally intended for use on teletypes; the meanings of these abbreviations are given in the *Meaning* column. Functions marked with a dagger (†) are implemented on the Apple II; the others are listed purely for historical interest.

> *Note:* Older model Apples (II, II Plus) don't have some of the keys listed in the *Type* column. To access these characters, use the CHR$ function.

Dec	= decimal ASCII code
Hex	= hexadecimal ASCII code
Char	= ASCII character name
Type	= what you type from the Apple computer keyboard

Dec	Hex	Char	Type	Meaning
0	00	NUL	CONTROL-@	null character †
1	01	SOH	CONTROL-A	start of heading
2	02	STX	CONTROL-B	start of text
3	03	ETX	CONTROL-C	end of text
4	04	EOT	CONTROL-D	end of transmission
5	05	ENQ	CONTROL-E	inquiry
6	06	ACK	CONTROL-F	acknowledge
7	07	BEL	CONTROL-G	bell †
8	08	BS	CONTROL-H or ←	backspace †
9	09	HT	CONTROL-I	horizontal tab
10	0A	LF	CONTROL-J or ↓	line feed †
11	0B	VT	CONTROL-K or ↑	vertical tab
12	0C	FF	CONTROL-L	form feed
13	0D	CR	CONTROL-M or RETURN	carriage return †
14	0E	SO	CONTROL-N	shift out
15	0F	SI	CONTROL-O	shift in
16	10	DLE	CONTROL-P	data link escape
17	11	DC1	CONTROL-Q	device control 1
18	12	DC2	CONTROL-R	device control 2
19	13	DC3	CONTROL-S	device control 3
20	14	DC4	CONTROL-T	device control 4
21	15	NAK	CONTROL-U or →	negative acknowledge
22	16	SYN	CONTROL-V	synchronous idle
23	17	ETB	CONTROL-W	end of transmission block
24	18	CAN	CONTROL-X	cancel †
25	19	EM	CONTROL-Y	end of medium
26	1A	SUB	CONTROL-Z	substitute
27	1B	ESC	CONTROL-[or ESC	escape
28	1C	FS	CONTROL-\	file separator
29	1D	GS	CONTROL-]	group separator
30	1E	RS	CONTROL-^	record separator
31	1F	US	CONTROL-_	unit separator

The following characters can be typed directly from the keyboards of most Apples. If you are using a model II or II Plus, use the CHR$ function to generate the “missing” characters:

Dec	Hex	Char	Dec	Hex	Char	Dec	Hex	Char
32	20	SPACE	64	40	@	96	60	
33	21	!	65	41	A	97	61	a
34	22	”	66	42	B	98	62	b
35	23	#	67	43	C	99	63	c
36	24	$	68	44	D	100	64	d
37	25	%	69	45	E	101	65	e
38	26	&	70	46	F	102	66	f
39	27	’	71	47	G	103	67	g
40	28	(	72	48	H	104	68	h
41	29	)	73	49	I	105	69	i
42	2A	*	74	4A	J	106	6A	j
43	2B	+	75	4B	K	107	6B	k
44	2C	,	76	4C	L	108	6C	l
45	2D	-	77	4D	M	109	6D	m
46	2E	.	78	4E	N	110	6E	n
47	2F	/	79	4F	O	111	6F	o
48	30	0	80	50	P	112	70	p
49	31	1	81	51	Q	113	71	q
50	32	2	82	52	R	114	72	r
51	33	3	83	53	S	115	73	s
52	34	4	84	54	T	116	74	t
53	35	5	85	55	U	117	75	u
54	36	6	86	56	V	118	76	v
55	37	7	87	57	W	119	77	w
56	38	8	88	58	X	120	78	x
57	39	9	89	59	Y	121	79	y
58	3A	:	90	5A	Z	122	7A	z
59	3B	;	91	5B	[	123	7B	{
60	3C	<	92	5C	\	124	7C	,
61	3D	=	93	5D	]	125	7D	}
62	3E	>	94	5E	^	126	7E	
63	3F	?	95	5F	_	127	7F	DELETE

Appendix D

Reserved Words

Table D-1 lists Applesoft's reserved words. In most cases these character sequences cannot be used as, or embedded in, variable names.

Applesoft converts all its keywords to one-byte codes, called **tokens**, to save memory. Refer to Section H.4 for a list of tokens. All other characters in a program occupy one byte each of program storage.

The ampersand character (&) is reserved for Applesoft's internal use and for user-supplied machine-language routines. When executed as an instruction, it causes a JSR to address $03F5 hexadecimal.

XPLOT is a reserved word that does not correspond to a current Applesoft statement.

Some reserved words are recognized by Applesoft only in certain contexts:

- COLOR, HCOLOR, ROT, SCALE, and SPEED are interpreted as reserved words only if the next nonspace character is an equal sign (=). This is of little benefit in the case of COLOR and HCOLOR, as the embedded reserved word OR prevents their use as variable names anyway.
- HIMEM and LOMEM are interpreted as reserved words only if the next nonspace character is a colon (:).
- IN and PR are interpreted as reserved words only if the next nonspace character is a number sign (#).
- SCRN, SPC, and TAB are interpreted as reserved words only if the next nonspace character is a left parenthesis, (.
- ATN is interpreted as a reserved word only if there is no space between the T and the N. If a space occurs between the T and the N, the reserved word AT is interpreted instead of ATN.
- TO is interpreted as a reserved word unless it is preceded by an A and there is a space between the T and the O. In that case, the reserved word AT is interpreted instead of TO.

Even if you don't embed reserved words in your variable names, they can sometimes pop up unexpectedly and cause problems. For example, the statement

```
100  FOR A = LOFT OR LEFT TO 15
```

is interpreted as

```
100  FOR A = LOF TO RLEFT TO 15
```

and causes a syntax error. To force the correct interpretation, use parentheses:

```
100  FOR A = (LOFT) OR (LEFT) TO 15
```

Table D-1. Applesoft Reserved Words

$	GET	NEW	SAVE
	GOSUB	NEXT	SCALE=
ABS	GOTO	NORMAL	SCRN(
AND	GR	NOT	SGN
ASC		NOTRACE	SHLOAD
AT	HCOLOR=		SIN
ATN	HGR	ON	SPC(
	HGR2	ONERR	SPEED=
CALL	HIMEM:	OR	SQR
CHR$	HLIN		STEP
CLEAR	HOME	PDL	STOP
COLOR=	HPLOT	PEEK	STORE
CONT	HTAB	PLOT	STR$
COS		POKE	
	IF	POP	TAB(
DATA	IN#	POS	TAN
DEF	INPUT	PRINT	TEXT
DEL	INT	PR#	THEN
DIM	INVERSE		TO
DRAW		READ	TRACE
	LEFT$	RECALL	
END	LEN	REM	USR
EXP	LET	RESTORE	
	LIST	RESUME	VAL
FLASH	LOAD	RETURN	VLIN
FN	LOG	RIGHT$	VTAB
FOR	LOMEM:	RND	
FRE		ROT=	WAIT
	MID$	RUN	
			XPLOT
			XDRAW

Appendix E

Error Messages

This appendix lists Applesoft's error messages and their causes. When an error occurs in immediate execution, Applesoft sounds a beep and displays a message of the form

```
?XX ERROR
```

where `XX` is the name of the particular error.

In deferred execution (during the course of a running program), the message takes the form

```
?XX ERROR IN YY
```

where `YY` is the line number of the statement in which the error occurred, the Applesoft prompt character ( ]) and the cursor are displayed, and control of the system is returned to the user. Variable values and the text of the program remain intact, but internal control information is erased and the program cannot be continued with the CONT command (refer to Section 1.3.3). An error in a deferred-execution statement is not detected until the statement is executed.

The error handling described can be overridden by an error-handling routine in the program itself, established with the ONERR GOTO statement (refer to Section 3.5.1). Error codes for use in such an error-handling routine are shown in square brackets following the error names. When an error occurs, the code listed is stored at location 222 decimal; it can be retrieved from that location with the PEEK function (refer to Section 7.1.1). Errors for which no code is given cannot occur in deferred execution.

Errors associated with the disk operating system also register at location 222; see the disk operating system manual for further information.

Debugging suggestions given under the individual error messages are not intended to be exhaustive or comprehensive; the causes of program bugs are as numberless as the sands of the sea and stars of the sky.

E.1 Error Messages by Number

See Section E.2 for an explanation of any error message listed below.

0	NEXT WITHOUT FOR
16	SYNTAX ERROR
22	RETURN WITHOUT GOSUB
42	OUT OF DATA
53	ILLEGAL QUANTITY
69	OVERFLOW
77	OUT OF MEMORY
90	UNDEF'D STATEMENT
107	BAD SUBSCRIPT
120	REDIM'D ARRAY
133	DIVISION BY ZERO
163	TYPE MISMATCH
176	STRING TOO LONG
191	FORMULA TOO COMPLEX
224	UNDEF'D FUNCTION
	CAN'T CONTINUE
	ILLEGAL DIRECT

E.2 Alphabetical List of Error Messages

See Section E.1 for a list of error messages by number.

BAD SUBSCRIPT [107]

A reference was made to an array element that is outside the dimensions of the array. This error can occur if the wrong number of dimensions are used in an array reference: for instance,

```
LET A(1, 1, 1) = Z
```

when A has been defined by

```
DIM A(2,2)
```

CAN'T CONTINUE

An attempt was made to continue a program with the CONT command when no program exists in memory, or after an error, or after a line has been changed, deleted from, or added to the program.

DIVISION BY ZERO [133]

An attempt was made to divide by 0; division by 0 is mathematically undefined. Often occurs when a variable is used in an arithmetic expression before being given a value (all numeric variables initially have the value 0). To debug, examine the divisor of the expression where the error occurred to see why it unexpectedly has a 0 value. Look particularly for variables that have inadvertently been used without having been given a nonzero value.

FORMULA TOO COMPLEX [191]

More than two statements of the form

```
IF "ZZ" THEN
```

were executed (where "ZZ" is any quoted string). The Applesoft IF...THEN statement wasn't intended to be used with strings, and the results of such statements are not meaningful. The wisest policy is to avoid this type of construction altogether.

ILLEGAL DIRECT

An attempt was made to use one of the following statements in immediate execution:

- DEF FN
- GET
- INPUT
- ONERR GOTO
- READ
- RESUME

ILLEGAL QUANTITY [53]

The argument supplied to a statement or function was out of the allowed range. This error can be caused by

- a negative array subscript (for example, LET A (-1) = 0)
- LOG with a negative or 0 argument
- SQR with a negative argument
- A ^ B with A negative and B not an integer
- use of LEFT$, MID$, RIGHT$, WAIT, PEEK, POKE, CALL, TAB, SPC, ON...GOTO, ON...GOSUB, or any of the graphics statements or functions with an improper argument.

NEXT WITHOUT FOR [0]

The variable named in a NEXT statement did not agree with the variable in the corresponding FOR statement, or a nameless NEXT was executed when no FOR was in effect. The most common causes of this error are forgetting a FOR or NEXT statement, typing the wrong variable in the NEXT statement, crossing loops, or accidentally branching into or out of the body of a FOR loop.

OUT OF DATA [42]

A READ statement was executed after all DATA statements in the program had already been read. A READ statement may have been executed more times than intended (for example, in an infinite loop), or one or more DATA statements may have been inadvertently omitted. Sometimes caused by accidentally leaving out a RESTORE statement.

OUT OF MEMORY [77]

Any of the following can cause this error:

- □ program too large
- □ too many variables
- □ FOR loops nested more than 10 levels deep
- □ subroutine calls nested more than 24 levels deep
- □ parentheses nested more than 36 levels deep
- □ too complicated an expression
- □ attempt to set LOMEM: too high
- □ attempt to set LOMEM: lower than present value
- □ attempt to set HIMEM: too low.

OVERFLOW [69]

The result of an arithmetic calculation was too large to be represented in Applesoft's internal number format.

REDIM'D ARRAY [120]

An attempt was made to define the same array twice in the same or different DIM statements. This error often occurs if an array has been referred to in a statement such as

```
LET A (I) = 3
```

before being defined in a DIM statement. At first reference, the array is automatically defined with an assumed dimension of 10; if such a statement is followed later in the program by

```
DIM A (100)
```

the `REDIM'D ARRAY` error results. Another common cause of the error is a program that loops back to a line before the DIM statement, consequently executing it a second time.

If you *must* define the same array twice in the same program, use CLEAR before redefining it. Remember that CLEAR initializes *all* variables (refer to Section 1.1.1). Before using CLEAR, save all essential data to disk (or to RAM) and close any open files.

Locating an Array Definition: This error message can prove useful if you wish to discover on what program line an array was defined. Just insert a DIM statement for the array in the first line, run the program, and the program halts with a `REDIM'D ARRAY` error when the original DIM statement is executed.

RETURN WITHOUT GOSUB [22]

A RETURN statement was encountered without a corresponding GOSUB having been executed. This error often occurs when control accidentally branches into a subroutine via a GOTO statement, or "falls into" a subroutine because there is no END or GOTO statement at the end of the program segment preceding the subroutine.

STRING TOO LONG [176]

An attempt was made by use of the concatenation operator (+) to create a string more than 255 characters long. This error tends to occur when a string variable is used more than once without being cleared (that is, without being reset to the null string).

SYNTAX ERROR [16]

A statement or expression doesn't conform to Applesoft's syntax rules. There are a myriad of possible causes for this error, such as a missing parenthesis, illegal character, or incorrect punctuation. Often results from a simple typing error.

TYPE MISMATCH [163]

The left side of an assignment statement was a numeric variable and the right side was a string, or vice versa; or a function that expected a string argument was given a numeric one or vice versa. Often caused by inadvertently leaving out the dollar sign ($) in a string variable or function name.

UNDEF'D FUNCTION [224]

A reference was made to a function that had never been defined. Can occur when you type something like `FN L(X)` when you meant to type `FN I(X)`; that is, a simple case of mistaken identifier.

UNDEF'D STATEMENT [90]

An attempt was made to transfer control, via GOTO, GOSUB, or IF...THEN, to a nonexistent line number. Common causes include accidentally deleting a line, changing a line number without changing references from other lines accordingly, and simple typing errors.

Appendix F

Peeks, Pokes, and Calls

This appendix discusses some of the many special features of the Apple II that you can use in your Applesoft programs by means of PEEK, POKE, or CALL statements (see Sections 7.1.1, 7.1.2, and 7.1.3, respectively). Notice that some of them duplicate the effects of other Applesoft features.

Many of these special addresses are **soft switches**—specific locations in memory that produce some special effect whenever the contents are read or written—any reference to them, whether a read (that is, a PEEK) or a write (a POKE), invokes the feature associated with the address. For instance, the sample given here for switching from text to graphics without clearing the graphics screen is

```
POKE -16304, 0
```

but you can get the same effect by executing

```
X = PEEK (-16304)
```

or by using POKE to address -16304 with a value other than 0. This does not apply in cases where you must use POKE to store a specific value into the special address, such as a margin setting or a cursor location.

> *For More Information:* For more information on special features accessible with PEEK, POKE, and CALL, see your Apple's reference manual.

F.1 Screen Text

The special locations described in this section are used for controlling the display of text on the screen:

- setting the boundaries of the text window within which characters are displayed and scrolled
- clearing all text from all or part of the screen
- scrolling text within the text window
- controlling the position of the cursor.

Setting the text window does not clear the remainder of the screen (for which you can use HOME) and does not move the cursor into the new text window (use HOME again, or HTAB and VTAB—see Section 5.2.4).

F.1.1 Setting the Text Window

This program lets you experiment with text windows:

```
10  HOME
20  PRINT " +---------------\+"
30  INPUT " | LEFT: ";L
40  INPUT " | WIDTH: ";W
50  INPUT " | TOP: ";T
60  INPUT " | BOTTOM: ";B
70  POKE 33,W
80  POKE 32,L
90  POKE 34,T
100  POKE 35,B
110  GOTO 10
```

POKE 32 L

Sets the left edge of the text window to the value specified by expression L. This value should be between 0 and 39 (or 0 and 79 if you're using 80 columns), where 0 represents the leftmost column of the screen.

The change doesn't become visible until the cursor attempts to return to the left edge of the window.

▲Warning The width of the window is not changed by this statement: this means that the right edge is moved by the same amount you move the left edge. To protect your program and Applesoft, first reduce the window width appropriately; *then* change the left edge.

POKE 33 W

Sets the width of the text window (number of characters per line) to the value specified by expression W. This value should be between 1 and 40 (or 1 and 80 if you're using 80 columns).

▲Warning

Make sure the right edge of the text window doesn't extend past the right edge of the display screen. The window width shouldn't be set greater than 40 (or 80) minus the current left edge of the window. For sample, if you've set the left edge of the window to 10, don't set the window width greater than 30 (or 70 if you're using 80 columns). Setting the window too wide causes display text to be written outside the usual memory area reserved for it, destroying parts of your program or vital system information.

Do not set the window width to 0! The statement

```
POKE 33, 0
```

causes the system to crash.

If W is less than 33, the TAB function (see Section 5.2.4.5) in a PRINT statement may cause characters to be displayed outside the text window.

POKE 34 T

Sets the top edge of the text window to the value specified by expression T. This value should be between 0 and 23, where 0 represents the top line of the screen.

▲Warning

Do not set the top edge of the window (T) lower than the bottom edge.

POKE 35 B

Sets the bottom edge of the text window to the value specified by expression B. This value should be between 0 and 23, where 23 represents the bottom line of the screen.

By the Way: No matter what you do to the left margin, width, top, and bottom of the text window, you can quickly restore it to the full screen with the TEXT statement.

▲Warning

Make sure the bottom of the text window doesn't extend past the bottom of the display screen. Setting the window bottom beyond line 23 causes display text to be written outside the usual memory area reserved for it, destroying parts of your program or vital system information.

Do not set the bottom edge of the window (B) higher than the top edge.

F.1.2 Text in Windows

These five CALLS are used to clear portions of the text window, and to move the cursor and scroll text.

CALL -936

Clears all text within the text window and moves the cursor to the top-left corner of the window. The effect is the same as that of the HOME statement or of pressing [ESC] [@] from the keyboard.

CALL -958

Clears all characters inside the text window from the current cursor position to the bottom-right corner. Characters above and to the left of the cursor are not affected. The effect is the same as that of pressing [ESC] [F] from the keyboard.

CALL -868

Clears all characters inside the text window from the current cursor position to the end of the line. The effect is the same as that of pressing [ESC] [E] from the keyboard.

CALL -922

Issues a line feed character, causing the cursor to move down one line without changing its horizontal position. If the cursor is on the bottom line of the text window, the contents of the window are scrolled up one line. The effect is the same as that of pressing [CONTROL]-[J] from the keyboard.

CALL -912

Scrolls all text within the text window up one line. The old top line is lost; the old second line becomes the top line; the bottom line becomes blank. Text outside the text window is not affected.

F.1.3 The Cursor in Windows

These PEEKs and POKEs move the cursor within the text window.

PEEK (36)

Yields the current horizontal position of the cursor, a number between 0 and 39 (0 and 79, if you're using 80 columns). The cursor position is given relative to the left edge of the text window, not the left edge of the screen. The effect is the same as that of the POS function (see Section 5.2.4).

POKE 36, CH

Moves the cursor to the horizontal position specified by expression CH, which is interpreted relative to the left edge of the text window, not the left edge of the screen. The value of this expression should be between 0 and the current width of the window, with 0 representing the leftmost column of the window. The effect is the same as that of the HTAB statement (see Section 5.2.4.6), but is not limited to 40 columns.

Like HTAB, this statement can move the cursor beyond the right edge of the text window, but only long enough to display one character.

> *80-Column Users:* You can use this POKE statement to position the cursor in columns 40 to 79 of the screen, which are inaccessible with HTAB.

▲Warning

> Don't move the cursor past the right edge of the display screen! The cursor position shouldn't be set greater than 40 (or 80) minus the current left edge of the window. For example, if you've set the left edge of the window to 10, don't set the cursor position greater than 30 (or 70 with 80 columns). Moving the cursor too far to the right may cause display text to be written outside the usual memory area reserved for it, destroying parts of your program or vital system information.

PEEK (37)

Yields the current vertical position of the cursor, a number between 0 and 23. The cursor position is given relative to the top edge of the screen, not the top edge of the text window. A value of 0 represents the top line of the screen, 23 the bottom line.

POKE 37, CV

Moves the cursor to the vertical position specified by expression CV, which is interpreted relative to the top of the screen, not the top of the text window. The value of this expression should be between 0 and 23, with 0 representing the topmost line of the screen. The effect is similar to that of the VTAB statement (see Section 5.2.4.7), except that

- □ screen lines are numbered from 0 to 23, not from 1 to 24 as with VTAB
- □ the specified cursor position is not limited to 24 lines.

Like VTAB, this statement can move the cursor beyond the bottom edge of the text window, but all subsequent text sent to the display screen then appears on that same line.

▲Warning Don't move the cursor past the bottom edge of the display screen! Setting the cursor position beyond line 23 causes display text to be written outside the usual memory area reserved for it, destroying parts of your program or vital system information.

F.2 Keyboard

The following special locations are used for reading input directly from the keyboard.

PEEK (-16384)

Reads the last character typed from the keyboard. If the high-order bit of this location is 1 (PEEK yields a result > 127), then a new character has been typed since the last POKE to address -16368; subtracting 128 from the value received gives the ASCII code for the character typed. If the high-order bit is 0 (PEEK yields a result <= 127), then no new character has been typed since the last POKE to -16368.

POKE -16368, 0

Clears the high-order bit of location -16384 to prepare for reading another keyboard character. This should be done immediately after reading the keyboard via PEEK (-16384).

F.3 Graphics

Four areas are reserved in the Apple II's memory for displaying text and graphics on the screen:

- □ Low-resolution page 1 is located at addresses $400 to $7FF hexadecimal (1024 to 2047 decimal). Information stored in this area can be interpreted and displayed on the screen in the form of either text or low-resolution graphics. This is the usual area of memory used for both these purposes, and is the area used by Applesoft's TEXT and GR statements.
- □ Low-resolution page 2, at addresses $800 to $BFF hexadecimal (2048 to 3071 decimal), can be used as an alternate area for either text or low-resolution graphics. Since this is the same area as the beginning of Applesoft's normal program storage space (see Section H.1), using it for text or graphics is tricky and is not recommended.
- □ High-resolution page 1, at addresses $2000 to $3FFF hexadecimal (8192 to 16383 decimal), is the usual area for high-resolution graphics, and is accessible via Applesoft's HGR statement.
- □ High-resolution page 2, at addresses $4000 to $5FFF hexadecimal (16384 to 24575 decimal), serves as an alternate area for high-resolution graphics, and is accessible via Applesoft's HGR2 statement.

soft switch: a location in memory that produces some special effect whenever its contents are read or written

To use the different text and graphics areas, you can use Applesoft's built-in text and graphics facilities or you can use PEEK and POKE to manipulate the soft switches that control the display of text and graphics. There are four such soft switches, each consisting of a pair of special locations in the Apple II's memory. Any PEEK or POKE to one of the locations in the pair sets the switch one way; a PEEK or POKE to the other location in the pair sets the switch the other way.

In the following list, the addresses shown in parentheses are those of the special locations that control the various settings of the switches. Each address is given first in hexadecimal (preceded by a dollar sign, $) and then in the equivalent decimal form.

The four soft switches controlling the display choose between

- □ text ($C051, -16303) and graphics ($C050, -16304)
- □ high ($C057, -16297) and low resolution ($C056, -16298)
- □ page 1 ($C054, -16300) and page 2 ($C055, -16299)
- □ full-screen graphics ($C052, -16302) and mixed text and graphics ($C053, -16301)

For Further Information: For further information on these and other soft switches in the Apple II's memory, see your Apple's reference manual.

F.3.1 Switching Graphics Screens

These POKEs let you switch from one text or graphics mode to another.

POKE -16304, 0

Switches the display from full-screen text to graphics without clearing the graphics screen. Depending on the settings of the other soft switches, the resulting display may be high- or low-resolution graphics, taken from page 1 or 2, and full-screen graphics or mixed text and graphics.

Similar Applesoft Statements: The GR statement switches to mixed text and low-resolution graphics from page 1 and clears the graphics screen to black. The HGR statement switches to mixed text and high-resolution graphics from page 1 and clears the graphics screen to black. The HGR2 statement switches to full-screen high-resolution graphics from page 2 and clears the entire screen to black.

POKE -16303, 0

Switches the display from any form of graphics to full-screen text without resetting the text window. Depending on the setting of the applicable soft switch, the text displayed may be taken from low-resolution page 1 or page 2.

The TEXT statement also switches to text display, but in addition selects page 1, resets the text window to the full screen, and positions the cursor in the bottom-left corner of the screen (column 1, row 24).

POKE -16302, 0

Switches the display from mixed text and graphics to full-screen graphics. Depending on the settings of the other soft switches, the resulting display may be either low- or high-resolution graphics and may be taken from either page 1 or page 2. If full-screen text is currently being displayed, there is no visible effect.

POKE -16301, 0

Switches the display from full-screen graphics to mixed text and graphics, with four lines of text at the bottom of the screen. Depending on the settings of the other soft switches, the upper portion of the screen may show low- or high-resolution graphics, taken from either page 1 or page 2. The text displayed in the bottom four lines is taken from the same page number as the graphics in the upper part of the screen. If full-screen text is currently being displayed, there is no visible effect.

POKE -16300, 0

Switches the display from page 2 to page 1, without clearing the screen or moving the cursor. Depending on the settings of the other soft switches, the resulting display may be text or low-resolution graphics taken from low-resolution page 1, or high-resolution graphics taken from high-resolution page 1; if graphics, it may be either full-screen graphics or mixed with four lines of text from low-resolution page 1.

Always execute this POKE statement before switching to Integer BASIC if you've been using page 2 in Applesoft; otherwise you'll be left still looking at text (low-resolution) page 2 while Integer BASIC is writing its screen output to page 1.

POKE -16299, 0

Switches the display from page 1 to page 2, without clearing the screen or moving the cursor. Depending on the settings of the other soft switches, the resulting display may be text or low-resolution graphics taken from low-resolution page 2, or high-resolution graphics taken from high-resolution page 2; if graphics, it may be either full-screen graphics or mixed with four lines of text from low-resolution page 2.

POKE -16298, 0

Switches from high- to low-resolution graphics, without clearing the screen. Depending on the settings of the other soft switches, the resulting display may be taken from low-resolution page 1 or page 2, and may be either full-screen low-resolution graphics or mixed with four lines of text from the same low-resolution page. If full-screen text is currently being displayed, there is no visible effect.

Always execute this POKE statement before switching to Integer BASIC if you've been using high-resolution graphics in Applesoft; otherwise Integer BASIC's GR statement incorrectly displays the high- instead of the low-resolution page.

POKE -16297, 0

Switches from low- to high-resolution graphics, without clearing the screen. Depending on the settings of the other soft switches, the resulting display may be taken from high-resolution page 1 or page 2, and may be either full-screen high-resolution graphics or mixed with four lines of text from the corresponding low-resolution page. If full-screen text is currently being displayed, there is no visible effect.

F.3.2 Clearing Graphics Screens

These CALLs clear graphics pages in various ways.

CALL -1998

Clears low-resolution page 1 to black if displaying low-resolution graphics, or to black-on-white at-signs (@) if displaying text. If displaying high-resolution graphics, or text or low-resolution graphics from page 2, there is no visible effect.

CALL -1994

Clears the upper 40 rows of low-resolution page 1 to black if displaying low-resolution graphics, or the upper 20 lines to black-on-white at-signs (@) if displaying text. If displaying high-resolution graphics, or text or low-resolution graphics from page 2, there is no visible effect.

CALL -3086

Clears the current high-resolution page to black. (Applesoft remembers which page you used last, regardless of the switch settings.)

CALL -3082

Clears the current high-resolution page to the color most recently used in an HPLOT statement. (Applesoft remembers which page you used last, regardless of the switch settings.)

F.4 Miscellaneous Input and Output

This section describes the special locations in the Apple II's memory for controlling a variety of input and output devices:

- reading the buttons on the hand controls
- controlling the annunciator outputs and the utility strobe
- producing sounds through the built-in speaker.

F.4.1 Hand Controls and Strobe

Three PEEKs read the status of the hand control buttons. Another PEEK triggers the utility strobe.

PEEK (-16287)

Reads the button on hand control 0; yields a result > 127 if the button is being pressed, <= 127 if it is not. The [Open Apple] key on the Apple IIe and Apple IIc keyboards is equivalent to this button and can be read in the same way.

PEEK (-16286)

Reads the button on hand control 1; yields a result > 127 if the button is being pressed, <= 127 if it is not. The [Solid Apple] key on the Apple IIe and Apple IIc keyboards is equivalent to this button and can be read in the same way.

PEEK (-16285)

Reads the button on hand control 2; yields a result > 127 if the button is being pressed, <= 127 if it is not.

> *Note:* Although there are provisions for connecting four hand controls (numbered 0 to 3) to the computer, there is no way to read the button on hand control 3.

PEEK (-16320)

Triggers the utility strobe (hand control connector, pin 5). This does not apply to the Apple IIc.

The utility strobe should always be controlled with PEEK, not with POKE. Using POKE triggers the strobe twice instead of once. See your Apple's reference manual for further information.

F.4.2 Annunciators

These eight POKEs control the annunciator output on hand control connectors.

> *Not for IIc Users:* The Apple IIc doesn't have easily-accessible annunciators. Apple IIc users can safely dispense with reading the next eight entries, but note that the locations discussed, POKE locations -16295 through -16290, are used by the system. They are generally not free locations.

> *What's an Annunciator?* The annunciators are four pins of the hand control connector that can each be set to either of two states (on or off) in the Apple II, Apple II Plus, and Apple IIe. The utility strobe is another pin of the connector that is normally at +5 volts but can be triggered to drop to 0 volts for one-half microsecond. These features are typically used to control devices such as lamps and relays connected to the computer through the hand control connector. See your Apple's reference manual for further information.

POKE -16295, 0

Turns on annunciator output 0 (hand control connector, pin 15).

POKE -16296, 0

Turns off annunciator output 0 (hand control connector, pin 15).

POKE -16293, 0

Turns on annunciator output 1 (hand control connector, pin 14).

POKE -16294, 0

Turns off annunciator output 1 (hand control connector, pin 14).

POKE -16291, 0

Turns on annunciator output 2 (hand control connector, pin 13).

POKE -16292, 0

Turns off annunciator output 2 (hand control connector, pin 13).

POKE -16289, 0

Turns on annunciator output 3 (hand control connector, pin 12).

POKE -16290, 0

Turns off annunciator output 3 (hand control connector, pin 12).

F.4.3 Loudspeaker

These PEEKs produce audible clicks.

PEEK (-16336)

Produces a single click from the built-in speaker; can be used in various combinations and frequencies to produce musical tones and other sounds.

The speaker should always be controlled with PEEK, not with POKE. Using POKE produces two clicks instead of one. See your Apple's reference manual for further information.

PEEK (-16352)

Produces a single click on a cassette recording or on an audio amplifier connected to the cassette output jack via the amplifier's auxiliary input jack; can be used in various combinations and frequencies to produce musical tones and other sounds. See Appendix M for further information on using a cassette recorder. (This does not apply to the Apple IIc.)

Cassette output should always be controlled with PEEK, not with POKE. Using POKE produces two clicks instead of one. See your Apple's reference manual for further information.

F.5 Error Handling

This section describes the special locations associated with Applesoft's error-handling mechanism. They can be used by user-supplied error-handling routines established with the ONERR GOTO statement. See Section 3.5 and Appendix E for further information.

PEEK (216)

Yields a result > 127 if an error-handling routine has been established with the ONERR GOTO statement, <= 127 if normal error handling is in effect.

POKE 216 0

Restores Applesoft's normal error-handling mechanism; cancels the effect of a previous ONERR GOTO statement.

PEEK (222)

After an error-handling routine has been called, yields the error code identifying the type of error detected. See Appendix E and Table 3-1 (Section 3.5.1) for further information on error codes.

Errors associated with the disk operating system also register at location 222; see the disk operating system manual for further information.

PEEK (219) * 256 + PEEK (218)

After an error-handling routine has been called, this expression yields the line number of the statement in which the error was detected.

CALL -3288

Clears from Applesoft's internal control stack information placed there when an error-handling routine was called. Should be used before exiting from any error-handling routine with a GOTO instead of a RESUME statement.

CALL 54915

Empties the internal control stack of all control information, without affecting the contents of any variables.

Appendix G

Hints for Program Efficiency

The information in this appendix can help you write programs that run faster or use less memory space.

- Section G.1, "Saving Space," gives tips you can follow if you need to conserve memory space.
- Section G.2, "Saving Time," suggests ways to speed up program execution.

G.1 Saving Space

Serious programmers often keep two versions of their programs: one expanded and heavily documented with REM statements, the other "crunched" to use the minimum memory space. There are a number of utility programs on the market that will make Applesoft programs more compact. They work by automatically removing REM statements, combining several statements onto a single program line, and eliminating optional semicolons in PRINT lists. Here are some tips for programmers who prefer to do the work themselves:

- Use multiple statements per line. There is a small amount of overhead (five bytes) associated with each line in the program. Two of these bytes contain the line number. This means that no matter how many digits you have in your line number (minimum line number is 0, maximum is 63999), it takes the same number of bytes (two). Putting as many statements as possible on each line cuts down on the number of bytes used by your program. (A single line can include up to 239 characters.)

  When combining statements into fewer lines, remember that when the condition in an IF...THEN statement is false, execution continues with the next line and not necessarily with the next statement.

  If you're counting bytes, remember to add in one byte for each colon used to separate statements.

  The Disadvantages: Combining many statements on one line makes editing and other changes much more difficult. It also makes a program more difficult to read and understand, not only for others but also for you yourself when you return to the program later on. Use this technique only in programs with serious space limitations.

Delete all REM statements. Each REM statement uses at least one byte (for the keyword REM itself), plus one byte for each character in the text of the remark. For instance, the statement

```
REM THIS IS A REMARK
```

occupies 18 bytes of memory. In the program line

```
140  X = X + Y : REM UPDATE SUM
```

the REM uses 12 bytes of memory, plus one for the colon separating it from the preceding statement.

Take care not to delete REM lines that are referred to by other lines. For example, if your program includes the lines

```
2[B00  GOTO 300
.
.
.
300  REM THIS IS THE NEXT ROUTINE
```

and you delete line 300, the program halts with an `UNDEF'D STATEMENT` error.

> ***The Disadvantages:*** Like programs with many statements on each line, those without detailed REM statements are difficult to read and understand, not only for others but also for you yourself when you return to the program later on. You should consider eliminating REM statements only when faced with a serious shortage of memory space.

- □ Use integer instead of real arrays wherever possible (see Section H.2).
- □ Use variables instead of constants. Suppose you use the constant 3.14159 ten times in your program. If you insert a statement

  ```
  PI = 3.14159
  ```

  and then use the variable PI instead of the constant 3.14159 each time it is needed, you save 40 bytes. This also results in a speed improvement.
- □ Applesoft programs need not end with an END statement, so you can save a little space by omitting it.
- □ Reuse the same variables. If you use a variable T to hold a temporary result in one part of the program and you need a temporary variable later in your program, use T again. Or if you're accepting a one-character input from the user in two different places in the program, use the same variable both times.

- Use subroutines and functions when the same action must be performed at different places in the program, to avoid having to write the identical code more than once.
- Use the zero elements of arrays—such as A(0) or B(0,X)—since space is allocated for them anyway.
- Semicolons are optional before and after TAB calls; leaving them out saves one byte per occurrence.
- Semicolons between items in a PRINT list are optional as long as the separate items are unambiguous. For instance, in line 50 of the following example all items are displayed separately (although concatenated), since the dollar signs at the ends of the string variable names make it clear they are three separate variables:

```
10  LET A$ = "WELL, "
20  LET B$ = "MARSHA, "
30  LET C$ = "IT LOOKS LIKE "
40  LET C = 10
50  PRINT A$ B$ C$ "FRED IS " C " HOURS
    LATE!"
```

  This program displays

```
WELL, MARSHA, IT LOOKS LIKE FRED IS 10 HOURS LATE!
```

  But in this example several of the variables are run together and interpreted as a single name:

```
10  LET A = 5
20  LET B = 10
30  LET C% = 15
40  LET D = 10
50  PRINT A B C% D
```

  Applesoft interprets line 50 as saying "display the value of integer variable ABC%, followed by the value of real variable D," and displays

```
010
```

  Since variable ABC% hasn't been assigned a value, its value is 0.
- If a quoted string is the last item in the last statement of a line, the closing quotation mark can be omitted, saving one byte:

```
10  PRINT "THIS IS THE WAY THE WORLD
    ENDS,
20  PRINT "NOT WITH A BANG BUT A WHIMPER
```

A Caution: This last technique should be used with caution. Bad things can happen if the omitted quotation mark comes somewhere other than at the end of a line:

```
10  PRINT "THIS WON'T WORK : PRINT "VERY
    WELL
```

This line displays

```
THIS WON'T WORK : PRINT 0
```

The final 0 is the value of the undefined variable VERYWELL.

G.2 Saving Time

Utility programs called *compilers* are now available that convert Applesoft programs to a form in which they run far faster than normally. However, a compiled program can take as much as 50 percent more space than a noncompiled one. The following hints should improve the execution speed of your Applesoft programs. Notice that some of these same hints were given in Section G.1 to save memory space. This means that in many cases you can both shorten and speed up your programs at the same time.

- This hint is probably ten times more important than any other in the list: *use real variables wherever possible instead of integer variables or constants.* It takes more time to convert an integer to its real-number representation than to fetch the value of a real variable. This technique is especially important within subroutines, loops, and other program segments that are executed repeatedly.
- Space for variables is allocated in the variable table in the order in which they are encountered during the execution of the program. A line such as

  ```
  5  A = 0 : B = A : C = B
  ```

  places A first in the variable table, B second, and C third (assuming this line is the first executed in the program). When these variables are referred to later in the program, Applesoft has to search only one entry in the variable table to find A, two entries to find B, and three entries to find C. Try to arrange for those variables that your program refers to most often to be located as early as possible in the variable table.

- □ Omit the index variable in NEXT statements. The statement

```
NEXT
```

is somewhat faster than

```
NEXT I
```

because no check needs to be made to see whether the variable named in the NEXT statement agrees with the index variable named in the corresponding FOR statement.

- □ When Applesoft encounters a backward reference from a later line of the program to an earlier one, such as

```
900  GOTO 100
```

it scans the entire program from the beginning until it finds the desired line number (100, in this example). So you can speed things up by placing frequently-referenced lines as early in the program as possible.

Appendix H

Implementation Details

This appendix contains information on various details of Applesoft's internal operation.

- Section H.1, "Apple II Memory Map," summarizes the use of memory in the Apple II and identifies areas of memory reserved for system use.
- Section H.2, "Applesoft Memory Allocation," describes the way Applesoft allocates memory for program and variable storage.
- Section H.3, "Zero Page Use," details Applesoft's use of special locations in page zero of the Apple II's memory.
- Section H.4, "Keyword Tokens," lists the internal codes Applesoft uses to represent keywords occurring in a program.

H.1 Apple II Memory Map

Table H-1 summarizes memory use in the Apple II. Addresses preceded by a dollar sign ($) are in hexadecimal; they are followed on the next line by their decimal equivalents.

Table H-1. Apple II Memory Use

Memory Range From	To	Used For
$0000 0	$01FF 511	System workspace; not advisable to use
$0200 512	$02FF 767	Keyboard character buffer
$0300 768	$03CF 975	Available for short machine-language programs
$03D0 976	$03FF 1023	Used by DOS and ProDOS
$0400 1024	$07FF 2047	Low-resolution graphics and text display, page 1
$0800 2048	0BFF 3071	Low-resolution graphics and text display, page 2
$0800 2048	$0XXX XXX	Applesoft program and variable space, where XXX is the setting of HIMEM:
$2000 8192	$3FFF 16383	High-resolution graphics display, page 1
$4000 16384	$5FFF 24575	High-resolution graphics display, page 2
$9600 38400	$BFFF 49151	DOS
$C000 49152	$CFFF 53247	Hardware I/O addresses
$D000 53248	$F7FF 63487	Applesoft
$F800 63488	$FFFF 65535	Apple II system Monitor

H.2 Applesoft Memory Allocation

Figure H-1 shows how Applesoft allocates the memory space between the start of program storage (normally $800 hexadecimal, 2048 decimal) and the end of variable storage (determined by the setting of HIMEM:). The boundaries between areas may vary; the left column gives *pointer* addresses at which the current settings of the boundaries can be found.

Figure H-1. Applesoft Memory Map

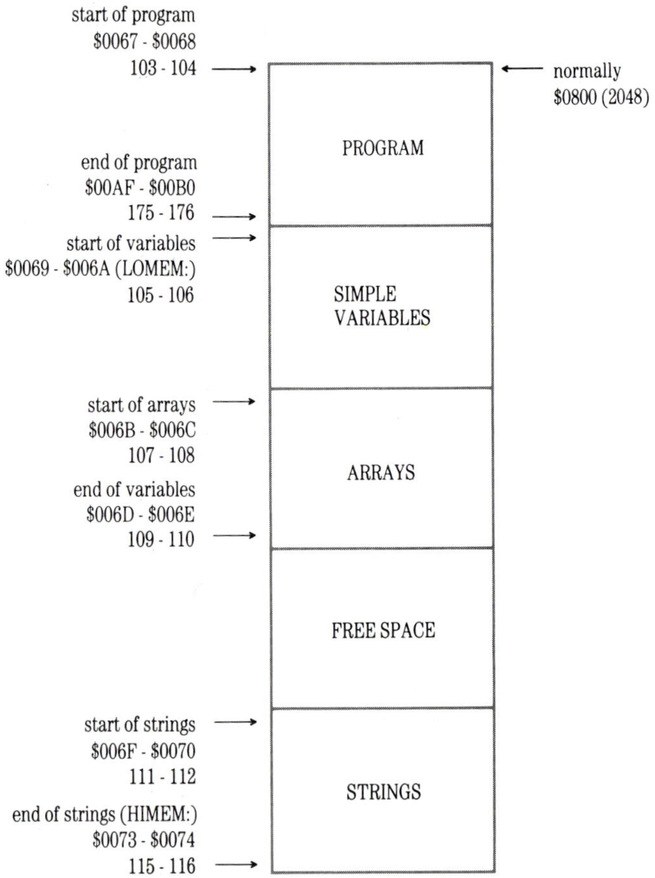

Pointer addresses are given in hexadecimal first, followed by their decimal equivalents. All pointers are stored with the low-order byte first. Thus, for example, the address of the beginning of string space can be calculated with the Applesoft expression

```
PEEK (112) * 256 + PEEK (111)
```

Table H-2 shows how space is allocated for individual variables and arrays. Simple real, integer, or string variables use seven bytes each. Real variables use two bytes for the variable name and five for the value (one exponent, four mantissa, most significant first). Integer variables use two bytes for the variable name, two for the value, and have zeros in the remaining three bytes. String variables use two bytes for the variable name, one for the length of the string, two for a pointer to the contents of the string in memory, and have zeros in the remaining two bytes.

Real arrays use a minimum of twelve bytes: two bytes for the array name, two for the size of the array in bytes, one for the number of dimensions, two for each dimension, and five for each element of the array. Integer array variables use only two bytes for each element. String array variables use three bytes for each element: one for the length of the string and two for a pointer to its contents. Multidimensional arrays are stored with the first subscript varying fastest.

String variables and arrays contain pointers (addresses) to the contents of the strings themselves, which are stored in order of creation from HIMEM: down, using one byte of memory for each character in the string. The pointer stored with the variable gives the address of the first character in the string.

When a new function is defined by a DEF FN statement, six bytes are used to store the pointer to the definition.

Reserved words occurring in a program are converted into one-byte tokens (see Section H.4. All other characters in a program occupy one byte of program storage each.

As a program is executed, space is allocated on the internal control stack as follows:

- Each active FOR/NEXT loop uses 16 bytes.
- Each active subroutine (one that has been called and has not yet returned) uses 6 bytes.
- Each pair of parentheses encountered in an expression uses 4 bytes.
- Each temporary result calculated in an expression uses 12 bytes.

Table H-2. Variable and Array Maps

Simple Variables

Real	Integer	String Pointers
NAME	NAME	NAME
(pos) 1st byte	(neg) 1st byte	(pos) 1st byte
(pos) 2nd byte	(neg) 2nd byte	(neg) 2nd byte
exponent: 1 byte	high byte	length: 1 byte
mantissa: m.s. byte †	low byte	address: low byte
mantissa	0	address: high byte
mantissa	0	0
mantissa: l.s. byte ‡	0	0

Array Variables

Real	Integer	String Pointers
NAME	NAME	NAME
(pos) 1st byte	(neg) 1st byte	(pos) 1st byte
(pos) 2nd byte	(neg) 2nd byte	(neg) 2nd byte
OFFSET pointer to next variable: add to address of this variable name	OFFSET pointer to next variable: add to address of this variable name	OFFSET pointer to next variable: add to address of this variable name
low byte	low byte	low byte
high byte	high byte	high byte
NO. OF DIMENSIONS 1 byte	NO. OF DIMENSIONS 1 byte	NO. OF DIMENSIONS 1 byte
SIZE Nth DIMENSION	SIZE Nth DIMENSION	SIZE Nth DIMENSION
high byte	high byte	high byte
low byte	low byte	low byte
SIZE 1st DIMENSION	SIZE 1st DIMENSION	SIZE 1st DIMENSION
high byte	high byte	high byte
low byte	low byte	low byte
REAL (0,0...0)	INTEGER% (0,0...0)	STRING$ (0,0...0)
exponent: 1 byte	high byte	length: 1 byte
mantissa: m.s.byte	low byte	address: low byte
mantissa		address: high byte
mantissa		
mantissa: l.s.byte		

Table H-2—Continued. Variable and Array Maps

Real	Integer	String Pointers
REAL (N,N...N)	INTEGER% (N,N...N)	STRING$ (N,N...N)
exponent: 1 byte	high byte	length: 1 byte
mantissa: m.s.byte	low byte	address: low byte
mantissa		address: high byte
mantissa		
mantissa: l.s.byte		

† m.s. = most significant

‡ l.s. = least significant

H.3 Zero Page Use

Table H-3 shows the locations that Applesoft uses in page zero of memory (locations $0000 through $00FF hexadecimal). Addresses are given first in hexadecimal, then in decimal. All pointers (memory addresses) are stored in the usual 6502 style, low-order byte first. To find the value of a pointer, use the Applesoft expression

```
PEEK (SECNDADDR) * 256 + PEEK (FIRSTADDR)
```

where FIRSTADDR and SECNDADDR are the addresses of the two bytes of the pointer itself.

Table H-3. Applesoft Zero Page Use

Locations	Used For
$0000 - $0005 0 - 5	Jump instructions to continue in Applesoft
$000A - $000C 10 - 12	Jump instruction for USR function (see Section 7.1.4)
$000D - $0017 13 - 23	General purpose counters/flags for Applesoft
$0020 - $004F 32 - 79	Reserved for system Monitor program
$0050 - $0061 80 - 97	General purpose pointers for Applesoft

Table H-3—Continued. Applesoft Zero Page Use

Locations	Used For
$0062 - $0066 98 - 102	Result of last multiplication or division
$0067 - $0068 103 - 104	Pointer to beginning of program; normally set to $0801
$0069 - $006A 105 - 106	Pointer to start of simple variable space; also points to the end of the program plus 1 or 2, unless changed with the LOMEM: statement
$006B - $006C 107 - 108	Pointer to start of array space
$006D - $006E 109 - 110	Pointer to end of array space
$006F - $0070 111 - 112	Pointer to start of string start; strings are stored from here to value of HIMEM:
$0071 - $0072 113 - 114	General pointer
$0073 - $0074 115 - 116	Highest location in memory available to Applesoft plus 1;on initial entry to Applesoft, set to the highest RAM memory location available
$0075 - $0076 117 - 118	Line number of line currently being executed
$0077 - $0078 119 - 120	"Old line number" at which execution was interrupted by END, STOP, or CONTROL-C
$0079 - $007A 121 - 122	"Old text pointer"; location in memory of statement to be executed next
$007B - $007C 123 - 124	Line number of DATA statement containing next item for READ
$007D - $007E 125 - 126	Absolute memory location of next item for READ
$007F - $0080 127 - 128	Pointer to current source of INPUT; set to $0201 during an INPUT statement; during a READ statement is set to the DATA item being read

Locations	Used For
$0081 - $0082 129 - 130	Name of last-used variable
$0083 - $0084 131 - 132	Pointer to value of last-used variable
$0085 - $009C 133 - 156	General usage
$009D - $00A3 157 - 163	Main floating-point accumulator
$00A4 164	General use in floating-point arithmetic
$00A5 - $00AB 165 - 171	Secondary floating-point accumulator
$00AC - $00AE 172 - 174	General usage flags/pointers
$00AF - $00B0 175 - 176	Pointer to end of program (not changed by LOMEN:)
$00B1 - $00C8 177 - 200	Character input routine; Applesoft calls here every time it wants another character
$00B8 - $00B9 184 - 185	Pointer to last character obtained through character input routine
$00C9 - $00CD 201 - 205	Random number
$00D0 - $00D5 208 - 213	High-resolution graphics scratch pointers
$00D8 - $00DF 216 - 223	ONERR pointers/scratch
$00E0 - $00E2 224 - 226	High-resolution graphics horizontal and vertical coordinates

Table H-3—Continued. Applesoft Zero Page Use

Locations	Used For
\$00E4 228	High-resolution graphics color code
\$00E5 - \$00E7 229 - 231	General use for high-resolution graphics
\$00E6 230	Current high-resolution page being drawn on (decimal 32 if page 1; decimal 64 if page 2)
\$00E8 - \$00E9 232 - 233	Pointer to beginning of shape table
\$00F0 - \$00F3 240 - 243	General-use flags
\$00F4 - \$00F8 244 - 248	ONERR pointers

H.4 Keyword Tokens

Applesoft converts all its keywords to one-byte codes, called *tokens*, to save memory space. Table H-4 is a list of the tokens representing the various keywords.

Table H-4. Applesoft Keyword Tokens

Hex	Dec	Keyword	Hex	Dec	Keyword
\$80	128	END	\$8D	141	PLOT
\$81	129	FOR	\$8E	142	HLIN
\$82	130	NEXT	\$8F	143	VLIN
\$83	131	DATA	\$90	144	HGR2
\$84	132	INPUT	\$91	145	HGR
\$85	133	DEL	\$92	146	HCOLOR=
\$86	134	DIM	\$93	147	HPLOT
\$87	135	READ	\$94	148	DRAW
\$88	136	GR	\$95	149	XDRAW
\$89	137	TEXT	\$96	150	HTAB
\$8A	138	PR#	\$97	151	HOME
\$8B	139	IN#	\$98	152	ROT=
\$8C	140	CALL	\$99	153	SCALE=

Table H-4—Continued. Applesoft Keyword Tokens

Hex	Dec	Keyword
$9A	154	SHLOAD
$9B	155	TRACE
$9C	156	NOTRACE
$9D	157	NORMAL
$9E	158	INVERSE
$9F	159	FLASH
$A0	160	COLOR=
$A1	161	POP
$A2	162	VTAB
$A3	163	HIMEM:
$A4	164	LOMEM:
$A5	165	ONERR
$A6	166	RESUME
$A7	167	RECALL
$A8	168	STORE
$A9	169	SPEED=
$AA	170	LET
$AB	171	GOTO
$AC	172	RUN
$AD	173	IF
$AE	174	RESTORE
$AF	175	&
$B0	176	GOSUB
$B1	177	RETURN
$B2	178	REM
$B3	179	STOP
$B4	180	ON
$B5	181	WAIT
$B6	182	LOAD
$B7	183	SAVE
$B8	184	DEF
$B9	185	POKE
$BA	186	PRINT
$BB	187	CONT
$BC	188	LIST
$BD	189	CLEAR
$BE	190	GET
$BF	191	NEW
$C0	192	TAB
$C1	193	TO
$C2	194	FN
$C3	195	SPC
$C4	196	THEN
$C5	197	AT
$C6	198	NOT
$C7	199	STEP
$C8	200	+
$C9	201	-
$CA	202	*
$CB	203	/
$CC	204	^
$CD	205	AND
$CE	206	OR
$CF	207	>
$D0	208	=
$D1	209	<
$D2	210	SGN
$D3	211	INT
$D4	212	ABS
$D5	213	USR
$D6	214	FRE
$D7	215	SCRN
$D8	216	PDL
$D9	217	POS
$DA	218	SQR
$DB	219	RND
$DC	220	LOG
$DD	221	EXP
$DE	222	COS
$EF	223	SIN
$E0	224	TAN
$E1	225	ATN
$E2	226	PEEK
$E3	227	LEN
$E4	228	STR$
$E5	229	VAL
$E6	230	ASC
$E7	231	CHR$
$E8	232	LEFT$
$E9	233	RIGHT$
$EA	234	MID$

Appendix I

Display Formats for Numbers

This appendix describes the formats in which Applesoft displays or prints numeric values. Numbers may not always be formatted in the way you might expect; this is particularly true for numbers more than nine digits long or for exceptionally small numbers.

Numeric values in Applesoft must be in the range -1*10 ^ 38 to 1*10 ^ 38. Any number whose absolute value is less than approximately 3*10 ^ -39 is converted to 0. True integer values to be assigned to integer variables (such as A%) must be in the range -32767 to +32767.

A number typed from the keyboard or a numeric constant used in an Applesoft program can have as many as 38 digits. However, only 9 digits are significant, and the last digit is rounded off. An Applesoft statement that you type as

```
PRINT 1.23456787654321
```

displays

```
1.23456788
```

on the screen.

Integers are always converted to real form before being used in arithmetic calculations, and the results are converted back to integer form when assigned to an integer variable. Conversion from real to integer form is by truncation to the next lower integer, not by rounding.

Applesoft displays and prints numbers according to the following rules:

- If the number is negative, it is preceded by a minus sign (-); if it is 0 or positive, no sign is used.
- If the number is an integer with an absolute value from 0 to 999 999 999, it is formatted as an integer.
- If the number is not an integer and its absolute value is between .01 and 999 999 999.2, it is formatted with a decimal point in the usual way.
- In all other cases, the number is formatted in scientific notation.

Table I-1 shows examples of the formats used for displaying and printing numbers.

Table I-1. Number Formats

Number	Output Format
+1	1
-1	-1
6523	6523
-23.460	-23.46
45.72 * 10 ^ 5	4572000
1 * 10 ^ 20	1E+20
-12.34567896 * 10 ^ 10	-1.2345679E+11
1000000000	1E+09
999999999	999999999

The format Applesoft uses for scientific notation is shown in Figure I-1.

Figure I-1. Format for Scientific Notation

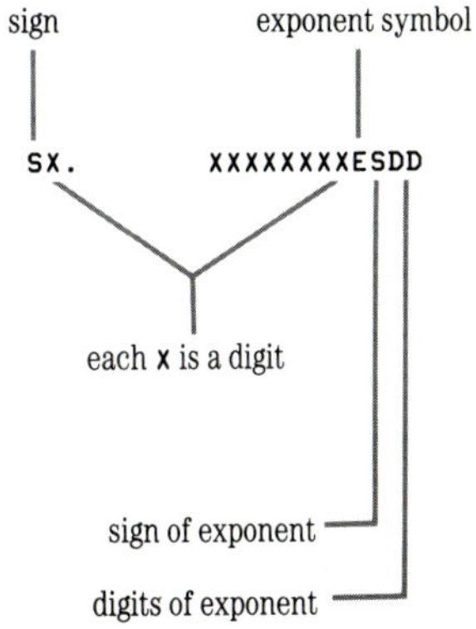

A sign is shown only if the number is negative. There is always exactly one nonzero digit before the decimal point and up to eight digits after it, with trailing zeros suppressed. There are never any leading zeros; the digit before the decimal point is always nonzero. If there is only one digit to print after all trailing zeros are suppressed, no decimal point is shown. The letter *E* (for exponent) is always followed by a sign and a two-digit exponent. The value of a number represented in this form is the number before the E times 10 raised to the power after the E.

For example,

`PRINT 35 * 345 ^ 14`	yields 1.18450085E+37
`PRINT -3.14159 * 567 ^ 5`	yields 1.84104669E+14
`PRINT 1 / 999`	yields 1.001001E-03
`PRINT -3 / 999`	yields -3.003003E-03

Appendix J

On-Screen Editing and Cursor Control

The figures and tables on the following pages summarize Applesoft's facilities for on-screen editing and cursor control. These features are discussed briefly in Section 1.4, "Editing What You Type," and at greater length in your Apple's owner's manual and the *Applesoft Tutorial.*

> ***80-Column Users:*** If your model has 80-column display capabilities, additional escape-mode features are available. If you have an Apple IIe 80-Column Text Card, see the manual that came with it. If you are an Apple IIc owner, you can find the information in your owner's manual.

Figure J-1. Single Cursor Moves

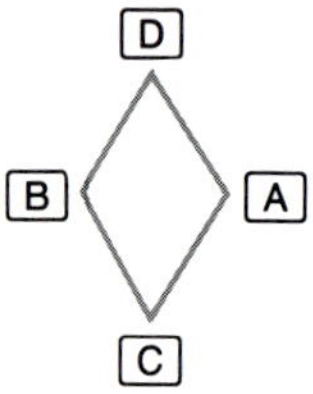

Figure J-2. Long-Range Cursor Moves

Note: Does not apply to original Apple II.

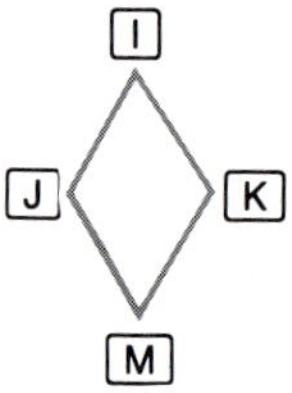

Table J-1. ASCII Equivalents of Arrow Keys

Note: Table applies to Apple IIc and Apple IIe only.

Key	**ASCII Code**	**Keyboard Equivalent**
[←]	8	[CONTROL]-[H]
[→]	21	[CONTROL]-[U]
[↑]	11	[CONTROL]-[K]
[↓]	10	[CONTROL]-[J]

Table J-2. Escape-Mode Functions

Note: Table applies to Apple IIc and Apple IIe only.

Key	**Function**
[A]	Moves cursor right one position; leaves escape mode
[B]	Moves cursor left one position; leaves escape mode
[C]	Moves cursor down one line; leaves escape mode
[D]	Moves cursor up one line; leaves escape mode
[I]	Moves cursor up one line; remains in escape mode
[J]	Moves cursor left one position; remains in escape mode
[K]	Moves cursor right one position; remains in escape mode
[M]	Moves cursor down one line; remains in escape mode
[←]	Moves cursor left one position; remains in escape mode
[→]	Moves cursor right one position; remains in escape mode
[↑]	Moves cursor up one line; remains in escape mode
[↓]	Moves cursor down one line; remains in escape mode
[E]	Clears from cursor to end of line; leaves escape mode
[F]	Clears from cursor to end of screen; leaves escape mode
[@]	Clears entire screen; moves cursor to top-left corner; leaves escape mode
[CONTROL]-[E]	Enables display of control characters
[CONTROL]-[D]	Disables display of control characters

Appendix K

40/80-Column Display Differences

The following table summarizes the differences in the Apple IIe's behavior with and without the Apple IIe 80-Column Text Card installed. Notice that even 40-column display behaves somewhat differently with the 80-Column Text Card installed and active than without it. See the *80-Column Text Card Manual* for further information.

Table K-1. 40/80-Column Display Differences

	Escape Mode	**Inverse**	**Inverse Home**	**Flash**	**Comma Tabbing**	**HTAB**
Card Inactive: 40-Column Display	Checkerboard cursor	Uppercase characters only	Clears text window to black: characters displayed in inverse	Uppercase characters only	Available	Available
Card Active: 40-Column Display	Plus-sign cursor; additional escape-mode features available	Upper- and lowercase	Clears text window to white; characters displayed in black	Not available *** DO NOT USE	Available	Available
Card Active: 80-Column Display	Plus-sign cursor; additional escape-mode features available	Upper- and lowercase	Clears text window to white; characters displayed in black	Not available *** DO NOT USE	Not available for second 40 columns	Not available for second 40 columns; use POKE 36, XX

Appendix L

Comparison With Integer BASIC

This appendix summarizes the differences between Applesoft BASIC and Apple's earlier Integer BASIC language. Section L.3 gives some hints on converting programs written in Integer or other versions of BASIC to Applesoft.

Applesoft BASIC can be used with two Apple disk operating systems: DOS 3.3 and ProDOS. ProDOS does not support Integar BASIC. If you must use Integer BASIC, you must use DOS 3.3. If you're using ProDOS only, you can disregard this appendix.

If Integer BASIC is loaded into your computer's memory, you can switch from Applesoft to Integer BASIC by typing the command

```
INT
```

To switch from Integer BASIC to Applesoft, type

```
FP
```

FP stands for floating-point, the name for the internal format used by languages like Applesoft to represent real numbers.

L.1 Differences Between Features

Table L-1 lists Applesoft statements and functions that are not available in Integer BASIC.

Table L-1. Applesoft Features Not Available in Integer BASIC

ATN	INT	SCALE=
	INVERSE	SHLOAD
CHR$		SIN
COS	LEFT$	SPC
	LOG	SPEED=
DATA	LOMEM:	SQR
DEF FN		STOP
DRAW	MID$	STORE
		STR$
EXP	NORMAL	
		TAN
FLASH	ON...GOSUB	
FN	ON...GOTO	USR
FRE	ONERR GOTO	
		VAL
GET	POS	
		WAIT
HCOLOR=	READ	
HGR	RECALL	XDRAW
HGR2	RESTORE	
HIMEM:	RESUME	
HOME	RIGHT$	
HPLOT	ROT=	

Table L-2 lists Integer BASIC statements and functions that are not available in Applesoft.

Table L-2. Integer BASIC Features Not Available in Applesoft

AUTO
DSP
MAN
MOD

Table L-3 lists Applesoft features that are expressed or accomplished differently in Integer BASIC.

Table L-3. Applesoft Features Expressed Differently in Integer BASIC

Applesoft	**Integer BASIC**
CLEAR	CLR
CONT	CON
HTAB	TAB
ON X GOTO 100, 110, 120	GOTO 100 + 10 * X
ON X GOSUB 1000, 1100, 1200	GOSUB 1000 + 100 * X
HOME	CALL -936
INVERSE	POKE 50, 127
NORMAL	POKE 50, 255
FLASH	POKE 50, 63
X% (integer variable)	X
<> or ><	#

L.2 Other Differences

As the name implies, the only numbers Integer BASIC can deal with are integers (whole numbers). Real variables and constants (numbers with decimal points or exponents) are available in Applesoft but not in Integer BASIC.

In Integer BASIC, the correctness of a statement's syntax is checked when the statement is typed (when you press RETURN). In Applesoft, such checking is not done until the statement is executed.

Integer BASIC permits the line number in a GOTO or GOSUB statement to be specified by an arithmetic variable or expression; in Applesoft they may be specified only by an actual line number. In Applesoft, only the first two characters in a variable name are significant (for example, GOOD and GOUGE are recognized as the same variable). In Integer BASIC, all characters in a variable name are significant.

String operations are differently defined in the two languages. In Integer BASIC, both strings and arrays must be defined in a DIM statement; in Applesoft, only arrays must be so defined.

Applesoft arrays can be multidimensional; Integer BASIC arrays are limited to one dimension. There are no string arrays in Integer BASIC.

Applesoft automatically sets all array elements to 0 or the null string on executing RUN or CLEAR. In Integer BASIC, your program must explicitly set all array elements to their initial values.

In Integer BASIC, if the condition specified in an IF...THEN statement is false, only the THEN portion of that statement is skipped. In Applesoft, all statements following the keyword THEN on the remainder of the same program line are skipped; program execution proceeds with the next numbered line.

In Applesoft, the TRACE statement displays the line number of each individual statement executed; in Integer BASIC, the line number is displayed just once for each program line.

In Applesoft, PEEK, POKE, and CALL can use the true range of memory addresses (0 to 65535). In Integer BASIC, locations with addresses greater than 32767 must be referred to by their corresponding negative values (location 32768 is called -32767-1; 32769 is called -32767; 32770 is called -32766; and so on).

If control reaches the last line of an Integer BASIC program without an END statement having been executed, an error message is displayed; in Applesoft, the END statement at the end of a program is optional.

In Integer BASIC, every NEXT statement must include a variable name; in Applesoft, the variable name is optional.

In the Integer BASIC INPUT statement, the string representing the optional prompting message is followed by a comma, not a semicolon as in Applesoft. If the first variable in the INPUT list is an arithmetic (integer) variable, a question mark (?) is displayed whether the optional prompting string is present or not; if the first variable in the list is a string variable, no question mark is displayed, again whether the prompting string is present or not. In Applesoft, the question mark is displayed only if no prompting string is specified.

L.3 Converting BASIC Programs to Applesoft

Although different versions of BASIC are generally similar, there are some incompatibilities that you should know about if you're planning to convert programs to Applesoft from Integer or other versions of BASIC. Here are some things to watch for:

- Some versions of BASIC use square brackets [ ] to denote array subscripts; Applesoft uses parentheses ( ).
- Many versions of BASIC require that you define the lengths of all strings in DIM statements before you use them. In converting a program to Applesoft, remove all such DIM statements; use DIM only to define arrays. In some of these other versions of BASIC, a statement of the form

  ```
  DIM A$ (I, J)
  ```

  defines a string array of J elements, each of length I. Convert DIM statements of this type to

  ```
  DIM A$(J)
  ```
- Some versions of BASIC use a comma (,) or an ampersand (&) for string concatenation; Applesoft uses a plus sign (+).
- Applesoft uses the string functions LEFT$, MID$, and RIGHT$ to extract substrings. Other versions of BASIC (such as Integer BASIC) use the expression

  ```
  A$ (I)
  ```

  to refer to character number I of string A$, and

  ```
  A$ (I, J)
  ```

  to designate the substring of A$ from character number I to character number J. These expressions occurring on the right side of an assignment statement can be converted to Applesoft as follows:

  Convert `A$(I)`
  to `MID$(A$, I, 1)`

  Convert `A$(I, J)`
  to `MID$(A$, I, J - I + 1)`

  When these expressions occur on the left side of an assignment statement, convert them as follows:

  Convert `A$(I) = X$`
  to `A$ = LEFT$(A$, I - 1) + X$ + MID$(A$, I + 1)`

  Convert `A$ (I, J) = X$`
  to `A$ = LEFT$(A$, I - 1) + X$ + MID$(A$, J + 1)`

Control

GOTO n	Branches to line n
ON *expr* GOTO $n1$, $n2$, $n3$...	Branches to line $n1$, $n2$, $n3$... depending on value of *expr*
IF *cond* THEN $s1$: $s2$: $s3$: ...	Executes statements $s1$, $s2$, $s3$... if condition *cond* is true
FOR $v = x$ TO y STEP z	Begins loop for all values of v from x to y by z; if STEP omitted, 1 is understood
NEXT v	Repeats loop for next value of v
GOSUB n	Branches to subroutine at line n
RETURN	Returns from subroutine to point of call
ON *expr* GOSUB $n1$, $n2$, $n3$...	Branches to subroutine at line $n1$, $n2$, $n3$... depending on value of *expr*
POP	Removes last return address from subroutine stack without branching
ONERR GOTO n	Establishes error-handling routine beginning at line n
RESUME	Reexecutes statement causing error
STOP	Halts execution with message identifying line
END	Halts execution with no message

String Operations

+	Concatenates strings
LEN (s)	Length of string s
LEFT$ (s, x)	Leftmost x characters of string s
MID$ (s, x, y)	y characters beginning at position $x$in string s
RIGHT$ (s, x)	Rightmost x characters of string s
STR$ (x)	String representing numeric value x
VAL (s)	Numeric value of string s
CHR$ (x)	Character with ASCII code x
ASC (s)	ASCII code for first character of string s

Input/Output

IN# n	Accepts input from slot n
IN# 0	Accepts input from keyboard
INPUT s; x, y, z	Prompts with string s, then reads values into variables x, y, z; if s omitted, ? is used
GET c	Reads one character into variable c
READ x, y, z	Reads values from DATA list into variables x, y, z
DATA x, y, z	Adds values x, y, z to DATA list
RESTORE	Restarts DATA list from beginning
RECALL a	Reads array a from tape
PDL (n)	Reads dial of hand control n
PR# n	Sends output to slot n
PR# 0	Sends output to display screen
PRINT x, y, z	Displays or prints values x, y, z
STORE a	Writes array a to tape
TEXT	Displays text
HOME	Clears screen and sends cursor to top
;	Starts next item at cursor position
,	Starts next item at next tab position
SPC (x)	Displays or prints x spaces (PRINT statement only)
TAB (x)	Moves cursor to column x (PRINT statement only)
HTAB x	Moves cursor to column x
VTAB y	Moves cursor to line y
POS (0)	Current horizontal cursor position
INVERSE	Displays text in black-on-white
FLASH	Displays flashing text
NORMAL	Displays text in white-on-black
SPEED= x	Sets text display rate to x (0 minimum, 255 maximum)

Graphics

GR	Displays low-resolution graphics
COLOR= x	Sets low-resolution display color to x
PLOT x, y	Plots single block at column x, row y
HLIN $x1$, $x2$ AT y	Draws horizontal line from column $x1$ to column $x2$ in row y
VLIN $y1$, $y2$ AT x	Draws vertical line from row $y1$ to row $y2$ in column x
SCRN (x, y)	Color on screen at column x, row y

Columns numbered from 0 to 39; rows from 0 to 39 in mixed text and graphics, 0 to 47 in full-screen graphics.

HGR	Displays high-resolution graphics, page 1; mixed text and graphics
HGR2	Displays high-resolution graphics, page 2; full-screen graphics
HCOLOR= x	Sets high-resolution display color to x
HPLOT x, y	Plots single point at column x, row y
HPLOT $x1$, $y1$ TO $x2$, $y2$ TO $x3$, $y3$	Draws high-resolution lines from column $x1$, row $y1$ to column $x2$, row $y2$ to column $x3$, row $y3$
HPLOT TO x, y	Extends previous line to column x, row y

Columns numbered from 0 to 279; rows from 0 to 159 in mixed text and graphics, 0 to 191 in full-screen graphics.

SHLOAD	Loads shape table from tape
DRAW n AT x, y	Draws shape number n at column x, row y
XDRAW n AT x, y	Erases shape number n at column x, row y
SCALE= x	Sets scale factor for drawing shapes to x
ROT= x	Sets rotation for drawing shapes to x

Utility Statements

PEEK (*addr*)	Contents of memory location *addr*
POKE *addr*, x	Stores value x at memory location *addr*
CALL *addr*	Executes machine-language subroutine starting at location *addr*
USR (x)	Executes user-supplied machine-language function routine with argument x
WAIT *addr*, $m1$, $m2$	Suspends execution until bit pattern specified by masks $m1$, $m2$ appears at location *addr*
HIMEM: *addr*	Sets highest memory address available for variable storage to *addr*
LOMEM: *addr*	Sets lowest memory address available for variable storage to *addr*
FRE (0)	Amount of available storage remaining
TRACE	Displays line number of each statement executed
NOTRACE	Stops displaying line number of each statement executed

Applesoft BASIC
Quick Reference Card

Editing and Cursor Control

←	Erases previous character
→	Recopies character under cursor
CONTROL-X	Cancels input line
ESC A	Moves right; leaves escape mode
ESC B	Moves left; leaves escape mode
ESC C	Moves down; leaves escape mode
ESC D	Moves up; leaves escape mode
ESC I	Moves up; remains in escape mode
ESC J	Moves left; remains in escape mode
ESC K	Moves right; remains in escape mode
ESC M	Moves down; remains in escape mode

After ESC, arrow keys are the same as I, J, K, M

ESC E	Clears to end of line
ESC F	Clears to end of screen
ESC @	Clears entire screen; moves cursor to top
DEL *n1*, *n2*	Deletes from line *n1* to line *n2*

Statements and Lines

Lines typed without a line number are executed immediately; those with a line number are saved for later (deferred) execution.

:	Separates multiple statements on same line
REM	Remarks for human reader

Operations on Whole Programs

NEW	Erases current program, resets all variables
CLEAR	Resets all variables
LIST	Displays current program
LIST *n1*-*n2*	Displays from line *n1* to line *n2*
RUN	Executes program from beginning
RUN *n*	Executes program starting at line *n*
RUN *name*	Loads and executes program *name* from disk
LOAD	Loads program from tape
LOAD *name*	Loads program *name* from disk
SAVE	Saves current program on tape
SAVE *name*	Saves current program on disk as *name*

Interrupting and Resuming

CONTROL-S	Suspends output (any key to resume)
CONTROL-C	Interrupts program execution
CONT	Continues execution after CONTROL-C, STOP, or END
CONTROL-RESET	Cancels program execution

Variables

Type	Name	Range
Real	AB	± 9.99999999 E+37
Integer	AB%	± 32767
String	AB$	0 to 255 characters

where A is a letter, B is a letter or digit. Name can be more than two characters, but only first two are significant.

Arrays

Type	Typical Element
Real	AB (x, y, z)
Integer	AB% (x, y, z)
String	AB$ (x, y, z)

where A is a letter, B is a letter or digit. Name can be more than two characters, but only first two are significant. Array size limited only by available memory.

DIM a (x, y, z)	Define array a with maximum subscripts x, y, z

Arithmetic Operators

=	Assigns value to variable (LET optional)
+	Addition
−	Subtraction
*	Multiplication
//	Division
^	Exponentiation

Relational Operators

=	Is equal to
<	Is less than
>	Is greater than
<= =>	Is less than or equal to
>= =>	Is greater than or equal to
<> ><	Is not equal to

Yield value 1 if true, 0 if false. Can also be used to compare strings.

Logical Operators

AND	Both true
OR	Either or both true
NOT	Is false

Interpret 0 as false, nonzero as true. Yield value 0 if false, 1 if true.

Precedence of Operators

( )	Parentheses (innermost first)
+ - NOT	Signed arithmetic, logical NOT
↑	Exponentiation
* //	Multiplication, division
+ −	Addition, subtraction
= < > <= =< >= => <> ><	Relational operators
AND	Logical AND
OR	Logical OR

Arithmetic Functions

ABS (x)	Absolute value of x
SGN (x)	Sign of x
INT (x)	Integer part of x
SQR (x)	Square root of x
SIN (x)	Sine of x radians
COS (x)	Cosine of x radians
TAN (x)	Tangent of x radians
ATN (x)	Arc tangent, in radians, of x
EXP (x)	Exponential of x
LOG (x)	Natural logarithm of x
RND (x)	If $x > 0$, generates random number between 0 and 1 If $x = 0$, repeats previous random number If $x < 0$, begins new repeatable sequence of random numbers
DEF FN (x) = *expr*	Defines function

- Some versions of BASIC allow "multiple assignment" statements of the form

  ```
  LET B = C = 0
  ```

  This statement would set both variables B and C to 0.

  In Applesoft, such a statement has an entirely different effect: all equal signs after the first are interpreted as logical comparison operators. Thus the statement above sets variable B to 1 (meaning true) if C equals 0, to 0 (meaning false) if it doesn't.

  The easiest way to convert such a multiple assignment statement into Applesoft is to rewrite it as

  ```
  C = 0 : B = C
  ```

  or

  ```
  B = 0 : C = 0
  ```

- Some versions of BASIC use a slash (/) instead of a colon (:) to separate multiple statements on the same line. In converting to Applesoft, change each such slash to a colon.
- Programs that use the MAT (matrix arithmetic) functions available in some versions of BASIC must be rewritten using FOR/NEXT loops to perform the corresponding matrix operations.

Appendix M

If You Have a Cassette Recorder

This appendix discusses Applesoft's facilities for storing programs and information on tape cassettes. For any of these features to work, all of the following conditions must be present:

- There must be a cassette tape recorder properly connected to the computer (Apple II, Apple II Plus, or Apple IIe only).
- The tape recorder must be turned on.
- There must be a tape cassette properly mounted in the recorder.
- The recorder must be set to RECORD or PLAY, depending on the statement being executed.

None of the Applesoft tape operations checks for these conditions; if any condition doesn't hold, the system may hang indefinitely. Only CONTROL-RESET can interrupt a tape operation.

Occasionally a tape recorder does not work properly when both input and output cables are plugged in at the same time. This problem originates from a ground loop in the tape recorder itself, which prevents making a good recording. The easiest solution is to unplug the output cable (usually labeled MONITOR on the tape recorder) when recording. Such a ground loop causes no trouble when reading a tape.

M.1 The SAVE Command

```
SAVE
```

The SAVE command writes the Applesoft program currently in memory onto a tape cassette. No prompting message or signal of any kind is given; the tape recorder must already be turned on and set to RECORD at the time the SAVE command is executed. Beeps signal the start and end of the recording. If your system is equipped with a disk drive and you have the disk operating system loaded and running, a SAVE command with a name following the keyword SAVE writes the current program onto a disk under that file name. Refer to Section 1.2.5 and your disk operating system manual for more information.

M.2 The LOAD Command

```
LOAD
```

The LOAD command reads an Applesoft program into memory from a tape cassette. No prompting message or signal of any kind is given; the tape recorder must already be turned on and set to PLAY at the time the LOAD command is executed. A beep signals when the beginning of information is detected on the tape; a second beep is sounded when the program has been successfully loaded.

If your system is equipped with a disk drive and you have the disk operating system loaded and running, a LOAD command with a name following the keyword LOAD reads a program from a disk under that file name. Refer to Section 1.2.6 and your disk operating system manual for more information.

M.3 The STORE Statement

```
STORE MX
```

The STORE statement writes the contents of an integer or real array onto a tape cassette. The name of the array (MX in the example above) follows the keyword STORE, without a subscript. No prompting message or signal of any kind is given; the tape recorder must already be turned on and set to RECORD at the time the STORE statement is executed. Beeps signal the start and end of the recording.

String arrays cannot be written with the STORE statement.

M.4 The RECALL Statement

```
RECALL MX
```

The RECALL statement reads information into an integer or real array from a tape cassette. The name of the array (MX in the example) follows the keyword RECALL, without a subscript. The designated array must have been previously defined in a DIM statement in the program issuing the RECALL.

No prompting message or signal of any kind is given; the tape recorder must already be turned on and set to PLAY at the time the RECALL statement is executed. A beep signals when the beginning of information is detected on the tape; a second beep is sounded when the information has been successfully transferred.

String arrays cannot be read with the RECALL statement.

The name of the array read with RECALL need not be the same name used in the STORE statement that wrote the information onto the tape. However, the dimensions of the array being read should be the same as those of the array originally written. For example, if the tape was written by the statement

```
STORE A
```

where array A had been defined by

```
DIM A (5, 5, 5)
```

it can be read back with the statement

```
RECALL B
```

where array B is defined by

```
DIM B (5, 5, 5)
```

If the dimensions of the two arrays differ, RECALL may scramble the information read into array B, or the program may halt with the message `?OUT OF MEMORY ERROR`.

M.5 The SHLOAD Statement

```
SHLOAD
```

The SHLOAD (for shape load) statement reads a shape table into memory from a tape cassette. The shape table is loaded just below the current setting of HIMEM: (see Section 7.2.1, "The HIMEM: Statement") and HIMEM: is reset to just below the shape table to protect it.

No prompting message or signal of any kind is given; the tape recorder must already be turned on and set to PLAY at the time the SHLOAD command is executed. A beep signals when the beginning of information is detected on the tape; a second beep is sounded when the shape table has been successfully loaded.

Section 6.3 contains extensive information on shape tables.

Appendix N

Complete Listing of the Postage Rates Program

The following is a complete listing of the postage rates program developed in Chapter 8. A copy of this program is included on the *ProDOS BASIC Programming Examples* disk.

`10 REM POSTAGE RATES`	Name of program.
`20 :`	Colon leaves line empty.
`30 REM DETERMINES POSTAGE FEES`	What program does.
`40 REM FOR EXPRESS, 1ST CLASS,`	
`50 REM AND PRIORITY MAIL`	Empty line inserted by embedding CONTROL-J (line feed) at end of REM statement in line 50.
`60 REM V3 10/15/83`	Number and date of this version
`70 REM BY JOHN SCRIBBLEMONGER & SCOT KAMINS`	Programmer's credit line.
`100 REM MENU OF POSTAGE CLASSES`	CONTROL-J here.
`110 HOME`	Begins with a clear screen.
`120 TITLE$ = "POSTAGE RATES"`	
`130 PRINT`	
`140 HTAB 21 - LEN (TITLE$) / 2`	Formula to center title.
`150 PRINT TITLE$`	
`160 VTAB 6`	
`170 PRINT "1. EXPRESS"`	
`180 PRINT "2. FIRST CLASS"`	
`190 PRINT "3. PRIORITY"`	
`200 PRINT`	
`210 PRINT "4. END THE PROGRAM"`	The escape hatch.
`300 REM`	CONTROL-J here,
`GET CLASS OF MAIL`	CONTROL-J here,
`310 VTAB 14`	
`320 PRINT "Press the number of your choice: ";`	Semicolon keeps response on same line,
`330 GET C$`	Only one keypress needed—cuts down on error possibilities; use of string variable to get number avoids type mismatch errors.

`335 REM`	CONTROL-J here.
`CHECKS FOR VALIDITY`	Another CONTROL-J (last time this is noted).
`340 IF C$ = "4" THEN END`	Ends program if user types a 4.
`350 IF VAL (C$) > 0 AND VAL (C$) < 4 THEN 380`	Skips next two lines if valid choice typed.
`360 PRINT CHR$(7); CHR$(7);`	Beeps twice to get attention.
`370 GOTO 330`	Response was invalid; try again.
`380 PRINT C$`	Since choice accepted via GET, it isn't displayed on the screen; displays it back to user.
`390 C = VAL (C$)`	Needs this value later to determine what section of program to branch to for proper processing.
`500 REM`	
`GET WEIGHT OF ITEM`	
`505 VTAB 16`	
`510 PRINT "Please enter the WEIGHT - a number plus an O for(ounces) or a P (for pounds) - and press the RETURN key: ";`	Prompting message to tell user what information to type and how to type it.
`520 CALL -868`	Clears to end of line; useful to erase any errors that might be typed.
`530 INPUT "";W$`	Empty string suppresses question mark.
`540 W1$ = RIGHT$ (W$, 1)`	Rightmost letter should be either O or P; use it later to see if weight is consistent with postal regulations.
`550 W = VAL (W$)`	How many ounces or pounds?
`555 REM`	
`WAS ENTERED WEIGHT VALID?`	
`560 IF W AND (W1$ = "O" OR W1$ = "P") THEN 710`	If a weight was typed, and if last character was either O for ounces or P for pounds, then proceeds.
`570 PRINT CHR$(7); CHR$(7);`	Beeps twice to get attention.
`580 GOTO 500`	Entry was invalid; tries again.

```
700 REM
    CHECK CONSISTENCY
```

```
710 ON C GOSUB 10000, 11000, 12000
```

Branches to appropriate subroutine to see if weight typed is within postal rules or program limitations for mail class chosen.

```
720 IF NOT EFLAG THEN 910
```

If no inconsistency detected in subroutine then proceeds with processing.

```
730 GOSUB 60000 : REM KEYSTALL
```

Waits for user to acknowledge message.

```
740 EFLAG = 0
```

Clears error flag set in subroutine.

```
750 CLEAR
```

Resets all variables, clears arrays, etc.

```
760 GOTO 100
```

Restarts program loop.

```
900 REM
    FIND APPROPRIATE CODE FOR PROCESSING
```

Everything is valid and consistent; now program can solve for the postage rate!

```
910 ON C GOSUB 1000, 2000, 3000
```

Branches to proper calculating routine.

```
920 GOSUB 61000 : REM FORMATTER
```

Formats result for display.

```
930 PRINT
935 REM
    DISPLAY RESULTS
```

```
940 PRINT "POSTAGE NEEDED: $ "; T$
```

Finally, the postage due!

```
950 GOSUB 60000 : REM KEYSTALL
```

Doesn't go on until user is ready.

```
960 CLEAR
```

Prepares for restart...

```
970 GOTO 100
```

...and does it.

```
999 REM
    SUBROUTINES BEGIN HERE
```

```
1000 REM
     EXPRESS MAIL CALCULATION
1010 W = INT (W + .99)           Weight must be increased to
                                 compensate for fractions; postal
                                 rates read "NOT MORE THAN x
                                 POUNDS."
1020 T = R (W)                   Rate array filled in express mail
                                 consistency-checking routine
                                 (line 10000).
1030 RETURN                      Ends routine.
2000 REM
     FIRST CLASS CALCULATION
2010 T = .20 + INT (W + .99 - 1) * .17
                                 First class rate is 20 cents first
                                 ounce plus 17 cents for each addi
                                 tional ounce or portion thereof
                                 (January 1984 rates).
2020 RETURN                      Ends routine.
3000 REM
     PRIORITY MAIL CALCULATION
3010 W = INT (W + .99)           Compensates for partial ounces or
                                 pounds.
3020 IF W > 10 THEN 3160         Goes to line 3160 for weights greater
                                 than 10 pounds (ounce weights
                                 converted to pounds in consistency
                                 subroutine starting at line 12000).
3025 REM
  PRIORITY RATES TO 10 POUNDS
3030 IF W <= 1 THEN T = 2.24
3040 IF W > 1 AND W <= 1.5 THEN T = 2.30
                                 Rates in half-pound increments.
3050 IF W > 1.5 AND W <= 2 THEN T = 2.54
3060 IF W > 2 AND W <= 2.5 THEN T = 2.78
3070 IF W > 2.5 AND W <= 3 THEN T = 3.01
3072 IF W > 3 AND W <= 3.5 THEN T = 3.25
3078 IF W > 3.5 AND W <= 4 THEN T = 3.49
3080 IF W > 4 AND W <= 4.5 THEN T = 3.73
```

```
3090 IF W > 4.5 AND W <= 5 THEN T = 3.97
3100 IF W > 5 AND W <= 6 THEN T = 4.44
```

Rates by the pound now!

```
3110 IF W > 6 AND W <= 7 THEN T = 4.92
3120 IF W > 7 AND W <= 8 THEN T = 5.39
3130 IF W > 8 AND W <= 9 THEN T = 5.87
3140 IF W > 9 THEN T = 6.35
3150 GOTO 3240
```

Branches to RETURN statement.

```
3160 REM
     PRIORITY RATES FOR OVER 10 POUNDS
3170 T1 = INT (W / 5 - 1) * 2.38 + 3.97
```

First 5 pounds cost $3.97; each added 5 pounds cost $2.38.

```
3180 W1 = W - INT (W / 5) * 5
```

How many odd pounds are there (pounds that are not multiples of 5 and must be charged at a special rate)?

```
3190 IF W1 = 1 THEN T2 = .47
3200 IF W1 = 2 THEN T2 = .95
3210 IF W1 = 3 THEN T2 = 1.42
3220 IF W1 = 4 THEN T2 = 1.90
3230 T = T1 + T2
```

Adds the 5-pound-multiples rate to the odd-pounds rate.

```
3240 RETURN
```

Ends routine.

```
10000 REM
      EXPRESS MAIL CONSISTENCY CHECK
10010 DATA 9.35, 9.35, 9.55, 9.90, 10.30, 10.65,
      11.00, 11.40, 11.75, 0
```

Express mail rates; 0 at end is "last item" flag.

```
10020 X = 0
```

Sets up counter to check how many rates are read from DATA list.

```
10030 X = X + 1
```

Increments counter.

```
10040 READ R (X)
```

Puts price into proper array element.

```
10050 IF R (X) = 0 THEN 10070
```

Price of 0 marks end of list.

```
10060 GOTO 10030
```

Gets next price.

```
10070 X = X - 1
```

X includes count of "last item" flag from 10050; subtracts it from count since it's a "dummy" item.

`10080 IF W1$ = "P" THEN 10100`	
	Next line is for ounces only.
`10090 W = W / 16`	Converts ounces to pounds.
`10100 IF W <= X THEN 10140`	If weight in pounds is covered by the rate chart, then goes ahead.
`10110 PRINT`	
`10120 PRINT CHR$ (7); CHR$ (7); "TOO HEAVY FOR MY TABLES - PLEASE CALL THE POST OFFICE"`	
	Sorry; can't help you.
`10130 EFLAG = 1`	Sets flag indicating inconsistent weight/type; will be checked at line 720.
`10140 RETURN`	Ends routine.
`11000 REM FIRST CLASS CONSISTENCY CHECK`	
`11010 IF W1$ = "O" AND W < 12.01 THEN 11060`	
	OK if not more than 12 ounces.
`11020 PRINT`	
`11030 PRINT CHR$ (7); CHR$(7); "TOO HEAVY FOR FIRST CLASS"`	Sorry—inconsistent!
`11040 PRINT "TRY PRIORITY MAIL"`	
	Suggests alternative.
`11050 EFLAG = 1`	Sets flag indicating inconsistent weight/type; will be checked at line 720.
`11060 RETURN`	Ends routine.
`12000 REM PRIORITY MAIL CONSISTENCY CHECK`	
`12010 IF W1$ = "P" THEN 12090`	
	If in pounds, then skips down.
`12020 IF W > 12 THEN 12080`	Skips down if weight is between 12 and 16 ounces.
`12030 PRINT`	
`12040 PRINT CHR$ (7); CHR$ (7); "TOO LIGHT FOR PRIORITY MAIL - "`	Too light!
`12050 PRINT "TRY FIRST CLASS"`	
	Suggests alternative.
`12060 EFLAG = 1`	Sets flag indicating inconsistent weight/type; will be checked at line 720.
`12070 GOTO 12150`	Branches to end of routine.
`12080 W = W / 16`	Converts ounces to pounds.
`12090 IF W <= 70 THEN 12150`	Final check: is item on the charts?

`12100 PRINT`	
`12110 PRINT CHR$ (7); CHR$ (7); "TOO HEAVY FOR PRIORITY MAIL -"`	Off the charts
`12120 PRINT "TRY ONE OF THE AIR EXPRESS COMPANIES"`	Too big for the Post Office!
`12130 EFLAG = 1`	Sets flag indicating inconsistent weight/type; will be checked at line 720.
`12150 RETURN`	Ends routine.
`59999 REM UTILITY ROUTINES`	Routines useful for various tasks but ancillary to rest of program.
`60000 REM KEYSTALL`	Routine to interrupt program until user presses a key.
`60010 VTAB 24`	Moves cursor to screen bottom.
`60020 INVERSE`	Sets text to appear black-on-white.
`60030 PRINT "PRESS ANY KEY TO GO ON...";`	
`60040 GET A$`	Waits for keypress.
`60050 NORMAL`	Restores ordinary white-on-black.
`60060 RETURN`	Ends routine.
`61000 REM MONEY FORMATTER`	Adds zeros after the decimal point where needed.
`61010 T$ = STR$ (T)`	Turns the calculated postage fee into a string.
`61020 IF T = INT (T) THEN T$ = T$ + ".00"`	If charge is in whole dollars, adds a decimal point and two zeros.
`61030 IF ASC (RIGHT$ (T$,2)) = 46 THEN T$ = T$ + "0"`	If second character from the right is a decimal point (ASCII code 46) then number has only one digit to right of decimal—so add a "0" to the string.
`61040 RETURN`	Ends the routine.

Appendix O

BASIC and the Mouse

It's not hard to write programs that use the mouse pointing device. This appendix is an introduction to what the mouse does and how to control it from BASIC programs. There are two sample programs at the end of this appendix.

▲Warning This appendix and the sample programs it contains assume you have a mouse attached to your computer either through the special mouse port (Apple IIc) or through port 4 (Apple II, Apple II Plus, Apple IIe). If you are using a computer with expansion slots and the mouse card is plugged into some port other than 4, adjust the port designation accordingly.

Also note that the sample code listed throughout this appendix sends information to the video screen using the command

```
PR#0
```

Some Apple II models capable of displaying 80 columns need a different command instead, in the form

```
PR#3
```

in order to keep the 80-column settings intact and to prevent meaningless garbage from being strewn randomly across the video screen. Check the appropriate manual, just to be sure.

Like the keyboard, the mouse is an input device for your computer. Programs you write and software you buy need special code to enable you to use the mouse, once it's plugged in. Typically with software written for the mouse, rolling the mouse along a flat surface moves a pointer or cursor on the video screen; pressing the button on top of the mouse sends a signal to the computer, usually (but not necessarily) meaning that the pointer is in the location you want.

O.1 Using the Mouse in BASIC

This section explains how to turn the mouse on and off so that you can use it in BASIC. You needn't try the commands out as you read; things will be clearer if you first read through this entire section to get a feel for what's going on. MOUSE.MOVE, the program that puts all these commands together for you, is listed at the end of this section.

Here's a list of all the commands you'll need in order to use the mouse from BASIC:

PR#4	directs the computer to send information to the mouse (if you are using an Apple with slots and your mouse card is in a port other than 4, the number after PR# should designate that port)
PR#0	directs the computer to send information to the video screen (but note the warning about 80-column displays)
IN#4	directs the computer to accept information from the mouse (if you are using an Apple with slots and your mouse card is in a port other than 4, the number after IN# should designate that port)
IN#0	directs the computer to accept information from the keyboard
CHR$ (1)	turns the mouse's firmware on and initializes coordinates to 0,0
CHR$ (0)	turns off the mouse's firmware, making it invisible to Applesoft

In Applesoft BASIC you use the CHR$ function to execute a DOS or ProDOS command within a program, specifically CHR$(4). The CHR$ function converts any valid code number to its corresponsing ASCII character; CHR$(4) returns the ASCII character code CONTROL-D. You use CONTROL-D to tell the computer that the next command should be interpreted as a DOS or ProDOS command.

All DOS and ProDOS commands work only if they are issued immediately following a CHR$(13)—that is, if they are not preceded by a semicolon or a response to a GET statement. One way to insure that this happens is to precede all disk operating system commands with a blank PRINT statement. For example:

```
40 PRINT : PRINT CHR$ (4);"PR#4"
```

See your DOS or ProDOS manual for more details.

O.1.1 Turning the Mouse On

The order of the following five steps is significant. Follow these steps whenever you're turning the mouse on in a BASIC program:

1. First, use the PR# command to tell the computer that you want to communicate with the mouse. Since PR# is an operating system command, it must be treated as an embedded disk operating system command:

```
PRINT CHR$ (4);"PR#4"
```

2. When you are hooked up to the mouse, turn it on:

```
PRINT CHR$ (1)
```

3. Then use PR# to tell the computer to send information to the screen instead of somewhere else. Note that you treat PR# like a DOS or ProDOS command:

```
PRINT CHR$ (4);"PR#0"
```

4. Next, direct the computer to accept input from the mouse with IN#, remembering again to treat it as a disk operating system command:

```
PRINT CHR$ (4);"IN#4"
```

5. Finally, use an INPUT statement to define variable names for mouse information. The statement should be in the form

```
INPUT X,Y,S
```

   where X is the horizontal location of the mouse, Y is the vertical position of the mouse, and S is the status of the mouse button. The possible values of these three variables are as follows:

   X = a number in the range 0 to +1023
   Y = a number in the range 0 to +1023
   S = a number in the range +1 to +4 or -1 to -4

   If S = ± 1 then the mouse button is still being pressed.
   If S = ± 2 then the mouse button has just been pressed.
   If S = ± 3 then the mouse button has just been released.
   If S = ± 4 then the mouse button has not been pressed.
   If S < 0 then a key on the keyboard has been pressed.

O.1.2 Turning the Mouse Off

The steps you use to turn the mouse off are similar to those you use to turn the mouse on.

1. `PRINT CHR$ (4);"IN#0"` directs the computer to accept information from the keyboard.
2. `PRINT CHR$ (4);"PR#4"` directs the computer to send information to the mouse (rather than the video screen).
3. `PRINT CHR$ (0)` turns the mouse firmware off.
4. `PRINT CHR$ (4);"PR#0"` directs the computer to resume sending information to the video screen.

The two BASIC programs that follow show you how to turn the mouse on and off, and how to use input from the mouse. Study these programs, play with them, and modify them to suit your own needs.

O.2 MOUSE.MOVE

The program named MOUSE.MOVE demonstrates the positions of the mouse. This program reads and displays the current location of the mouse and the status of the mouse button (whether it was just pressed, is currently being pressed, and so on). Type in and run the program, then move the mouse over your desk top and watch the coordinates change. Press the mouse button and see the status change. Press any key to stop the program.

O.2.1 MOUSE.MOVE Program Listing

```
10  HOME
20  PRINT "This is a demonstration of the
      Mouse"
30  PRINT  CHR$ (4);"PR#4": PRINT  CHR$ (1)
40  PRINT  CHR$ (4);"PR#0"
50  PRINT  CHR$ (4);"IN#4"
60  INPUT "";X,Y,S
70  VTAB 10: PRINT X;"   ",Y"   ",S"   "
80  IF S > 0 THEN GOTO 60
```

```
90  PRINT  CHR$ (4);"IN#0"
100  PRINT  CHR$ (4)"PR#4": PRINT CHR$ (0)
110  PRINT  CHR$ (4);"PR#0"
120  POKE -16368,0: REM Clears keyboard
      strobe
130  END
```

O.2.2 How MOUSE.MOVE Works

1. Line 10 clears the screen to black.
2. Line 20 prints a message.
3. Line 30 turns on the mouse.
4. Line 40 redirects the computer to send information to the video screen.
5. Line 50 tells the computer to accept input from the mouse.
6. Line 60 uses an empty string as a prompt to suppress the question mark, then reads the mouse position and status of the mouse button.
7. Line 70 prints the mouse position and status of the mouse button.
8. Line 80 goes to line 60 if no key has been pressed.
9. Line 90 tells the computer to accept input from the keyboard.
10. Lines 100 and 110 turn off the mouse.
11. Line 120 resets the keyboard strobe so that the next time a key is pressed BASIC can check for it (see Appendix F, Section F.2 for details).
12. Line 130 ends the program.

O.3 MOUSE.DRAW

This program is an expanded version of MOUSE.MOVE. With this program, you can cause the mouse to draw pictures on the low-resolution graphics screen. Pressing the mouse button clears the screen and lets you produce a new picture.

O.3.1 MOUSE.DRAW Program Listing

```
10  REM  Uses mouse to draw low-resolution
     graphics
100  GOSUB 1000:  REM  Turn on the mouse
110  PRINT  CHR$ (4);"IN#4"
120  INPUT "";X,Y,S: REM  Read mouse
     position
130  IF S = 1 THEN 100: REM  Clear the
     screen
140  IF S < 0 THEN 300:  REM Time to quit?
150  REM  Scale the position
160  X =  INT (X / 25.575)
170  Y =  INT (Y / 25.575)
180  PLOT X,Y
190  GOTO 120

300  REM  Check if time to quit
310  POKE -16368,0: REM Clear keyboard
     stobe
320  PRINT  CHR$ (4);"IN#0"
330  VTAB 22: PRINT "Press RETURN to cont
     or ESC to quit"
340  VTAB 22: HTAB 39: GET A$: PRINT
350  IF A$ =  CHR$(13) THEN HOME : GOTO 110
360  IF A$ < >  CHR$ (27) THEN 340
370  REM  Clear screen and turn off mouse
380  TEXT : HOME
390  PRINT  CHR$ (4);"PR#4": PRINT  CHR$ (0)
400  PRINT  CHR$ (4);"PR#0"
410  END

1000  REM Clear screen and initalize mouse
1010  HOME : GR
1020  COLOR= 15
1030  PRINT  CHR$ (4);"PR#4": PRINT  CHR$ (1)
1040  PRINT  CHR$ (4);"PR#0"
1050  RETURN
```

O.3.2 How MOUSE.DRAW Works

1. Line 10 reminds you what the program does.
2. Line 100 goes to the subroutine at line 1000 to turn on the mouse and the low-resolution graphics page.
3. Line 110 tells the computer to accept input from the mouse.
4. Line 120 uses an empty string to suppress the question mark, then reads the mouse position and status of the mouse button.
5. If the mouse button is pressed, line 130 sends program to line 100 to begin again.
6. If a key is pressed, line 140 sends program to line 300 to check for an end.
7. Line 150 reminds you what the next two lines do.
8. Lines 160 and 170 convert the mouse position to low-resolution graphics coordinates.
9. Line 180 plots a point on the low-resolution screen.
10. Line 190 goes back to line 120 and does it all again.
11. Line 300 reminds you what the next group of statements does.
12. Line 310 resets the keyboard strobe so that the next time a key is pressed BASIC can check for it (see Appendix F, Section F.2 for details).
13. Line 320 tells the computer to accept input from the keyboard.
14. Line 330 prints a line of instructions on the screen.
15. Line 340 gets a character from the keyboard.
16. If you press [RETURN], line 350 returns to the main program for more graphics; otherwise program goes to the next line.
17. If you didn't press [ESC], line 360 sends the program back to line 340 to get another character.
18. Line 370 reminds you of what happens next.
19. Line 380 sets the screen to text and clears it.
20. Lines 390 and 400 turn off the mouse.
21. Line 410 ends the program.
22. Line 1000 reminds you what this subroutine does.
23. Line 1010 clears the screen and turns on the low-resolution graphics screen.
24. Line 1020 sets the graphics color to white.
25. Lines 1030 and 1040 turn on the mouse.
26. Line 1050 returns to the main program.

An Idea: You might write a program that uses the mouse to move a pointer on the screen. Then, when the pointer reaches a certain area on the screen and the user presses the mouse's button, the program could open up a new text window that displays a menu or other information. Refer to Appendix F for details on windows.

Glossary

acronym: A word formed from the initial letters of a name or phrase, such as laser, from *l*ight *a*mplification by *s*timulated *e*mission of *r*adiation.

address: A number used to identify something, such as a location in the computer's memory.

algorithm: A step-by-step procedure for solving a problem or accomplishing a task.

AND: A logical operator that produces a true result if both of its operands are true, a false result if either or both of its operands are false; compare **OR**, **NOT**.

Apple II: A personal computer in the Apple II family, manufactured and sold by Apple Computer; generic name for all computers in the series.

Applesoft: An extended version of the BASIC programming language used with the Apple II family of computers and capable of processing numbers in floating-point form. An interpreter for creating and executing programs in Applesoft is built into the Apple II system in firmware. Compare **Integer BASIC**.

application program: A program that puts the resources and capabilities of the computer to use for some specific purpose or task, such as word processing, data-base management, graphics, or telecommunications. Compare **system program**.

application software: The component of a computer system consisting of application programs.

argument: The value on which a function operates.

arithmetic operator: An operator, such as +, that combines numeric values to produce a numeric result; compare **relational operator**, **logical operator**.

array: A collection of variables referred to by the same name and distinguished by means of numerical subscripts.

ASCII: American Standard Code for Information Interchange; a code in which the numbers from 0 to 127 stand for text characters, used for representing text inside a computer and for transmitting text between computers or between a computer and a peripheral device.

assembler: A language translator that converts a program written in assembly language into an equivalent program in machine language.

assembly language: A low-level programming language in which individual machine-language instructions are written in a symbolic form more easily understood by a human programmer than is machine language itself.

BASIC: Beginner's All-purpose Symbolic Instruction Code; a high-level programming language designed to be easy to learn and use. Two versions of BASIC are available from Apple Computer for use with the Apple II: Applesoft (built into the Apple II in firmware) and Integer BASIC (provided on the DOS 3.3 SYSTEM MASTER disk).

binary: The representation of numbers in terms of powers of 2, using the two digits 0 and 1. Commonly used in computers, since the values 0 and 1 can easily be represented in physical form in a variety of ways, such as the presence or absence of current, positive or negative voltage, or a white or black dot on the display screen.

binary file: A file containing "raw" information not expressed in text form; compare **text file**.

binary operator: An operator that combines two operands to produce a result; for example, + is a binary arithmetic operator, < is a binary relational operator, and OR is a binary logical operator. Compare **unary operator**.

bit: A binary digit (0 or 1); the smallest possible unit of information, consisting of a simple two-way choice, such as yes or no, on or off, positive or negative, something or nothing.

bit bucket: The final resting place of all information; see **write-only memory**.

body: The statements or instructions making up some construct in a program, such as a loop or a subroutine.

boot: To start up a computer by loading a program into memory from an external storage medium such as a disk. Often accomplished by first loading a small program whose purpose is to read the larger program into memory. The program is said to "pull itself in by its own bootstraps"; hence the term bootstrapping or booting.

boot disk: See **startup disk**.

bootstrap: See **boot**.

branch: To send program execution to a line or statement other than the next in sequence.

buffer: An area of the computer's memory reserved for a specific purpose, such as to hold graphical information to be displayed on the screen or text characters being read from some peripheral device. Often used as an intermediary "holding area" for transferring information between devices operating at different speeds, such as the computer's processor and a printer or disk drive. Information can be stored in the buffer by one device and then read out by the other at a different speed.

bug: An error in a program that causes it not to work as intended.

byte: A unit of information consisting of a fixed number of bits; on the Apple II, one byte consists of eight bits and can hold any value from 0 to 255.

call: To request the execution of a subroutine or function.

card: See **peripheral card**.

catalog: A list of all files stored on a disk; sometimes called a directory.

cathode-ray tube: An electronic device, such as a television picture tube, that produces images on a screen coated with phosphors that emit light when struck by a focused beam of electrons.

central processing unit: See **processor**.

character: A letter, digit, punctuation mark, or other written symbol used in printing or displaying information in a form readable by humans.

character code: A number used to represent a text character for processing by a computer system.

code: (1) A number or symbol used to represent some piece of information in a compact or easily processed form. (2) The statements or instructions making up a program.

command: A communication from the user to a computer system (usually typed from the keyboard) directing it to perform some immediate action.

compiler: A language translator that converts a program written in a high-level programming language into an equivalent program in some lower-level language (such as machine language) for later execution. Compare **interpreter**.

component: A part; in particular, a part of a computer system.

computer: An electronic device for performing predefined (programmed) computations at high speed and with great accuracy.

computer system: A computer and its associated hardware, firmware, and software.

concatenate: Literally, "to chain together"; to combine two or more strings into a single, longer string containing all the characters in the original strings.

conditional branch: A branch that depends on the truth of a condition or the value of an expression; compare **unconditional branch**.

constant: A symbol in a program representing a fixed, unchanging value; compare **variable**.

control: The order in which the statements of a program are executed.

control character: A character that controls or modifies the way information is printed or displayed. Control characters have ASCII codes between 0 and 31 and are typed from the Apple II keyboard by holding down the [CONTROL] key while typing some other character. For example, the character [CONTROL]-[M] (ASCII code 13) means "return to the beginning of the line" and is equivalent to the [RETURN] key.

controller card: A peripheral card that connects a device such as a printer or disk drive to the Apple II, and controls the operation of the device.

control variable: See **index variable**.

CPU: Central processing unit; see **processor**.

crash: To cease operating unexpectedly, possibly damaging or destroying information in the process.

CRT: See **cathode-ray tube**.

current input device: The source, such as the keyboard or a modem, from which an Applesoft program is currently receiving its input.

current output device: The destination, such as the display screen or a printer, to which an Applesoft program is currently sending its output.

cursor: A marker or symbol displayed on the screen that marks where the user's next action will take effect or where the next character typed from the keyboard will appear.

data: Information; especially information used or operated on by a program.

debug: To locate and correct an error or the cause of a problem or malfunction in a computer system. Typically used to refer to software-related problems; compare **troubleshoot**.

decimal: The common form of number representation used in everyday life, in which numbers are expressed in terms of powers of 10, using the ten digits 0 to 9.

default: A value, action, or setting that is automatically used by a computer system when no other explicit information has been given. For example, if a command to run a program from a disk does not identify which disk drive to use, the disk operating system automatically uses the same drive that was used in the last operation.

deferred execution: The saving of an Applesoft program line for execution at a later time as part of a complete program; occurs when the line is typed with a line number. Compare **immediate execution**.

delimiter: A character that is used for punctuation to mark the beginning or end of a sequence of characters, and that therefore is not considered part of the sequence itself. For example, Applesoft uses the double quotation mark (") as a delimiter for string constants: the string "DOG" consists of the three characters D, O, and G, and does not include the quotation marks. In written English, the space character is used as a delimiter between words.

device: (1) A physical apparatus for performing a particular task or achieving a particular purpose. (2) In particular, a hardware component of a computer system.

digit: (1) One of the characters 0 to 9, used to express numbers in decimal form. (2) One of the characters used to express numbers in some other form, such as 0 and 1 in binary or 0 to 9 and A to F in hexadecimal.

dimension: The maximum size of one of the subscripts of an array.

directory: A list of all files stored on a disk; sometimes called a catalog.

disk: An information storage medium consisting of a flat, circular magnetic surface on which information can be recorded in the form of small magnetized spots, similarly to the way sounds are recorded on tape.

disk drive: A peripheral device that writes and reads information on the surface of a magnetic disk.

Disk II drive: A model of disk drive made and sold by Apple Computer for use with the Apple II family of computers; uses 5-1/4-inch flexible ("floppy") disks.

disk operating system: A software system for the Apple II that enables the computer to control and communicate with one or more Disk II drives.

disk-resident: Stored or held permanently on a disk.

display: (1) Information exhibited visually, especially on the screen of a display device. (2) To exhibit information visually. (3) A display device.

display color: The color currently being used to draw high- or low-resolution graphics on the display screen.

display device: A device that exhibits information visually, such as a television receiver or video monitor.

display screen: The glass or plastic panel on the front of a display device, on which images are displayed.

edit: To change or modify; for example, to insert, remove, replace, or move text in a document.

element: A member of a set or collection; specifically, one of the individual variables making up an array.

embedded: Contained within. For example, the string "HUMPTY DUMPTY" is said to contain an embedded space.

ending value: The value against which the index variable is tested after each pass through a loop, to determine when to stop repeating the loop.

error code: A number or other symbol representing a type of error.

error message: A message displayed or printed to notify the user of an error or problem in the execution of a program.

escape mode: A state of the Apple II family of computers, entered by pressing the ESC key, in which certain keys on the keyboard take on special meanings for positioning the cursor and controlling the display of text on the screen.

escape sequence: A sequence of keystrokes beginning with the ESC key, used for positioning the cursor and controlling the display of text on the screen.

execute: To perform or carry out a specified action or sequence of actions, such as those described by a program.

expansion slot: A connector inside the Apple II, II Plus, and IIe computers in which a peripheral card can be installed; sometimes called peripheral slot or port.

expression: A formula in a program describing a calculation to be performed.

FIFO: First in, first out.

file: A collection of information stored as a named unit on a peripheral storage medium such as a disk.

file name: The name under which a file is stored on a disk.

firmware: Those components of a computer system consisting of programs stored permanently in read-only memory. Such programs (for example, the Applesoft interpreter and the Apple II Monitor program) are built into the computer at the factory; they can be executed at any time but cannot be modified or erased from main memory. Compare **hardware**, **software**.

fixed-point: A method of representing numbers inside the computer in which the decimal point (more correctly, the binary point) is considered to occur at a fixed position within the number. Typically, the point is considered to lie at the right end of the number, so that the number is interpreted as an integer. Fixed-point numbers of a given length cover a narrower range than floating-point numbers of the same length, but with greater precision. Compare **floating-point**.

flag: A variable whose contents (usually 1 or 0, standing for true or false) indicate whether some condition holds or whether some event has occurred, used to control the program's actions at some later time.

floating-point: A method of representing numbers inside the computer in which the decimal point (more correctly, the binary point) is permitted to "float" to different positions within the number. Some of the bits within the number itself are used to keep track of the point's position. Floating-point numbers of a given length cover a wider range than fixed-point numbers of the same length, but with less precision. Compare **fixed-point**.

format: (1) The form in which information is organized or presented. (2) To specify or control the format of information. (3) To prepare a blank disk to receive information by dividing its surface into tracks and sectors; also **initialize**.

function: A preprogrammed calculation that can be carried out on request from any point in a program.

GAME I/O connector: A special 16-pin connector inside the Apple II, II Plus, and IIe computers, originally designed for connecting hand controls to the computer, but also used for connecting some other peripheral devices. Compare **hand control connector**.

graphics: (1) Information presented in the form of pictures or images. (2) The display of pictures or images on a computer's display screen. Compare **text**.

hand control: An optional peripheral device that can be connected to the Apple II's hand control connector and has a rotating dial and a pushbutton; typically used to control game-playing programs, but can be used in more serious applications as well.

hand control connector: A 9-pin connector on the Apple II's back panel, used for connecting hand controls to the computer. Compare **GAME I/O connector**.

hang: For a program or system to "spin its wheels" indefinitely, performing no useful work.

hardcopy: Information printed on paper for human use.

hardware: Those components of a computer system consisting of physical (electronic or mechanical) devices. Compare **software**, **firmware**.

hertz: The unit of frequency of vibration or oscillation, also called cycles per second; named for the physicist Heinrich Hertz and abbreviated Hz. The current provided by a standard power outlet alternates at a rate of 60 hertz; that is, it changes polarity 60 times each second. The Apple II's 6502 microprocessor, for example, operates at a clock frequency of 1 million hertz, or 1 megahertz (MHz).

hexadecimal: The representation of numbers in terms of powers of 16, using the sixteen digits 0 to 9 and A to F. Hexadecimal numbers are easier for humans to read and understand than binary numbers, but can be converted easily and directly to binary form: each hexadecimal digit corresponds to a sequence of four binary digits, or bits.

high-level language: A programming language that is relatively easy for humans to understand. A single statement in a high-level language typically corresponds to several instructions of machine language.

high-order byte: The more significant half of a memory address or other two-byte quantity. In the Apple II's 6502 microprocessor, the low-order byte of an address is usually stored first and the high-order byte second.

high-resolution graphics: The display of graphics on the Apple II's display screen as a six-color array of points, 280 columns wide and 192 rows high.

Hz: See **hertz**.

immediate execution: The execution of an Applesoft program line as soon as it is typed; occurs when the line is typed without a line number. Compare **deferred execution**.

implement: To realize or bring about; for example, a language translator implements a particular language.

index: (1) A number used to identify a member of a list or table by its sequential position. (2) A list or table whose entries are identified by sequential position.

index variable: A variable whose value changes on each pass through a loop; often called control variable or loop variable.

infinite loop: A section of a program that repeats the same sequence of actions indefinitely.

information: Facts, concepts, or instructions represented in an organized form.

initialize: (1) To set to an initial state or value in preparation for some computation. (2) To prepare a blank disk to receive information by dividing its surface into tracks and sectors; also **format**.

input: (1) Information transferred into a computer from some external source, such as the keyboard, a disk drive, or a modem. (2) The act or process of transferring such information.

instruction: A unit of a machine-language or assembly-language program corresponding to a single action for the computer's processor to perform.

integer: A whole number, with no fractional part; represented inside the computer in fixed-point form. Compare **real number**.

Integer BASIC: A version of the BASIC programming language used with the Apple II family of computers; older than Applesoft and capable of processing numbers in integer (fixed-point) form only. An interpreter for creating and executing programs in Integer BASIC is included on the DOS 3.3 SYSTEM MASTER disk, and is automatically loaded into the computer's memory when the computer is started up with that disk. Compare **Applesoft**.

interactive: Operating by means of a dialog between the computer system and a human user.

interface: The devices, rules, or conventions by which one component of a system communicates with another.

interpreter: A language translator that reads a program written in a particular programming language and immediately carries out the actions that the program describes. Compare **compiler**.

inverse video: The display of text on the computer's display screen in the form of black dots on a white (or other single phosphor color) background, instead of the usual white dots on a black background.

I/O: Input/output; the transfer of information into and out of a computer. See **input**, **output**.

I/O device: Input/output device; a device that transfers information into or out of a computer. See **input**, **output**, **peripheral device**.

K: Two to the tenth power, or 1024 (from the Greek root *kilo*, meaning one thousand); for example, 64K equals 64 times 1024, or 65,536.

keyboard: The set of keys built into the Apple II computer, similar to a typewriter keyboard, for typing information to the computer.

keystroke: The act of pressing a single key or a combination of keys (such as CONTROL-C) on the Apple II keyboard.

keyword: A special word or sequence of characters that identifies a particular type of statement or command, such as RUN or PRINT.

kilobyte: A unit of information consisting of 1K (1024) bytes, or 8K (8192) bits; see **K**.

language: See **programming language**.

language translator: A system program that reads a program written in a particular programming language and either executes it directly or converts it into some other language (such as machine language) for later execution. See **interpreter**, **compiler**, **assembler**.

LIFO: Last in, first out.

line: See **program line**.

line number: A number identifying a program line in an Applesoft program.

load: To transfer information from a peripheral storage medium (such as a disk) into main memory for use; for example, to transfer a program into memory for execution.

location: See **memory location**.

logical operator: An operator, such as AND, that combines logical values to produce a logical result; compare **arithmetic operator**, **relational operator**.

loop: A section of a program that is executed repeatedly until some condition is met, such as an index variable reaching a specified ending value.

loop variable: See **index variable**.

low-level language: A programming language that is relatively close to the form that the computer's processor can execute directly. Low-level languages available for the Apple II include 6502 machine language and 6502 assembly language.

low-order byte: The less significant half of a memory address or other two-byte quantity. In the Apple II's 6502 microprocessor, the low-order byte of an address is usually stored first and the high-order byte second.

low-resolution graphics: The display of graphics on the Apple II's display screen as a sixteen-color array of blocks, 40 columns wide and 48 rows high.

machine language: The form in which instructions to a computer are stored in memory for direct execution by the computer's processor. Each model of computer processor (such as the 6502 microprocessor used in the Apple II) has its own form of machine language.

main memory: The memory component of a computer system that is built into the computer itself and whose contents are directly accessible to the processor.

mask: A pattern of bits for use in bit-level logical operations.

memory: A hardware component of a computer system that can store information for later retrieval; see **main memory**, **random-access memory**, **read-only memory**, **read-write memory**, **write-only memory**.

memory location: A unit of main memory that is identified by an address and can hold a single item of information of a fixed size; in the Apple II, a memory location holds one byte, or eight bits, of information.

memory-resident: (1) Stored permanently in main memory, as firmware. (2) Held continually in main memory even while not in use, as the disk operating system.

menu: A list of choices presented by a program, usually on the display screen, from which the user can select.

MHz: Megahertz; one million hertz. See **hertz**.

microcomputer: A computer, such as the Apple II, whose processor is a microprocessor.

microprocessor: A computer processor contained in a single integrated circuit, such as the 6502 microprocessor used in the Apple II.

mode: A state of a computer or system that determines its behavior.

modem: Modulator/demodulator; a peripheral device that enables the computer to transmit and receive information over a telephone line.

monitor: See **video monitor**.

Monitor program: A system program built into the Apple II in firmware, used for directly inspecting or changing the contents of main memory and for operating the computer at the machine-language level.

nested loop: A loop contained within the body of another loop and executed repeatedly during each pass through the containing loop.

nested subroutine call: A call to a subroutine from within the body of another subroutine.

nibble: A unit of information equal to half a byte, four bits, or fifty cents; can hold any value from 0 to 15. Sometimes spelled *nybble*.

NOT: A unary logical operator that produces a true result if its operand is false, a false result if its operand is true; compare **AND**, **OR**.

null string: A string containing no characters.

operand: A value to which an operator is applied.

operating system: A software system that organizes the computer's resources and capabilities and makes them available to the user or to application programs running on the computer.

operator: A symbol or sequence of characters, such as + or AND, specifying an operation to be performed on one or more values (the operands) to produce a result; see **arithmetic operator**, **relational operator**, **logical operator**, **unary operator**, **binary operator**.

OR: A logical operator that produces a true result if either or both of its operands are true, a false result if both of its operands are false; compare **AND**, **NOT**.

output: (1) Information transferred from a computer to some external destination, such as the display screen, a disk drive, a printer, or a modem. (2) The act or process of transferring such information.

page: (1) A screenful of information on a video display, consisting on the Apple II of 24 lines of 40 or 80 characters each. (2) An area of main memory containing text or graphical information being displayed on the screen.

pass: A single execution of a loop.

peek: To read information directly from a location in the computer's memory.

peripheral: At or outside the boundaries of the computer itself, either physically (as a peripheral device) or in a logical sense (as a peripheral card).

peripheral card: A removable printed-circuit board that plugs into one of the Apple II, II Plus, or IIe's expansion slots and expands or modifies the computer's capabilities by connecting a peripheral device or performing some subsidiary or peripheral function.

peripheral device: A device, such as a video monitor, disk drive, printer, or modem, used in conjunction with a computer. Often (but not necessarily) physically separate from the computer and connected to it by wires, cables, or some other form of interface, typically by means of a peripheral card.

peripheral slot: See **expansion slot**.

plotting vector: A code representing a single step in drawing a shape on the high-resolution graphics screen, specifying whether to plot a point at the current screen position and in what direction to move (up, down, left, or right) before processing the next vector. See **shape definition**, **shape table**.

point of call: The point in a program from which a subroutine or function is called.

pointer: An item of information consisting of the memory address of some other item. For example, Applesoft maintains internal pointers to (among other things) the most recently stored variable, the most recently typed program line, and the most recently read DATA item.

poke: To store information directly in a location in the computer's memory.

pop: To remove the top entry from a stack.

precedence: The order in which operators are applied in evaluating an expression.

printed-circuit board: A hardware component of a computer or other electronic device, consisting of a flat, rectangular piece of rigid material, commonly fiberglass, to which integrated circuits and other electronic components are connected.

printer: A peripheral device that writes information on paper in a form easily readable by humans or literate monkeys.

processor: The hardware component of a computer that performs the actual computation by directly executing instructions represented in machine language and stored in main memory.

program: (1) A set of instructions describing actions for a computer to perform in order to accomplish some task, conforming to the rules and conventions of a particular programming language. In Applesoft, a sequence of program lines, each with a different line number. (2) To write a program.

program line: The basic unit of an Applesoft program, consisting of one or more statements separated by colons (:).

programmer: The human author of a program; one who writes programs.

programming: The activity of writing programs.

programming language: A set of rules or conventions for writing programs.

prompt: To remind or signal the user that some action is expected, typically by displaying a distinctive symbol, a reminder message, or a menu of choices on the display screen.

prompt character: (1) A text character displayed on the screen to prompt the user for some action. Often also identifies the program or component of the system that is doing the prompting; for example, the prompt character] is used by the Applesoft BASIC interpreter, > by Integer BASIC, and * by the system Monitor program. Also called prompting character. (2) Someone who is always on time.

prompt message: A message displayed on the screen to prompt the user for some action. Also called prompting message.

push: To add an entry to the top of a stack.

queue: A list in which entries are added at one end and removed at the other, causing entries to be removed in FIFO (first-in-first-out) order; compare **stack**.

RAM: See **random-access memory**.

random-access memory: Memory in which the contents of individual locations can be referred to in an arbitrary or random order. This term is often used incorrectly to refer to read-write memory, but strictly speaking both read-only and read-write memory can be accessed in random order. This misuse of the term random-access is an attempt to confuse new users, creating a rite of passage and an excellent market for glossaries of computer terms. Compare **read-only memory**, **read-write memory**, **write-only memory**.

read: To transfer information into the computer's memory from a source external to the computer (such as a disk drive or modem) or into the computer's processor from a source external to the processor (such as the keyboard or main memory).

read-only memory: Memory whose contents can be read but not written; used for storing firmware. Information is written into read-only memory once, during manufacture; it then remains there permanently, even when the computer's power is turned off, and can never be erased or changed. Compare **read-write memory**, **random-access memory**, **write-only memory**.

read-write memory: Memory whose contents can be both read and written; often misleadingly called random-access memory, or RAM. The information contained in read-write memory is erased when the computer's power is turned off, and is permanently lost unless it has been saved on a more permanent storage medium, such as a disk. Compare **read-only memory**, **random-access memory**, **write-only memory**.

real number: A number that may include a fractional part; represented inside the computer in floating-point form. Compare **integer**.

relational operator: An operator, such as >, that compares numeric values to produce a logical result; compare **arithmetic operator**, **relational operator**.

reserved word: A word or sequence of characters reserved by a programming language for some special use, and therefore unavailable as a variable name in a program.

resident: See **memory-resident**, **disk-resident**.

return address: The point in a program to which control returns on completion of a subroutine or function.

ROM: See **read-only memory**.

routine: A part of a program that accomplishes some task subordinate to the overall task of the program.

run: (1) To execute a program. (2) To load a program into main memory from a peripheral storage medium, such as a disk, and execute it.

save: To transfer information from main memory to a peripheral storage medium for later use.

scientific notation: A method of expressing numbers in terms of powers of 10, useful for expressing numbers that may vary over a wide range, from very small to very large. For example, the number of atoms in a gram of hydrogen is approximately 6.02E23, meaning

6.02 times 10 to the 23rd power. (The letter *E* stands for exponent.) The number is easier to understand in this form than in the form 602000000000000000000000.

screen: See **display screen**.

scroll: To change the contents of all or part of the display screen by shifting information out at one end (most often the top) to make room for new information appearing at the other end (most often the bottom), producing an effect like that of moving a scroll of paper past a fixed viewing window. See **viewport**, **window**.

seed: A value used to begin a repeatable sequence of random numbers.

shape definition: A coded description of a shape to be drawn on the high-resolution graphics screen, consisting of one or more plotting vectors. See **shape table**, **plotting vector**.

shape table: A collection of one or more shape definitions, together with their indices.

shape table index: A list giving the memory addresses of the shapes in a shape table.

simple variable: A variable that is not an element of an array.

soft switch: A means of changing some feature of the Apple II from within a program; specifically, a location in memory that produces some special effect whenever its contents are read or written.

software: Those components of a computer system consisting of programs that determine or control the behavior of the computer. Compare **hardware**, **firmware**.

space character: A text character whose printed representation is a blank space, typed from the keyboard by pressing the SPACE bar.

stack: A list in which entries are added or removed at one end only (the top of the stack), causing them to be removed in LIFO (last-in-first-out) order; compare **queue**.

starting value: The value assigned to the index variable on the first pass through a loop.

startup disk: A disk containing software recorded in the proper form to be loaded into the Apple II's memory in order to set the system into operation. Sometimes called a boot disk; see **boot**.

statement: A unit of a program in a high-level language specifying an action for the computer to perform, typically corresponding to several instructions of machine language.

step value: The amount by which the index variable changes on each pass through a loop.

stepwise refinement: A technique of program development in which broad sections of the program are laid out first, then elaborated step by step until a complete program is obtained.

string: An item of information consisting of a sequence of text characters.

strobe: (1) An event, such as a change in a signal, that triggers some action. (2) A signal whose change is used to trigger some action.

subroutine: A part of a program that can be executed on request from any point in the program, and that returns control to the point of the request on completion.

subscript: An index number used to identify a particular element of an array.

substring: A string that is part of another string.

syntax: The rules governing the structure of statements or instructions in a programming language.

system: A coordinated collection of interrelated and interacting parts organized to perform some function or achieve some purpose.

system program: A program that makes the resources and capabilities of the computer available for general purposes, such as an operating system or a language translator. Compare **application program**.

system software: The component of a computer system consisting of system programs.

text: (1) Information presented in the form of characters readable by humans. (2) The display of characters on the Apple II's display screen. Compare **graphics**.

text file: A file containing information expressed in text form; compare **binary file**.

text window: An area on the Apple II's display screen within which text is displayed and scrolled.

truncate: To shorten by discarding a part; specifically, to convert a real number to the next lower integer.

unary operator: An operator that applies to a single operand; for example, the minus sign (-) in a negative number such as -6 is a unary arithmetic operator. Compare **binary operator**.

unconditional branch: A branch that does not depend on the truth of any condition; compare **conditional branch**.

user: The person operating or controlling a computer system.

user interface: The rules and conventions by which a computer system communicates with the person operating it.

value: An item of information that can be stored in a variable, such as a number or a string.

variable: (1) A location in the computer's memory where a value can be stored. (2) The symbol used in a program to represent such a location; compare **constant**.

video: (1) A medium for transmitting information in the form of images to be displayed on the screen of a cathode-ray tube. (2) Information organized or transmitted in video form. (3) An early space pioneer.

video monitor: A display device capable of receiving video signals by direct connection only, and that cannot receive broadcast signals such as commercial television. Can be connected directly to the Apple II computer as a display device.

viewport: All or part of the display screen, used by an application program to display a portion of the information (such as a document, picture, or worksheet) that the program is working on. Compare **window**.

window: (1) The portion of a collection of information (such as a document, picture, or worksheet) that is visible in a viewport on the display screen; compare **viewport**. (2) A viewport. (3) A flat, rectangular panel, usually made of silica, used in many archaic structures as a human-to-nature interface.

wraparound: The automatic continuation of text from the end of one line to the beginning of the next, as on the display screen or a printer.

write: To transfer information from the computer to a destination external to the computer (such as a disk drive, printer, or modem) or from the computer's processor to a destination external to the processor (such as main memory).

write-only memory: A form of computer memory into which information can be stored but never, ever retrieved, developed under government contract in 1975 by Professor Homberg T. Farnsfarfle. Farnsfarfle's original prototype, approximately one inch on each side, has so far been used to store more than 100 trillion words of surplus federal information. Farnsfarfle's critics have denounced his project as a six-million-dollar boondoggle, but his defenders point out that this excess information would have cost more than 250 billion dollars to store in conventional media. Compare **read-only memory**, **read-write memory**, **random-access memory**.

Index

D

E

F

G

H

I

J, K

L

M

N

O

P

S

T

U

Tell Apple About Your ...... *Applesoft BASIC Programmer's Reference*

☐ Please contact your authorized Apple dealer when you have questions about your Apple products. Dealers are trained by Apple Computer and are given the resources to handle service and support for all Apple products. If you need the name of an authorized Apple dealer in your area, call toll-free: 800-538-9696.

☐ Would you like to tell Apple what you think about this product? After you have had an opportunity to use this product, we would like to hear from you. You can help us to improve our products by responding to the questionnaire below and marking the appropriate boxes on the card at the right with a #2 **lead pencil**. If you have more than one response to a question, mark all the boxes that apply. Please detach the card and mail it to Apple. Include additional pages of comments if you wish.

Please Do Not Mark Above This Line

1. How would you rate the *Applesoft BASIC Programmer's Reference* manual overall? (**1**=poor. . .**6**=excellent)
2. Where did you buy this manual? (**1**=dealer, **2**=bookstore, **3**=other)
3. Was it easy to find a copy of this manual? (**1**=no, **2**=yes)
4. Which Apple computer are you using? (**1**=Apple II, **2**=Apple II Plus, **3**=Apple IIe, **4**=Apple IIc, **5**=Apple IIGS, **6**=other)
5. How much experience have you had with computers? (**1**=none. . .**6**=extensive)
6. Which of the following best describes your programming? (**1**=college class requirement, **2**=job requirement, **3**=hobby, **4**=source of income, **5**=other)
7. How much of this manual have you read? (**1**=entire manual, **2**=specific chapters, **3**=reference only)
8. How easy was this manual to read and understand? (**1**=difficult. . .**6**=very easy)
9. How would you rate the organization of this manual? (**1**=poor. . .**6**=excellent)
10. How easy was it to find the information you needed? (**1**=difficult. . .**6**=very easy)
11. To what degree did the technical material in the manual meet your expectations? (**1**=low. . .**6**=high)
12. What did you like best about the manual?
13. What did you like least about the manual?
14. Please describe any errors or inconsistencies you may have encountered in this manual. (Page numbers would be helpful.)
15. What suggestions do you have for improving the *Applesoft BASIC Programmer's Reference* manual?

Thanks for your time and effort.

1. ☐1 ☐2 ☐3 ☐4 ☐5 ☐6
2. ☐1 ☐2 ☐3
3. ☐1 ☐2
4. ☐1 ☐2 ☐3 ☐4 ☐5 ☐6
5. ☐1 ☐2 ☐3 ☐4 ☐5 ☐6
6. ☐1 ☐2 ☐3 ☐4 ☐5
7. ☐1 ☐2 ☐3
8. ☐1 ☐2 ☐3 ☐4 ☐5 ☐6
9. ☐1 ☐2 ☐3 ☐4 ☐5 ☐6
10. ☐1 ☐2 ☐3 ☐4 ☐5 ☐6
11. ☐1 ☐2 ☐3 ☐4 ☐5 ☐6
12. ______
13. ______
14. ______
15. ______

Return Address: ______________________

____

____

____

Place
First Class
Postage
Here

Apple Computer, Inc.
P.O. Box 1143
Cupertino, CA 95014
USA

All Language Pub